THE MIND

A USER'S MANUAL

THE MIND

A USER'S MANUAL

John Taylor

WILEY

Published in 2006 by John Wiley & Sons, Ltd, The Atrium, Southern Gate, Chichester, West Sussex, PO19 8SQ, England

Other Wiley Editorial Offices

John Wiley & Sons, Inc. 111 River Street, Hoboken, NJ 07030, USA

Jossey-Bass, 989 Market Street, San Francisco, CA 94103-1741, USA

Wiley-VCH Verlag GmbH, Pappellaee 3, D-69469 Weinheim, Germany

John Wiley & Sons Australia, Ltd, 33 Park Road, Milton, Queensland, 4064, Australia

John Wiley & Sons (Asia) Pte Ltd, 2 Clementi Loop #02-01, Jin Xing Distripark, Singapore 129809

John Wiley & Sons Canada Ltd, 22 Worcester Road, Etobicoke, Ontario, Canada, M9W 1L1

Wiley also publishes its books in a variety of electronic formats. Some content that appears in print may not be available in electronic books.

ISBN-13 978-0-470-02222-1 (PB)

Printed in the U.S.A.

To my grandson Jack, who inspired me to write this book

Acknowledgments

I gratefully acknowledge material from other publications that has been used in the text to help illustrate various points. The sources are as follows:

Author photo   Michael Woods.

p. 77   Quote from the Journal of Experimental Psychology: Human Perception and Performance. Reproduced by permission of the American Psychological Association and the author. From *Journal of Experimental Psychology: Human Perception and Performance*, 24, 1656–1674.

p. 88   Quote from J. H. Reynolds et al. from the Journal of Neuroscience. Reproduced with permission from the Society of Neuroscience. From J. H. Reynolds *et al.* (1999). Competitive Mechanisms Subserve Attention in Macaque Areas V2 and V4, *J. Neuroscience*, 19(5), 1736–1753.

p. 90   Quote from Corbetta and Shulman article from *Nature Reviews Neuroscience*. Reproduced by permission from Nature Reviews Neuroscience, 3:201–215, copyright 2002, Macmillan Magazines Ltd.

p. 102   Chambers Dictionary definition of 'efferent'. © Chambers Harrap Publishers Ltd: *The Chambers Dictionary* (2003).

p. 162   Quote from Parnas article. Reproduced with permission from Joseph Parnas.

p. 165   Quote from Temple Grandin website. Reproduced with permission from Temple Grandin. From *An Inside View of Autism*.

p. 173   Anosognosia report. Reproduced with permission from Psychology Press. Berti, A. *et al.* (1998) Anosognosia for motor impairments and dissociations with Patients' Evaluation of the Disorder: Theoretical Considerations. *Cognitve Neuropsychiatry*, 3(1), 21–44.

p. 161   Quote taken from *Antonin Artaud: Selected Writings*

p. 176   Quote from Deborah Wearing's book Forever Today. Quote from Clive Wearing's diary reproduced from *Forever Today* by Deborah Wearing.

p. 223   Robert Pater in Industrial Safety and Hygiene News. Reproduced with permission from Robert Pater. www.masteringsafety.com.

p. 226   Olivia Carter on BBC News Report 13/06/05. Reproduced with permission from Olivia Carter.

p. 229   Seymour Papert quotation from article in Game Developer magazine. Reproduced from Does Easy Do It? Children, Games and Learning, *Game Developer*, 1998, p. 88.

p. 230   John Beyer quotation. Reproduced with permission from John Beyer, Mediawatch UK.

p. 236   Lucy Bending quote. Reproduced by permission of Lucy Bending from http://www.wellcome.ac.uk/en/pain/microsite/history1.html

p. 254   Marc Hauser quote. Reproduced with permission from Marc Hauser, from *Wild Minds: What Animals Really Think*.

Contents

WHY A MIND-USER'S MANUAL?

My Grandson Jack

I realised I had to write a mind-user's manual when I first saw my grandson Jack. He was only two days old and as amazing as is any new human life to see and hold. To begin with, Jack was deeply embedded in his own little needs and desires, but other than food and drink he seemed almost completely on automatic, and even where food and drink were concerned, he didn't appear to have any repertoire – just guzzle it down and then back to near oblivion. Or so it seemed to me. However, I knew that out of this little bundle of flesh and blood would arise a decisive individual with his own thoughts, his own desires and his own emotional life. I wanted Elizabeth and Sam, Jack's parents, to give Jack all the best possibilities to grow into a thinking, creative person, one most able to respond effectively to whatever life can throw at him. Yet there are so many possible ways to get him to develop – send him to a Jesuit seminary, teach him intensively at home, try a boarding school – whatever. On top of that are an enormous number of unhelpful pressures from outside – drugs, religious fanaticism, alcoholism, and so on. How could I help Jack not to get bogged down sooner or later in some dead-end job or idea or a fanaticism of some sort considerably worse? Maybe even becoming an academic like me!

Jack's mind, which seemed to me almost completely blank at two days old, would be imprinted over the next years, both by Elizabeth and Sam, as well as by teachers at his school. But how could he be helped to avoid the wrong and recognise the right in both content and in ways of thinking? When he became his own man, where would this lead him? Would he have the time or inclination to experience the beauty of the amazing world around him, or the creativity of his own soul? Learn to create and show his spark of genius in whatever area best suited him, and be a thrusting young man able to think for himself and able to handle the dubious and the gold-plated real creations of life equably? Or would he end up needing drugs (legal or illegal) or other crutches to help him face up to what had become for him a threatening world?

Even more importantly, how would he avoid the claims of so many about how to live? Charlatans and the misguided cry their wares from the rooftops – using human stupidity, from that of air-headed celebrities to that of the weak and needy, to get people to kneel down and worship whatever they claim as gospel. These amazing flimflams arise from a misdirected hold on the nature of our existence. To have some road forward in life's complexity, many will take on board amazing rubbish explaining ourselves. At root the problem is to find an explanation of how our minds fit into the external reality pressing in on us. Instead of the gods of old – all of whom were realised not to be effective and were discarded one after the other – there are still 'gods' to appeal to, some dressed up in clothes to fit them to the modern world. People even call on bits of the sciences – the god of quantum mechanics has been particularly popular recently – to give that all-embracing explanation. But flight to the loony and the not-so-loony but still wrong explanations of ourselves boils down to fear that can only be prevented by understanding the true nature of mind in the material world.

I had to help Jack past the whirlpools and quagmires of those numerous easy solutions to the hard problem of the nature of the mind in the real world. They would strew his path with potholes for him to fall into. What better than if I could present him with a 'user's manual' for his mind? If he can keep his mind clean and bright then he should be able to handle the rest. He should be able to fight off the principles of absolute faiths. He would be able to avoid being bribed by the promise of absurd rewards in heaven into becoming a suicide bomber. He would be able to face up to the nature of his own mind and try to work out his own destiny in a way consistent with the reality in which he is ineradicably present. I could thereby help prevent him allowing others to put blinkers on his mind, making him listen only to what is in their claimed sacred writings. If he doesn't get his mind up to scratch, then he could really fail by falling in with some such bum crowd, imbuing him with crackpot ideas of religious fanaticism or whatever, and give his mind (and his soul) totally to them.

There are many people out there in a similar position to Jack. They also need to get their minds as clear and bright as a searchlight, just to be able to hold their own in the cut and thrust of daily life. But where is their mind-user's manual? Nowhere that I could see. There were lots of exhortations to do this and to follow that, but none of them seemed to have any rigorous scientific underpinning. Only by using rigorous scientific testing of the claims made about the mind can these claims begin to be justified. There is already a growing understanding of brain and mind coming from the hard work of many neuroscientists. Let us employ that knowledge to move forward to understand the scientific basis of the mind. The story that is about to be unfolded is about the most subtle and beautiful object in the universe – the human brain – and how it ever so subtly creates our inner experience. It is a truly amazing device, but one needing care in its maintenance as much as do our bodies. So I am also writing this manual for those of you who have noticed the absence of a scientifically justified mind-user's manual for your own guidance. Not that one mind fits all, but at least one good mind-user's manual should do you all to begin with. More specialised manuals, like those distinguishing between a Ford, a Rolls Royce or a Ferrari type of mind, hopefully will come later.

My manual is different from others because it is an absolute first. Not only will it tell you how to keep your mind clean and bright, and how to deal with minor difficulties in its smooth running, most importantly, it will tell you what your mind is for, so that you can then develop your own ways of handling it with more efficiency and in a manner best suited to yourself.

To obtain a trustworthy answer to the sixty-four thousand dollar question, 'What is the mind?', with the subordinate but closely associated question, 'What is the mind for?', I have developed an approach based on the latest scientific evidence about its nature. This allows me to focus on the most important components of the mind, leading to understanding of how the minds of children might best be developed, and what might be going wrong in various sorts of mental illnesses. The theory also has important implications across society, as well as in our treatment of animals, be they pets, farm animals or those in the wild.

The need for a suitably rewarding but disciplined environment is one feature arising from the theory for children, in an environment that could be called 'guided creative fun'. For adults, the need for a similar mixture of intellectual stimulation and fun as for children is to be expected, but now with guidance coming from bosses, colleagues, friends and loved ones. This can be most efficiently achieved if based on a guided creative fun upbringing from infancy. Tentative scientific answers to the much deeper questions of the nature of free will and its implications for society in terms of resulting moral responsibility are also corollaries of the theory. In addition, animal experience has the beginnings of a scientific understanding from the theory. All this is founded on scientific results and arguments out of which the theory has been developed.

Science is the framework inside which the theory is developed. That is because science gives answers that can be tested again and again, to ultimate destruction or acceptance. Only by such a standard of verifiability can we hope to discover the true nature of our own reality. As an example of the strictness of testing used by science, some years ago I was asked to vouch for the authenticity of a piece of A4 paper covered on one side with equations. These were rejected scribbles of the great scientist Albert Einstein. I looked at them with care, and advised that these equations were consistent with his attempts to construct a unified theory of matter and gravity solely from his ideas of gravity. They would have been developed in the mid- to late-1930s. Einstein had great hopes for these equations and the associated ideas. But they just did not work out. So in the end he had thrown the piece of paper away – just crumpled it up and dropped it in his waste paper basket. Apparently it had then been saved for posterity by someone who recognised his handwriting. And here it was in my hands, with a reserve price of tens of thousands of pounds on it for a forthcoming auction. But this was only of value to memorabilia-hunters, not to science. It was consigned to the dustbin of science. It was just no good. Like so many other ideas. Neither the piece of paper with Einstein's scribbled equations, nor all the other ideas that have passed through scientists' waste paper baskets across the world, matched with reality. It is reality that is the ultimate truth – the 'ground truth' on which all knowledge must reside.

Let me emphasise again that I am providing for you the first scientifically based mind-user's manual. Most importantly, and to distinguish it from others on the market, its truth can be tested by the rigorous methods of science. At the same time, it has led me to a remarkable discovery: the theory gives a possible fusion of science and religion through the basic experience of 'stillness' – emptiness in the mind of all content – claimed by mystics as a route to God. This fusion is achieved by an explanation from my scientific approach of how the stillness experience could arise in the brain by suitable preparation, such as through meditation or fasting. In this way, my manual can cover a vast range of the forces that tug and pull at society today, even to the extent of threatening to rend it asunder. Only by a scientifically based fusion of science and religion can there be a strong enough mixing of the multi-differentiated parts of society into a universal whole, based on scientific truth about the nature of the human mind.

What I provide for you here, and I hope for Jack and his parents as he grows up, is a new way of looking at your mind. The bottom line is that the mind is a mean, lean, attention machine. It certainly is an attention machine, allowing you to focus your attention rapidly on those things around you which you need to focus on, with rapidity and efficiency. How rapidly and efficiently depends on how mean and lean your attention machine actually is. So I will include various ways of getting your attention machine leaner and meaner. You can essentially treat this book as your attention gym, for attention workouts. At an even deeper level, attention is the gateway to consciousness, and I will tell you how that gateway is crossed, leading to the amazingly subtle inner 'you'. That story is still to be properly unfolded, but even the glimpse I can give you of it in this book indicates that my proposal begins properly to make sense across all our experience – of inner self, of soul, of supposed contact with God – and all the trials and tribulations of living in this world so full of conflicting ideas and other minds. This book is thus a paean – and a practical prayer – to the subtlety of your mind. Cherish it with ever greater attention!

All of us need a mind-user's manual. For anyone who can now read (Jack can't yet, but his parents stand in *loco parentis*), there are still books and courses on more efficient reading (such as speed reading) that could be attended. So how about some sort of user's manual or course of lectures on using your mind? Lots of books have been written claiming they explain the mind scientifically. In the end either the author admits that he/she hasn't a clue, or removes any hard problem about your mind by denying there is any such a thing as 'I' to explain, or alternatively gives an explanation imbued with ancient wisdom but unrelated to modern science.

So we all have a problem: either accept that there is no inner self, or struggle on with no clue as to how it is made – and it would seem presently with no clue from modern science. This is emphasised by writers who claim that science and religion are separate, and must remain ever so. Science handles matter, religion the soul. But the soul is what the inner centre of mind is all about. Yet given the vast variety of religions that could be for sale at your local religious supermarket, there is no agreement among them either as to the nature of the mind or how it is made.

In the present situation, Jack must therefore work it out for himself like you have done so far for your mind. But I think it's going to get more and more difficult for the children of Jack's generation to get through unaided. The competition to catch minds is getting fiercer from all sides: from fanatical religions, from drugs, from relentless hedonism, and from all together in some cases. And all of us are embedded in an ever more complex and fragmented society that our minds have to encompass and come to terms with, in order that we can be effective.

That there is no specific mind-user's manual – with a title very similar to this book – may make you still suspect that you really don't need one. You may have felt all along, consciously or unconsciously, that you know how to handle your mind without too much trouble. After all, it's yours, which you were born with and grew up with, so why any problem? Why worry about it when you seem to be doing all right just forging ahead? As the saying goes, 'ignorance is bliss'. So you are happy to stay ignorant of what your mind is really for and how best to use it.

But wait a moment – are you really so disinterested? We all have problems in life, with its emotional and intellectual turmoil, the cut and thrust of daily life, and the difficulty of interpersonal communication. Given life's ups and downs (especially the downs), you must sooner or later have realised that you could make good use of a mind-user's manual – provided it is a really good one that you can fully trust and which helps by answering the questions about your mind that have been piling up ever since you were born (or thereabouts). And I want to give one to Jack for that reason.

User's manuals usually leave unsaid the purpose of the system that the manual is explaining. The purpose of a car is obvious, and although the standard car manual does not give all the gory details of the functioning of the internal combustion engine, that is because the car's purpose is known – to get its driver and passengers from point A to point B under their own steam as fast and efficiently as possible. The same holds for a manual about a washing machine or a dishwasher. So what is different about the mind? Why not a user's manual for the mind that leaves the purposes of the mind unsaid? Yet in terms of the material world, all religions leave the purpose of mind unsaid. Mind – equated with a non-material soul – is in general implicitly assumed to be a mechanism for our communication with God. Modern books trying to explain the mind also seem not to provide any convincing argument for its presence (in terms of the possible existence of an inner self or soul). So why should we expect one now?

There are many controversial views about the mind – from religions imbuing it with an eternal soul with which to contact God to modern Western neuroscience denying anything other than that the mind is just there for better information processing but has no 'inner self'; from those claiming one must live the austere life (the 'early to bed' folks) to those saying 'go out and get stoned every night to really experience the world and blow your mind'. So there appears to be no fully accepted and scientifically tested use for the mind as there is for the machines I mentioned above – those wonders of the modern world, such as the car, the washing machine, the mobile, the microwave, and all the other things that make our lives so much more efficient.

However, ignorance about the function of mind has led to there being many, many different 'manuals' on the mind, containing exhortations to expand experience through drugs (as egged on by Aldous Huxley's *Doors of Perception*), religion (as in the relevant sacred texts), and so on. These are the 'mind-expanding' user manuals presently on offer to Jack, his parents and all of us, including those claiming that part of the mind is immaterial – a soul, as many religions would have. This has produced the confusing world of many different mind-user's manuals now on offer.

The existence of this plethora of mind manuals is because of the sadly undeniable fact that no one has brought forward a proper explanation of the purpose of the mind – except their own, as they stridently proclaim! But theirs are explanations – even if only implicit – as yet untested by science. If no scientifically proven understanding of the purpose of the mind is available, then how can any of these user's manuals be trusted? They may all be false. Following them could really screw you up. And I don't want that to happen to Jack, his parents or the rest of us. So beware of mind-user's manuals. Read the small print with great care, if such small print exists (and it usually doesn't). Of course, that same careful scrutiny should also be applied to this user's manual. So let me give a brief look at what my mind-user's manual contains.

This user's manual is in four parts. In the first part I consider in more detail the dangers arising from what can be termed 'mind-user's manuals' presently available, after a description of what is usually meant by 'mind'. Mind-user's manuals usually claim to be an explanation of all experience seen through specific eyes. Thus, those seen through religions, which claim to bring your mind to God, those through drugs, which lead to a wonderful new view of the world (and even to new worlds only viewable under drugs), and finally those through emotions allowed to run riot and felt to the full, are considered in successive chapters. This first part concludes with a set of criteria that need to be possessed by a valid and effective mind-user's manual.

In the second part, I give a description of a scientific approach to the mind that extends the common-sense view, and which enables a crucial set of functions to be developed for our consciousness. This is explored in terms of normal experience on the basis of attention. It leads to a control model of consciousness providing an explanation of the basic construction of our subtle and beautiful consciousness, in the most complex machine in the world, our own brains.

Part III contains an explanation of a broad range of distorted experiences, which test and further explore the consciousness model presented in Part II. This covers religious mystical experiences across all the world's religions, and for the first time helps to fuse these religions with a scientific view of the universe.

Finally, I apply my model of consciousness to the world of everyday experience. This covers our own world of adulthood, Jack's developing world of infancy and childhood, our animals (pets, farm animals or wild animals), and finally advice, along the lines of a car user's manual, encompassing the scientific justification I have written before: how to use your attentive brain to get the best out of it.

I would like to conclude by acknowledging my wife for her trenchant criticism, my daughter Elizabeth for helpful discussions, and my younger research colleagues for their constant stimulation on the nature of the brain and how it works to create the various faculties of mind.

PART I

BEWARE THE IDES OF MIND

Soothsayer: *Beware the Ides of March.*

Julius Caesar: *He is a dreamer; let us leave him. Pass.*

Julius Caesar, Act I, Scene 2

CHAPTER ONE

WHAT'S IN YOUR MIND?

The Black Depths of A Mind

A man was quietly walking his dog along a secluded pathway, with nature's bounty all around. But as he walked he suddenly noticed something that he could not at first believe. Closer up, he had the horrifying vision of a young girl's naked body lying near the path, exposed in all its innocence. She had been stripped, tied up and stabbed more than 20 times in a brutal attack that had the hallmarks of a ritual killing. The body was later identified as that of a schoolgirl, Jodi Jones, only 14 years of age. Who had committed such a terrible crime on a defenceless young girl? She had not fought back, so she very likely knew her attacker. Police finally tracked down a likely suspect. He was a social misfit but apparently one of Jodi's closest friends.

A bleak report appeared in *The Times* of 22 January 2005, some months after the body had been found, saying baldly, 'Luke Mitchell, 16, was found guilty by a majority verdict of murdering Jodi Jones, 14, as she ran to meet him on a summer's evening in 2003. The judge, Lord Nimmo Smith, told Mitchell: "It lies beyond any skill of mine to look into the black depths of your mind. I can only look at what you have done." '

The Times report on the trial, and some analysis of Luke Mitchell's life, helped go a little way towards probing into that black depth of his mind. He had become a Satanist, and used to boast, 'Once you have shaken hands with the Devil you then have truly experienced life'. He claimed he smoked hundreds of cannabis joints a week and carried knives to school. He was even recalled as having said to another boy at the school, 'I can just imaging myself going out and getting stoned and killing somebody and how funny it would be'.

How did he get into this dreadful state of mind? He had very little parental guidance, his mother doing nothing to curb his behaviour and his father having removed himself from his life. His mother apparently did nothing to discourage his obsession with the occult, nor was she concerned about his use of drugs or under-age sex. He had little caring guidance so his gothic fantasies were allowed to spiral downwards. He wrote in a schoolbook 'Satan lives' and in another 'I have tasted the devil's green blood'. Driven on by these drug-inspired fantasies, he committed this heinous crime. He was totally impassive at his trial, uncaring for the young lover he had slaughtered so savagely, a teenage killer without remorse.

Society has to prevent such fantasists from developing so far, possibly to go on to murder, and being a terrifying danger to those around them. Details of the 'guided creative fun' I mentioned earlier are needed to help ensure such prevention. It is a very difficult issue in a free society to achieve such creative guidance without apparent over-control. But the bottom line in our increasingly interactive society is that parents and all others involved must prevent their children becoming such a danger. All parents must make efforts to ensure this at every stage of their children's upbringing, as well as giving them a feeling of the joy of their own lives, in their own creations and endeavours.

A first step in that direction is to consider what the mind actually consists of, in order to know how the resulting components should develop and be helped to develop. This should allow us to produce individuals able to function without being a danger to others, but instead an enjoyment to themselves and all who know them. Note that the word 'development' occurs here. It is the developmental process, in which parents and teachers are crucially involved, where this process is going on. But it is the mind of the child that is being developed. So a deep enough understanding of that mind, especially of what it is for, is essential to enable proper definition of the overall framework of that guidance. That is why I talked earlier about the scenario of child upbringing I termed 'guided creative fun'. The proper understanding of the nature of mind must play a crucial role in helping flesh out the substance of that scenario.

The Nature of Mind

You may suspect your mind is not a machine, or at least not a simple one. You accept that it is a very complex system – not one you want just anyone to look at under the hood to check your oil level or uncover why your little red light on your dashboard is blinking away. But that leads to the question: what is this manual-free but very complicated device – our minds – that we have in our heads? It closes down like clockwork when we go to sleep, and in the morning it starts up again when the birds (or our kids or our wife, husband or partner) shout at us to get up and not lie there doing nothing. Then our mind feels that we are still the same self:

still the same pet loves and hates, no change there – it is a remarkably good personality-keeper.

But how can this mind of yours – which you feel is not in your head at all, but expanding over all you can see – be able to work like that? It just cannot be made from a piece of stone or lump of earth. They have no mentality at all, never have and never will do. A stone doesn't even squeal when you step on it or kick it. Never has done, never will do. You are the one that squeals, from the pain you experience in your mind.

So perhaps your mind is not material at all. It is perhaps made of something else – whatever that is. But a non-material mind can lead to all sorts of weird and wonderful possibilities: from life after death, relationship to God (whoever that is), paranormal phenomena like viewing things at a distance, to ghosts, magic, and so on – not the Harry Potter sort, which is fictional fun, but instead the sort claimed by some to be real. Do you really want to go down that weird and wacky route? I ventured down there for a distance myself some decades ago, and only found credulity and lies. I managed to hold onto my scientific standards of evidence. But some never return to the land of the verifiably real.

But surely an immaterial mind makes more sense than the material one, you ask. How can my ethereal-like mind be made from two fistfuls of porridge, as the brain appears to be? Even more surely, the mind cannot be made out of the same stuff as my left toe. Or so popular thinking would lead us to expect.

Finding out how the mind works seems to have the same apparent impossibility as that other old chestnut: 'How did the universe begin?'. But while the question of how the universe began looks really impossible to answer (because whatever it grew out of had still to be part of the whole universe – so either it had always been growing, or it came from a primordial egg which had no way of knowing when to start growing – time had not even started then), why should discovering how our own minds work turn out to be as bad? A simple-minded naturalistic view would make our minds be created purely by the activity in our brains. If we cannot get to the bottom of the 'two fistfuls of porridge' of the brain to break its code, then any scientific tools we used to do the probing are not the vaunted polished chisels they had been claimed to be. They would not be able to uncover all the dark secrets of the universe. The minds inside our heads would be impenetrable.

From this point of view the only way forward is to follow the scientific way as strongly as we can to see if it can succeed. We have to probe the brain ever more carefully, and try to make it give up its secrets. We have still a long way to go along that route, as compared to the several hundred more years we have taken probing into stones and rocks, then into molecules, atoms and nuclei, further down into elementary particles, and thence to superstrings, presently the smallest parts we know of matter. In this progress material science has raced ahead of brain/mind science. Let us hope brain science will catch up soon. In the end, of course, we may find there is something about the mind that is left over after all possible science has been done. But we have a long way to go until we reach that situation. The history of science tells us that many previously unexplained and subtle natural phenomena have finally fallen under the domain of scientific explanation – life as based on organic matter that could be artificially created, heredity as from the genetic code and the structure of DNA, illness as due to microbes, earthquakes as caused by clashing tectonic plates – the list goes on and on, and nor is it finished.

So the steps we take in initially trying to understand the brain must follow the scientific method, which means attempting to understand what is actually there, probing the brain down to its smallest units and trying to see how these units could give it the functionality it possesses, especially that of mind. Until that has been done exhaustively – and for a further several hundred years, as has already occurred in studying the science of matter – we do not expect to have done the job properly. This book can be seen as a progress report on the attempt to understand that highest and most subtle function of all we can posit is created by our brains – that of consciousness.

At the same time, the book also reports on the implications of the resulting knowledge about the mind. For there are implications for how we can use such understanding to make our minds as effective as possible, and similarly how our society could be developed to help all the minds belonging to it to achieve their maximum potential. The design principles of the mind are being discovered to depend heavily on interactions of minds with each other in society. Hence the need for 'guided creative fun' as a general mode of development, where the guidance comes from parents, teacher and peers, and more generally from society. If we do not get this guidance right then our society will keep on producing its Luke Mitchells.

The Science of Mind

When we look more closely at the brain, it is certainly very different from two fistfuls of porridge. It is made of billions of 'living atoms' called nerve cells (or neurons). Each of these is a minute information communication system, taking in bits of information from thousands of other like-minded nerve cells and sending out a response to thousands of others. The response of any nerve cell is also very simple – a brief pulse, called a spike, of electrical activity saying 'yes, there are enough inputs to switch me on' or no spike, saying 'no, not enough activity to arouse me – stay off'. The spike itself is a very brief pulse of electricity, lasting no more than a thousandth of a second, sent down the communication channel (the axon) leaving the cell and branching to inform thousands of other cells of the cell's response.

In spite of the simplicity of the basic neuron-to-neuron communication, the overall complexity of the total communication across all the billions of neurons in the brain is awe inspiring. Excitations spark like lightning showers across the gulfs between neurons. The nature of the functions carried out by these communications is beginning to be unravelled by modern brain imaging machines, which can look at the brain in its ceaseless activity without disturbing the subject whose brain is being probed. I even helped develop a system that is so fast in reading out and analysing brain activity, that a subject lying in one of the machines could move his fingers and see the region of his brain being active shone back on to a screen he could view. Surely not just two fistfuls of porridge! Far, far, more complicated.

This complication is compounded by the ability of the connections between nerve cells to be modified by experience. There appear to be two general form of this. First, there are changes impressed on the connections between the nerve cells in the brain by incoming activity or feedback from responses. These changes of connectivity are therefore to be regarded as a way of learning about the environment, trying to make sense of what is out there or what is in one's own bodily responses. The second way that connections between nerve cells can change is by a crucial mechanism that allows us to put meaning and value into our surroundings, on top of what it looks like. The changes in this second learning route are based on rewarded responses to particular stimuli. If there is a reward, say of delicious tasting food when you eat it, then not only the stimulus – the food – and its response are increased in likelihood by increasing the connections between the relevant input and response, but also value maps are set up to allow predictions to be made about the value of a particular stimulus the next time it is encountered. So you will choose that delicious piece of food on the plate if it tasted so good before. This reward, or reinforcement learning, as it is sometimes called, is at the basis of learning our goals – those that have the good rewards – and their use in planning and making decisions. As such, it is at the basis of the 'guided creative fun' scenario I am advocating for child development, and even more through the whole of life for adults. The guidance is from rewarding valued responses that children make to things around them.

But was I not too simple-minded to claim that our minds are created purely by the activity in our brains? Much of modern humanity believes completely the opposite when they think about it. Religion shouts the opposite at you. So how can it be as simple as I just claimed, that the brain is ticking away like some simple machine, with nerve cells sending spikes between each other like mad? If God can reach into your brain and stir it up, then it cannot be such a simple machine. If He can get at the spiking of the neurons in some way or other, then there is more to the mind than neurons and spikes.

Even more strongly, if the mind is not all material then it is just not a machine at all. It is not a machine if there really is a non-material soul as part of the mind, as billions of humans still believe in our 'modern' age. And if mind is not material then all bets on using science to understand it are off. Other approaches must be followed. But I said that only by following a scientific approach, in which we start by assuming that the mind is all in the brain, can we begin to tackle the problem of mind in a verifiable way. Only when we exhaust this should we then turn to completely alternate approaches, with their greater problem of verifiability.

CHAPTER TWO

DEFINING YOUR MIND

Exploring Your Mind

The voices going through his head were insistently repeating over and over again: 'Kill him, kill him' until he shouted, 'Shut up!' But they kept on saying it. Perhaps he shouldn't have stopped taking his medicine. Yet it was the only way he could get out of the hospital – under the pills he was completely zonked out and couldn't play the 20 questions game about his sanity when the health workers interviewed him for release. By then he knew he had to get out. And he couldn't go back on the pills when he was outside since it was too scary and he needed all his wits about him. 'Kill him, kill him,' the voice shouted again in his ears. So he did – the poor fool cycling down the hill in the leafy park had no time to swerve as the knife plunged sharply into his chest and stopped his heart dead. But the voices still went on.

What is in the mind? How can it become so befuddled by a 'voice in its head' that it loses sight of external reality, even so far as to kill innocent bystanders? Knowing the answer to these questions should help us begin to attack the problem of the nature of the mind itself. It will hopefully let us ground our development on the reality of the mind, and begin to resolve the puzzle about its apparent non-material nature. How can a pill have any control over the 'voice in the head' if the voice and the mind listening in to that voice are not material? We can only find this knowledge by turning to what has been understood by psychologists and brain scientists over the past hundred years or so, and relating that knowledge to our own inner experience as we go about our daily lives. We can thereby start from a reasonably secure and verifiable knowledge base. This will give us an idea of what the mind does, although we must remember that we still have the uphill climb to discover *how* it does it from a purely material but subtly beautiful brain.

Let me start by trotting out some dictionary definitions of mind, so at least we're plugged into the standard meanings. As we should expect, these are complex, with many possibilities. The Collins dictionary, for example, requires us to choose the most appropriate from a total of twenty-nine different definitions it gives of mind. I chose the one that encapsulates what I regard as most relevant: 'The human faculty in which there are ascribed thoughts, feelings, etc., often regarded as an immaterial part of a person'. In a similar vein, but more succinctly, Chambers dictionary states that mind is: 'that which thinks, knows, feels, wills'.

These definitions still indicate a breadth of meaning of the concept of 'mind'. It has narrowed down our overall set of possibilities, but we still have a number of facets of mind that we need to explore further. We will do that in terms of the most important aspect of mind: how it is used. Looking into its uses and abuses and exploring all its faculties should help us begin to put together a story of what the mind is for. Only then, when that script has been filled out and all the characters introduced and begun their play, can we hope to create a suitably scientifically based mind-user's manual, which indicates the beauty and power of what is purely inside our own heads as the subtlest and most powerful lean, mean attention machine.

Uses of the Mind

From the definitions of mind I have just extracted, and with a little further thought, we can set up a list of the more specific functions of mind that I think we would all agree are important:

- Perceiving
- Thinking
- Remembering
- Imagining
- Planning
- Reasoning
- Speaking and understanding words said to us
- Emotional experience
- Unconscious processing.

All of these involve bona fide mental activities except possibly for the last two, those of emotions and of unconscious processing. Of course, what is mental is debatable – the mind is a complex phenomenon in its own right, whose meaning itself has changed over the past few decades. It has become ever more embracing – as my list shows. Both the Collins and Chambers dictionaries back my inclusion of feeling in the attributes of mind.

In spite of these claims, it is still somewhat controversial that emotions and unconscious processing are really part of mind. Yet each is crucial in the operation of mind. Without any emotions, a mind will become a pretty dreary thing, just chundering on with the dull routine of life. And without any unconscious processing going on underneath it all, only raw unprocessed images and sensations could be in the mind. The mind would have to work that much harder to be able to do all the things in the list above that it is called upon without a grumble and with considerable efficiency. So I will include these two final but important aspects of the mental life as part of the furniture of mind.

Let me introduce at this point the further term *cognition*, and to separate cognition from mind. Cognition is a term that has itself spread its wings over the past few decades, so it has come almost to cover the same functions as those of mind. Here I want to distinguish those functions of mind that involve awareness or consciousness as a crucial component – the cognitive components – from those which do not – the non-cognitive. This usage is close to the original meaning of cognition – only involving conscious processing – before it was expanded to include any mental function, even those without consciousness.

In the above bullet-pointed list we see that all but the last two are involved in cognitive processes. It is these – emotion and unconscious processes – which I take to be part of the furniture of the mind, but which are not clearly cognitive. That is obvious for the last item – unconscious processes. It is not so clear for emotion. In fact conscious emotional experiences arise in the feelings of happiness or anger, for example. But on the other hand there are lots of emotions being aroused outside consciousness, as many examples demonstrate. For example you could be shown a happy face subliminally – so you are unaware of it due to it being shown to you too briefly – but find that its emotional state influences how you respond to later stimuli: you do so in a more positive manner. So you initially had an unconscious emotion elicited by the subliminal stimulus, only later finding that it modified your conscious experience.

To summarise, I suggest that the mind has both conscious and un-conscious components. Some of these components are what I term cognitive – those involving awareness (equated with consciousness) – while some are completely non-cognitive and outside awareness, such as unconscious processing. There is also at least one component of mind – emotion – that has some cognitive and some non-cognitive components.

Let me consider in more detail each of these mental functions, to help clarify the enormous complexity of mind – and even why we have one in the first place.

I perceive the paper on which I am writing notes for this chapter. My perception is of a white oblong, smooth to the touch. I perceive other things around my study – the window, the desk and so on. These percepts are made sense of in terms of higher-level concepts. I make sense of my perception of the specific piece of paper before me in terms of my general concept of 'pieces of paper', which I have built up by my earlier experiences of them. The concept does not involve particular shapes or sizes or colours of paper. My perception of the piece of paper now in front of me certainly does. So the crucial difference between percepts and concepts in the brain is that a percept is the ongoing and fleeting experience associated to a given external stimulus, while a concept is a memory of a range of somewhat similar percepts.

Having clothed my present perception inside the relevant concept of pieces of paper coded in my brain, I can then prepare to make a desired action on this specific piece of paper in terms of motor actions on concepts, guided by the shape, size, colour or other specific properties of my particular percept of piece of paper. Alternatively, I could make a quite different response, like getting up out of my chair (another mixture of percept embedded in the concept of a chair), going down the stair (yet again a mixture of percept and concept) and making myself a cup of coffee – a concept with an associated delicious experience of value that I hold in my mind, especially that of its smell and of its taste and after-effect. When I actually experience the coffee I have made, then I do so through the relevant percept. So I seem to be surrounded by percepts, given meaning in terms of their embedding concepts. But while that may be true, remember all these percepts and concepts are only in my brain; the real objects are outside in the environment. The concepts I possess are also arranged in sets of categories, possessing a powerful hierarchical structure. For example, consider the chain: animals, dogs, terriers, Yorkshire terriers, my little Yorkie Pippa, sadly no longer with us, but a bundle of fun to my family in her life.

Thinking uses concepts and also their more specific re-creations as percepts. My thinking uses the concepts I have learnt in my brain, especially the more easily remembered ones, to help me plan, for example, what should be the further chapters of this book. Besides thinking involving planning and remembering, it can also involve imagining myself in all sorts of situations, as well as their consequences. This is where the powers of imagination allow me to recreate percept-like experiences to create an imaginary world with a degree of veracity that helps me use it to develop its consequences. That is at the basis of planning – where I work out the consequences of imagined acts and carry out the one with the most rewarding outcome. Thinking can also be seen to contain the faculty of reason. So if I were asked a puzzle of some sort to do in my mind, such as the latest Sudoku, I would have to reason out how to do it, working through in my mind what would happen if I made that move – no, it doesn't work; start again – thinking through the consequences of another move, and so on.

Speech is a different faculty altogether, as we see from the fact that initially none of us, when we first came on the scene, were born with any powers of speech. Speech takes some time to develop in an infant. My grandson Jack now recognises about 150 words and that number is increasing fast, at his present age of 14 months. He will move on next to say single words about the objects he sees or wants to play with. He has already said his first word: 'baa'. No wonder he's said that – there are over 50 Wensleydale sheep in the field behind his house, which he sees several times a day as he goes for a walk with his mother, and each time she points them out to him.

Infants' initial one-word statements are created, usually by the end of their first year, by picking up their own version of words the adults speak to them. This imitation is helped by rewarding responses to the infants' initial babblings and simple one-syllable attempts at complex words they hear. Two- or three-word strings of words then begin to be produced at about two years of age. Within a further year, infants will start an enormous expansion of their language powers, with a number of new words learnt every day and an increasingly complex syntax in terms of function words, like 'the', 'a' and so on, inserted phrases and much more. Language is one of the great powers that we seem to acquire effortlessly through our early lives, but about which we still know only too little. Yet brain science is putting on the pressure and improving our understanding of it.

Turning now to emotions, these are extremely important to help motivate us to scale the heights, as well as plumb the depths. Heights and depths seem to come sequentially, especially for certain people. Some of the most creative people have periods of bleak depression, as did the great Winston Churchill. He called those periods his 'black dog days', and they were a great trial to him. The enormous level of activity he kept up throughout his life was partly to keep such bad days away. There are those who are even deeper in the pit of despair, with waves of self-disgust or hopelessness sweeping over them. For them emotions weigh them down to the bottom of the ocean, and they are helpless in their grip. Yet once out of it, and like you or me in a happy mood, all can be conquered. There are no impossible tasks. There are only pessimistic fools who try to put us off scaling these heights. Such manic–depressive cycles can now be controlled by suitable drugs. But one has to be careful that the whole of life is not then a flat road with no ups and downs at all.

More generally, emotions are now seen as aroused through some sort of appraisal process that we each go through in assessing a situation and its possible outcomes for us. This process need not be conscious, as in the development of anger in a situation in which we feel threatened or under attack in some way and respond by preparing for attack in response. Fear would arise from a situation in which we realise that we must withdraw from a perceived threat, it being too great to do otherwise. And so on through the range of emotions.

How many different emotions can we discern in ourselves or in other people? A very hard question to answer, with some researchers suggesting six, others ten basic emotions, others even more. An alternative approach is to consider emotions as just labels attached to certain states made up of a mixture of different combinations of levels of activation and of value (and possibly other factors). By the term 'value' we mean how rewarding a stimulus has been discovered to be from past experience – its value being made up from past experiences of it. So emotions are particular combinations of pairs of levels of activation and rewards. Fear has low activation and negative reward, anger high activation but also negative reward. And there are similar pairs of values for the other basic emotions of happiness, etc. This method of assignment allows the many more emotions that have been named (and any that haven't yet) to be fitted together in its overall scheme, giving it an edge of superiority over taking a basic list of emotions and stopping there. It doesn't leave out any possible emotions that may be dreamt up in the future.

I have recently been involved in a European Commission-funded project called ERMIS, to build a machine that can recognise emotions in people from their faces and their speech. In the process we have found that it has given us considerable flexibility to use this idea of specific emotion states as embedded in an activation–value continuum. Such flexibility is especially relevant because we observe people to glide smoothly from one emotional state to another during a conversation.

We now come to more difficult mental events: the unconscious processes. Can they be said to be in our minds at all? Surely our minds are only made up of things of which we are conscious? However, it would be very limiting to take such an attitude towards the processes going on inside our heads of which we are not conscious. We now realise that unconscious processing can be at a high level: it can involve representations inside our brains even up to the level of concepts. This makes their exclusion quite unwarranted.

I have already defined the mind as involving such unconscious processes. But that they could be going on up to such a high level of meaning in the mind is both remarkable and until quite recently controversial. The controversy was over the two extreme possibilities:

(i) attention and resulting awareness arising late in time when processing a stimulus by the brain, or (ii) attention occurring at a low level, and at the very earliest time when the stimulus first activates the brain. The battle between the two sides has raged for some decades, but now has subsided, with decisive evidence being discovered that shows that stimuli are processed up to a high level of meaning without being attended to or becoming conscious.

One phenomenon that has shown that a lot of processing occurs at an unconscious level in the brain has been the 'attentional blink'. This is a remarkable phenomenon, in which attention is shown to take a certain amount of time to process a stimulus. During this processing, other stimuli are not able to be attended to. It is as if attention 'blinks its eye shut' to anything else during the period it is processing a particular stimulus.

The attentional blink lasts about one third of a second after the first of two stimuli being presented. During that period it is not possible to be conscious of any other stimulus. Yet it has been shown that a second stimulus, presented during the blink, is processed to a high level, even though there has been no awareness of it. This has been done by a number of methods. One is by looking at the activity in the brain brought about by the second stimulus. Of particular importance here is the so-called N400, an electrical signal in the brain that can be measured on the scalp by sticking electrodes onto it and magnifying the result. The N400 is characteristic of semantic-level processing, occurring at about 400 milliseconds (or 2/5 of a second) after the second stimulus has been presented. The N400 has been observed for the second stimulus presented during the blink, showing it has indeed been processed up to semantic level.

Alternatively, it has been shown that the second stimulus, when presented in the blink of an earlier stimulus, can leave a trace of itself – so-called priming – behind, to affect the speed of processing of a third stimulus. Thus if the second stimulus was the word 'nurse', there was speed-up of recognition time for a third stimulus 'doctor' as a word among a set of stimuli made up of meaningless strings of letters. So the stimulus 'nurse' was processed up to its level of meaning, even though the subject was unaware of it.

There are numerous other ways of showing that processing of stimuli in the brain goes on without consciousness up to a high level. It has even been suggested that up to 90% of the brain is involved in processing material at an unconscious level. That seems to be the source of the exhortation to try to use that 90% of the brain otherwise not being used. That is clearly a most unwise demand. If you could break into that brain space devoted to unconscious processing, then such processing would cease, or at least be severely damaged. Once again, we come back to a brain without unconscious processing facilities. It would put an enormous load on the conscious processing part.

But perhaps that would not now matter because you would have much more brain space to work with at conscious level, and could thereby handle the chaos of raw images and everything else. Here we come to an important aspect of consciousness and attention: I only have one thing in my conscious mind at once. More than one and I really have to juggle hard, constantly going back to the earlier item to ensure I remember it – I rehearse it, go back to the later item, come back to the first, and so see-saw back and forth between the two items in my mind. But if all of the brain were working at a conscious level then I would have many things in my mind at once. In fact, I would have the whole of my environment in my mind. I would not be focusing attention on one small area or object. That would make my thinking very hard – everything would have to be thought about at once. I think I would truly go out of my mind in that situation.

For that reason attention filters out all of the unconsciously processed material, leaving 90% of it outside my filter gateway to consciousness. If you suggest that I could still do that filtering using all my brain at conscious level, it would seem that a new filter level would then have to be introduced, called higher-level attention, for example, to single out that item I wish to use for further processing. But the gateway of the higher-level attention would lead to a higher-level consciousness, since attention and consciousness seem so closely coupled. So we are back to a two-level system as before, with attention and higher-level attention replacing unattended and attended. Nothing gained at all.

I have now covered my list of functions of mind. However, some of them do not function in the damaged brain, and so studying these deficits as they occur should also help us understand better the functions of the various components of the mind.

Hidden Depths

Unconscious activities are very important in the human brain. I have already noted that they take up about 90% of the processing space in the brain. Do damages to particular bits of that processing lop off components of conscious experience? And can there still be some form of knowledge available to the subject, without consciousness attached?

The prime example of this is the phenomenon called 'blindsight'. A person may suffer damage to their visual cortex, from a blow to the head, say, making them blind in one particular region of space. But in some cases the person can still 'guess' above chance that a light is or is not shining in that blind part of their vision. Thus they are said to have blindsight. It is a remarkable phenomenon, since they seem to be able to conjure knowledge of the external world out of total darkness. How could this knowledge arise?

It is known, in certain blindsight subjects, that in spite of the damage to the cortical region that acts as entry in the brain to visual information, there is still activity in higher regions. It is as if this information has jumped over the entry gate to visual cortex and entered the hallowed areas of higher (though still unconscious) visual processing. How this occurs is still under debate, but could be either by direct lines of communication from the outside into these higher processing levels or by the information going through an alternate gate to reach these higher areas. The latter can occur in monkeys, but it is still under debate if that is also true in humans. Either way, the information gets to the higher visual levels.

However, the rub is that this information cannot easily be acted on spontaneously. The blindsighted subject is loath to say where the spot of light may be or if it is on or off, and only makes a response after some urging to make a guess. It is at a different level of certainty than aware knowledge; it is not veridical. More generally we can say that the blindsight knowledge is not reportable, where reportability is a sine qua non of consciousness. It seems as if the loss of the very early visual brain tissue, acting as the initial cortical processing area, does not give the activity enough support to be reported and acted on as conscious activity normally is.

This leads to a very important feature that emerges about con-sciousness: it arises through brain activity that can be reported on, and so used promiscuously throughout the brain by other processing systems involved, for example, in response. Without reportability there is no consciousness. It is as if there is some gateway to consciousness, with the gate possessing an entry barrier that can only be raised provided the incoming activity to the gate is above some basic threshold. This corresponds to a so-called binary system: one in which the output is either on or off. When it is on there is consciousness of the stimulus; when it is off there is none. Let me emphasise this result as basic to the nature of consciousness – a gateway to its production, with a barrier to be jumped in order for stimulus-driven neural activity to become conscious.

A set of results were obtained by the American scientist Benjamin Libet in the 1960s and 1970s, which have been the source of considerable controversy but more especially of further insight into the nature of the emergence of consciousness in the brain. The first of these was discovered during medical treatment of patients with otherwise intractable movement problems. Dr Libet and his medical colleagues placed small electrodes on the bare surface of the motor cortex of the brain of a patient (when the top of the patient's skull had been removed preparatory to the necessary operation). A remarkable result was found when only a very small amount of electrical current was passed through the electrode into the patient's brain, on a spot which caused them to feel as if the back of their hand had been touched. It was discovered that it took up to half a second to achieve such awareness of the touching process. In other words, consciousness is a very slow process in the brain, not occurring at the drop of the first activity entering the cortex, for example. The threshold gate, which I introduced in relation to blindsight earlier, must be some way up the processing hierarchy, and certainly not close to the entry into cortex. I even wrote a scientific paper in 1996 which was based on this, and on related work on the effects of subliminal stimuli, with the title 'Breakthrough to awareness', a very apposite description of the manner in which the neural activity underpinning consciousness suddenly jumps out of neural activity of which there is no direct conscious experience.

A further result has caused even more surprise about the nature of consciousness. A decade or so after Libet gave us his first surprise about the slowness of the emergence of consciousness, he found that it was also delayed by several hundred milliseconds in comparison to unconscious activity presaging a movement. He found this out by an experiment in which the brain activity of a subject was monitored as they prepared to make a voluntary movement of their finger, as well as the subject estimating, by looking at the hands of a specially designed clock (allowing short spaces of time to be noted from the clock hand position) when exactly they became aware of the movement itself. The brain activity measured over the motor and associated prefrontal cortical areas began to rise significantly above its pre-activity value about 200–300 milliseconds before the exact time estimated by the subject when they became conscious they were making the movement.

This result has sparked a vast range of assessments of the function of consciousness. One side concludes that it is to be expected, since the subject has an over-riding, conscious goal to move their finger at some time. This then will cause, at some specific time, enough activity to be sent to the motor cortex from some decision centre to cause the movement. The timing result just shows that decision is out of consciousness, and only the somatic features of it may arise in consciousness. The other extreme claims that consciousness has no function in active processing, but is just a helpless looker-on at the feast of neural activity in the brain. It may later, after a crucial movement has begun, send out a veto to stop the movement in its tracks.

Some have even gone so far as claiming that these and similar results imply that consciousness gets in the way of creative processes and should be suppressed as strongly as possible. That is a dangerous suggestion, especially since taking drugs or alcohol is often said to be a way of getting out of your mind (in this case read 'conscious mind' for mind). However, note that a high proportion of car accidents, for example, are now claimed to arise from those under the influence of drugs (it used to be under alcohol before laws were tightened up in various countries). This is only one example of the dangers of being out of attention/conscious control when going about your daily business in this increasingly crowded world.

In summary, consciousness breaks through to awareness by some sort of thresholded neural activity, and it arises only slowly after an input stimulus – some 200–300 or so milliseconds after a stimulus input or a decision has been made. This does not mean consciousness is too late to have any function. But a model of that function must be developed consistent with these results of Libet and his colleagues.

Search for the Self

It is often claimed that all that needs to be done to create a conscious system is to build one that is able to 'look at' itself suitably carefully. The notion of self is central to the nature of consciousness I will develop in this user's manual. So let me consider what it can be composed of.

To begin with, there is a notion of self that we each build gradually as we grow older, being composed of our attributes of various sorts. Thus you can answer 'yes' or 'no' if I ask you 'Are you impatient?' or 'Are you a shy person?'. These self-attributes gradually change as we pass along life's highways and byways, brushing shoulders with others in a way that may shake off the shyness or mellow the impatience (or possibly not, in either case). I can write down a list of many possible attributes that you could say yea or nay to, but I trust you have got my message.

Recently there have been studies to discover if there are specific sites in the brain where there exist representations of such self-attributes. In particular it has been asked if these attributes are of a similar sort to those we apply to our friends or to well-known people like celebrities such as the footballer David Beckham or the pop star Madonna. It has been discovered that in fact there are two quite different places for such memories to be stored, one for self and one for others' attributes. In other words, we look at our own peculiarities differently than we look at those of other people.

A self composed of reportable attributes can be seen by reflecting on oneself. So it is naturally called the 'reflective' self. Other aspects of that reflective self are the images of your face you see each time you look in a mirror. Those have crucially to be updated by your episodic memory from those glances in the mirror. If you lose the ability to update your episodic memory, say by loss of your hippocampus (the crucial brain site for the laying down of such memories), then you could lose the ability to update your facial image as part of your reflective self.

Exactly this happened to the subject H.M., who had a severe loss of the cortex in his temporal lobe brought about by an operation to treat his otherwise intractable epilepsy, caused, it was thought, by a lesion in his hippocampus. After his operation he was completely unable to update any episodic memory. He could meet someone and talk with them for a while very sensibly, and then meet them again a few minutes later and have no knowledge at all of ever having met them or talked with them. In H.M.'s case he had the added burden that every time he looked in a mirror, some twenty years after his operation, he said 'Who's that grey-haired old man in the mirror? That's not me – I'm black haired and look so much younger'. Clearly this is a very sad commentary on ageing, yet understandable. But in any case it is an even more tragic commentary on the nature of loss of one's sense of self as it is in real time, and how that sense is updated constantly.

Development of Mind

There are other aspects of self that have even been studied in animals, since they are components that are amenable to assessment without the use of language. An important case is the test introduced by the animal behaviourist Gordon Gallup. He drugged a chimpanzee and put a mark on its forehead. The animal had already become accustomed to using a mirror, learning to look at parts of its body – its back, for example – otherwise unobservable.

The question Gallup asked was about the response of the chimpanzee when it woke up and saw the coloured spot on its forehead when it looked at itself again in the mirror. Would it react in any way to the sudden appearance of the spot on its forehead? The answer is that it really did matter to the chimpanzee. When it looked at its face in the mirror it noticed the spot, and touched its forehead, as if to see if the spot was really on its forehead. In other words, it could recognise its own image in a mirror. This faculty is called mirror self recognition, or MSR for short. MSR has been observed in a few other animals (dolphins in particular) but not in macaque monkeys or lower down the animal scale. Infants also develop MSR, this occurring at about 2–3 years of age. It was this faculty of MSR which was sadly frozen in time in the patient H.M.

Theory of Mind

As adults we also possess powers of recognition of the nature of self in others. In particular, we can ascribe states of mind to other people. This is a very important faculty for such highly social animals. It starts to develop at about 3–4 years of age in children. A lot of studies have been performed detecting exactly when this develops. Children are asked questions about a variety of situations in which this faculty would be expected to be used. For example, a child is shown a chocolate box full of crayons, and asked what another person would expect to find if they saw this particular box for the first time. Very young children say 'crayons', but children older than about 3–4 years old correctly say 'chocolates' – since until a person has opened the box they do not know what it contains, except by its outer label.

Again, this is a form of knowledge which is tied to the nature of one's experience of the world inside one's own head, and also to the fact that other people have similar encounters and experiential knowledge.

The Nature–Nurture Divide

I have advised you so far to be careful of any mind-user's manual, even this one. But at least one – the correct one, whatever it is – is needed. A baby is born with a brain containing the most remarkable seeds of its own development, but without the detailed program worked out. As a well-known saying states: 'a child's mind can be moulded into any shape if you catch the child young enough' – when their brain is still effectively a tabula rasa – a blank sheet. It is empty of content, so that anything can be written on it – as it could on my grandson Jack's when I held him in my arms when he was two days of age. That may be a little premature, since the nature versus nurture controversy is not yet completely settled. But nature – as determined by the genes in a baby's make-up – does contribute an important amount to its future behavioural and skill levels. Some would even say about 50% of our personalities are genetically and 50% environmentally determined. If 50% of a person's personality and response capabilities can be affected by their upbringing – a very significant amount – the environment certainly cannot be left to chance in any infant's development.

From the earliest days, infants are completely at the mercy of their parents or other caregivers. They are helpless, and initially will have little control over their responses, other than using reflexes to satisfy their most primitive needs for food, drink and prevention of pain. As infants grow, their highly malleable brains suck in information from all sides by their developing senses, like a piece of blotting paper.

As infants look about at the stimuli they can see or touch, they begin to build up internal representations of the objects and sounds around them. That is why it has been recognised as important to surround infants with a reasonable number of alerting stimuli, such as mobiles of butterflies, as well as with pictures over the walls of their rooms, so they can build these early sense impressions into percepts and later concepts they can then use in developing their response and thinking powers. For example, an infant's room being full of animal pictures, and his/her parents spending time pointing to the various animal pictures and saying the animal's name would lead to the infant developing an extensive vocabulary of the animals' names.

In due course, infants begin to take more notice of things around them, and will attend to stimuli for longer and longer times. They will begin to notice special things they find of interest and will look at them, especially if they are named and their attention is reinforced by their mother or father talking about the object.

The vocabulary starts to mount, up to a hundred or so words, which they understand but cannot speak.

Growing into Adulthood

The number of brain cells was thought, until recently, to have been fixed in number after the first few years of age. However, that idea now appears to be at fault. In particular, it has been shown that London taxi drivers have an increased number of brain cells in their hippocampus. I mentioned the dramatic problems caused by the loss of hippocampus earlier in the case of H.M. Now it seems that not only should you keep all your hippocampal cells, but if you are a taxi driver you can increase their number as you grow older. This very likely happened for the taxi drivers by their constant battling with remembering their way about the multitude of streets and place names in London. Each taxi driver has to pass a test called 'The Knowledge', in which they have to tell their examiner the fastest route from one site A in London to another B. Acquiring this skill and its continued usage clearly sparked off the increased size of the hippocampus. This would involve either an increase in the number of nerve cells contained by the hippocampus, and either in addition, or in place of, an increase in the number of connections between these hippocampus cells. So their hard work really paid off. Who knows what can be achieved of increased nerve cell complexity by hard mental work!

One area of remarkably slow development in the adult is the prefrontal cortex. It is usually still maturing up to the age of 40 years or more. Such slow maturation is to be expected to be of value in building a powerful and sophisticated controller of posterior cortical activity. This controller in prefrontal cortex can begin to learn to do its control work after the posterior sites have learnt most of their representations. Such a delay of the prefrontal cortex coming online may expose teenagers to increased risks. It is in the prefrontal cortices that the internal rules of social behaviour are encoded over the years. But until they are in place, teenagers will find themselves vulnerable to riskier responses than their more mature adult colleagues in society. That may explain why young males (and increasingly young females) suffer fatalities from dangerous exploits like racing their cars on normal roads. Yet there is clear value in the flexibility of a brain system that allows them to experiment and also be moulded by their society as they grow older.

Summary on the Mind

There are various functions of mind I have explored: perceiving, thinking, remembering, imagining, feeling and unconscious processing. Beyond these assorted functions are even more specialised ones involved in the production of a sense of self. This was itself found to have various components, some of which were noted as also being possessed by other animals close to us on the evolutionary tree.

With this understanding under our belts, we are ready to venture out into the far murkier world of the variety of users' manuals that claim to help the mind reach its ultimate fruition.

CHAPTER THREE

A GUIDE TO MIND-USER'S MANUALS

There are numerous competing mind-user's manuals presently on offer. Most of these approaches to the mind contain features of the truth of the mind's nature and understanding. So I will not dismiss them but try to incorporate what we will see as essential elements.

The Common-Sense Mind-User's Manual

This is based on the answer to the question about the nature of mind expected from the proverbial man (or woman) in the street. It goes along the lines of the purpose of the mind being to think with, so you can be more efficient in your interaction with the world. Such mind power is supposed to arise from the brain. This becomes obvious if you meet people with mental disabilities due to a variety of brain injuries, so they can no longer plan or make decisions or do the things people do with their minds. The famous case of Phineas Gage shows the problem faced by anyone if the functioning of their mind is disturbed by brain damage.

Phineas Gage was the hard-working foreman of a railway gang building one of the great railway lines across the United States from east to west, opening up the North American continent to millions of pioneers. Gage was careful and methodical, attributes of great value in preventing him from injury in his profession, which was the dangerous one of blowing up outcrops in the way of the railway line he was helping build. But one time he made a bad mistake, thinking an explosive charge had failed whereas the fuse was burning slowly. As he went back to investigate what had happened, the explosive charge went off, blowing the tamping iron he used to prepare the explosive right through the frontal part of his brain. It carried parts of his brain away with it, leaving a hole through the front of his skull. Amazingly, he did not lose consciousness, but was able to be assisted onto a wagon and taken to the nearby town where he was seen by a doctor. He survived apparently intact physically, although suffered a terribly debilitating personality change. He became reckless and had to be sacked by his company. His life went from bad to worse, and he ended up touring the halls showing the hole in his skull and the tamping iron which started it all. He was divorced by his wife, and was said in the end to have been killed in a knife brawl. His tragic loss of self-control was already echoed in my comments at the end of the previous chapter about controls not yet encoded in young brains. Phineas Gage's tragedy was that he very likely had no brain capacity remaining from which to develop new self-control after the tamping iron took away that which he had already developed so effectively as he grew up.

There are many other cases which show how much we are under the control of our brains. And the whole variety of human experience seems to be controlled by one part or another of the brain. Think of the millions whose minds are crumbling away from Alzheimer's disease or who are unable to move due to Parkinson's disease, or have difficulty in relating to others due to autism. All of these effects are seen now as due to brain defects. In the common-sense view, then, the brain is *the* arbiter of a person's personality and mind. It is amazingly beautiful when it works, but literally soul-destroying as it crumbles away.

Yet this common-sense view of the mind is under threat from all sides. From religions you are exhorted not to think but to 'have faith', for which intelligence gets in the way. Moreover, religions only make sense in terms of a relation with an infinite supernatural being if some part of the mind can communicate with that being. If not, but instead the brain generates the mind solely by a set of nerve cells working subtly together but in a well-defined scientific manner, the supernatural being's fingers would find no place to manipulate the user's mind. From the viewpoint of religion, the common-sense view must give way, in some undefined manner, to let the supernatural into our brains.

From the arts it is claimed that consciousness, that highest power of each of our minds, gets in the way of creativity. A recent popular book *The User Illusion* has claimed 'Consciousness plays a far smaller role in human life than Western Culture has tended to believe. The epoch of the I is drawing to a close'. From this perspective, which is also apparently backed up by results from recent neuroscience that I mentioned in the previous chapter, the common-sense view is under strong attack.

From the clubbers are those who say 'carpe diem' – live for the day – go and expand your experience by alcohol, sex and drugs. You should explore your own mind by distorting its normal ways of perceiving. Aldous Huxley termed the use of drugs as a way to open 'The Doors of Perception'. But it can become a route to death through heroin or crack addiction, with its ability to turn normal people into drug-starved criminals, willing to steal or even kill others for a few dollars for the next fix, until they themselves are dead of an overdose or from disease from a shared needle.

As a personal example of this, some years ago I went to live for a time in a delightful apartment (lent me by a friend) just below Times Square in

New York. He warned me not to walk along the sidewalk too close to the houses. This surprised me – was there some sort of sidewalk cycling or skating near the houses? 'No,' said my friend, 'it's the drug addicts – they will pull you into an alleyway, slit your throat, and rob you'. He was right – that did happen occasionally. But it also occurred away from the alleyways. To underline the more general danger, the 'Good Humor' man (innocuously selling ice cream from his barrow) at the end of the street was knifed to death by a drug addict the day I arrived at the apartment. So I always kept my eyes open and walked well away from alleyways when I was out and about there. There are dangers on all sides in life, but drug addiction drives people to extreme measures, just to 'get out of their minds'. But why not stay in them? It is these minds that are crafted so delicately and obediently to lead to a mind able to do its owner's bidding – the most subtle and beautiful entity, I claim, in the whole universe. Why distort it?

So on many sides the common-sense view seems to be rejected, leading to dangerous and restricted views on the mind, or to its denigration, or to attempts to reduce its control. I will not give up on the common-sense view, since it contains a lot of sense (as a common-sense view usually has). But it needs a careful development, helped by better evidence, to which I will return later.

The Religious Mind-User's Manual

There are of course as many religious answers about why we have a mind as there are religions. And even in a given religion there may be different detailed answers from different sects. I will turn to this in more detail in the next chapter, but overall I will consider religion as the supposition that there is a supernatural power which controls the universe, usually identified with its creator. The major religions of the world (Islam, Hinduism, Buddhism, Judaism and Christianity) claim that there is a god somehow in control of the material world. The crucial part of our mind – our soul – is then to be considered as that part created from god or the eternal mind, and to possess some form of eternal life.

Most religions believe there to be such an immortal part to the mind – the soul. The idea of the soul goes back at least to the ancient Egyptians with their notion of Ka, as a copy of the person, developing as they themselves develop through life (and beautifully portrayed by Philip Pullman in his trilogy *His Dark Materials*). The soul was also discussed by Plato and Aristotle. As Plato wrote, 'If ... absolute ideas existed before we were born, then our souls must have existed before we were born. And if the soul existed before birth, the soul must continue to exist after death, since she has to be born again'. More generally nearly all religions share the conviction that the soul as man's essential nature is able to survive the body, since it is the essence of consciousness or awareness.

From the religious viewpoint the proper way to protect your mind is to ensure it is on good terms with god. Such is the case in all religions, with prayers and votive offerings to your god in order that you are granted eternal life by keeping in your god's good books. Your soul will then be able to return to a good body (as in the Hindu faith, by your karma) or go to heaven and have eternal sherbet or ice cream or whatever (as in Islam or Christianity). These are the essential contents of the religious mind-user's manual. But does your mind really work like that?

The only sure-fire way I know to answer such a leading question is to look at the facts, if there are any. So what is the evidence that life goes on after death, so there could be an eternal soul? To some there is strong evidence. To many, however, there is none.

In my own career I have investigated many cases of claimed 'life after death' or of transference from one life to another. The John Fletcher/Edward Ryall case is a good example. Edward Ryall wrote a book called *Second Time Round*, in which he claimed he had an earlier life as John Fletcher, who lived in Somerset at the time of Oliver Cromwell and the English Civil War. Fletcher, according to Ryall, lived a lusty life, but was caught on the side of the King and very soon thereafter killed as a traitor by the Roundheads.

Second Time Round was a good read, and I interviewed Edward Ryall for a BBC Radio 4 programme about it, finding him pleasant but firm in his view that he had lived an earlier life as Fletcher – based on all the evidence he produced in his book, not only about John Fletcher himself but also about other families in the area. Interesting, I thought, but not conclusive. Nor was the strong endorsement by Professor Stephenson, the then great authority on reincarnation.

To check out this story further, I took a trip with my wife to Western Zoyland in Somerset, where John Fletcher had been claimed to live, and visited the parish church. By good luck the vicar was there, and was able to show us the Parish registry dating back to those days. We searched in vain for the name of any Fletcher – there were none, in spite of there needing to be at least six such entries, according to the claims in his book – his marriage, baptisms of his children, funeral of one of his relatives, etc. I found nothing there at all – not a trace.

However, there was a clue in the church – a one shilling and three pence booklet (in old money – the booklet was printed many years before my visit) containing a history of the surrounding area in the time of the Civil War. It contained the names of the main families, most of whom appeared in Ryall's book. So what more natural than to suspect that somehow this booklet had crept into Ryall's keeping and he had imagined having a life in those earlier days, a far better life than he had lived in this one.

Dream on, Edward Ryall – I just cannot accept there is any evidence that he had actually lived that earlier lusty life of John Fletcher. It was all made up in his mind. The lack of the evidence in the church registry was the first bit of damning evidence. The second was the booklet in the church. The third, which negated the advocacy of the 'expert witness' Professor Stephenson, was that Stephenson had never visited the parish church to check out Ryall's story at first hand, according to the helpful vicar.

This is only one of a number of cases I investigated of claims of communion with the dead or of reincarnation. I wrote about them in my book *Science and the Supernatural* that was published in 1980, summarising the results of my attempt to bring science to bear on the supernatural – on all the supernatural phenomena on which I could lay my hands. These phenomena – dowsing, spoon bending, distant viewing, looking into the future, haunting, and so on – all had the same problem: a closer look at the evidence showed it was flawed in one way or another. So no proof that I could find stood up to solid investigation. No voices from the dead. No reincarnation. Just death. Finis.

The Philosopher's Mind-User's Manual

Philosophers have debated and argued over the mind for millennia, ever since the beginning of philosophy and even of recorded civilisation. They have totally failed to reach any consensus about the nature of the mind and soul.

There are several extremes. One claim is that there is no real awareness – we are all zombies with nothing going on in our heads other than information processing. Nobody is at home. No inner self. Which is totally contrary to my experience and, I trust, to yours.

Another extreme is that there is only mind – all is awareness and the physical world is an illusion. That also seems doubtful on the basis of how important is the brain to create the experiences of the mind. My father used to be a strong believer that all was mind. We used to argue most vehemently about this, ever since I was trained as a theoretical physicist. But when I challenged him to explain, for example, Newton's laws of motion, which provide such an accurate descriptor of so much of the material world, purely in terms of 'mind', he failed to see the point. There is a material world out there of great complexity. To replace its understanding by claiming 'All is mind' but not be able to replace the detailed explanations of many complex real phenomena is just not on. It cannot be true. Nor has any other believer that all is mind come up with any purely mental explanation of our present remarkably accurate understanding of the world around as provided by modern 'all is material' science – down to the level of the unified $SU3 \times SU2 \times U1$ gauge theory of matter, based on quarks and gluons, and its awesome extension into the ten-dimensional world of superstrings.

A further approach was suggested: mind and matter coexist in two parallel universes. However attractive that is (allowing an immortal soul as well, in the mental universe) no one has ever solved the problem of how these two universes interact. Some philosophers have even claimed that, in fact, they do not interact, so the mental universe is just an epiphenomenon – it does not have any impact on the active and dynamic material world. It is just a mirror of the physical world. So our minds are somehow just a powerless reflection of what is going on in our bodies, so making the mind superfluous: truly a user illusion!

Again, this cuts right against our inner experience – my thoughts do influence what I do next. They act as a very powerful control system for my further thoughts and the actions that then ensue. To downplay a person's mind would make that control useless. That still leaves a lot to explain in more detail about how the mind works, but we will come to that in due course.

Finally, one approach, already described as the common-sense view, is that there is only matter but with a very subtle creation by that matter, when miraculously distributed in the 'two fistfuls of porridge' of the brain, to produce mind. How that is achieved is yet beyond us, most say. Some pessimistic philosophers even claim it never will be understood. Our minds are so constructed it will always be beyond the powers given us. Again, we will come back to that in due course.

So the gamut of the philosopher's mind-user's manual is as extensive as that of the religious one. It also covers those who only wish to enjoy life (the hedonists) and those who think that existence has to be fought hard by expressing the impossibility of ever understanding it (the existentialists). In other words, there is no unique way forward from the philosophers to help guide the development of an infant's mind or continue ours on the straight and narrow; only many more different user's manuals.

The Animal's Mind-User's Manual

Since animals cannot talk, their description of their inner experience is very difficult to decipher. But if we are, as Darwin and Wallace rightly showed, descended from a common ancestor of ourselves and the apes, and that from earlier animals, then undoubtedly there are vestiges of mind in many lower animals. This is an old argument, but one difficult to deny. The continuity of genetic content and the fossil record is too strong for us to ignore the animal mind.

Arguments concerning animals' minds generate much controversy, especially about animal experiments. I will return to this much later, when we are better equipped to make progress on the arguments.

The Scientist's Mind-User's Manual

A mind-user's manual might most obviously be thought to be one involving at least some scientific explanation of what the mind is for. Science has had a number of views on the mind. They all attempt to discover how it might be created from activity in the brain.

At least one basic feature appears clear from the scientific point of view: the mind is the supreme controlling system in the brain, itself the controller of the body. Let me expand a little.

As the body needs to be properly controlled by the brain, so does the controlling brain need an overall controller to control it. There are many processes going on in the brain that are unconscious – up to about 90%, as estimated by neuroscientists (which is what has led to the often-quoted but incorrect claim that I mentioned earlier, that we only use 10% of our brains). So this majority of activity needs to be coordinated by some controlling centre. That is where consciousness and mind come in. Consciousness is the ultimate controller. It even sits on top of the system, allowing us to focus attention on specific stimuli. Attention is already a very powerful filter to cut down on all the distracters around us in our complex world.

So that is why consciousness is needed – as the supreme controller. But consciousness goes beyond attention. For attention can be focused on events in their surroundings by people who cannot even see – they have what is called 'blindsight' because they are technically blind (due to brain damage), but can guess much better than chance that something is in a particular direction in front of them. I described a case of blindsight in the previous chapter. Such subjects can be shown to be attending to unseen stimuli, even though they are not aware of the objects they can attend to.

Given that attention is not enough for awareness, there must be some extra 'oomph' that allows us to be conscious in this marvellously private way, and that can make the world vigorously spark into life inside us when we wake up in the morning. The extra 'pizzazz' that makes attention zing into awareness is something special. I suggest that it is a signal saying 'You are about to move your attention', not 'You have moved your attention' because that would be too late. It would already have happened. And if you were standing in front of a fast-moving car bearing straight down on you then it would indeed be too late for you. It is the pre-attention signal that you need to speed you to jump out of the way. What a valuable little signal that would be, wouldn't it?

That is what, I claim, consciousness is all about. It involves a crucial signal that speeds up the entrance of content into consciousness, as well as giving an ownership seal on the stimulus about to enter consciousness. Bring on your experience, it says – and it helps it along. This speed-up is happening in each one of us, with a similar mechanism. There is some partial scientific evidence that such is the basis of conscious experience, as well as more general evidence from the world's religions, and especially its mystics, as I will expand on shortly.

What an amazing and beautiful world to lead to the evolution of this delicate control mechanism with such power, but inside what looks like two handfuls of porridge! We could still be like a distant relative of ours, the flatworm *Xenoturbella*, which lives at the bottom of lakes. *Xenoturbella* is a long-distant cousin of ours, and belongs to the rather exclusive group of animals, including ourselves, that descended from the same ancestor some 500 million years ago. But poor little *Xenoturbella* has rather little in the way of the porridge-like grey matter that we have so crucially lots of in our brains. We have enough to support our wonderful conscious experience, of which we now have the beginnings of a scientific understanding.

What is more, emotions can be folded into the overall equation by infusing emotional colour into our conscious experience. How this occurs in our consciously controlled brain is still being probed, but what is known will be described later. It will lead to an explanation of emotions and feelings that should allow us to have a better appreciation of these important aspects of our experience, and lead us to value them as they, in their turn, give value to our lives.

In conclusion, all consciousness, I claim, requires this precursor signal to moving your attention, and then actually achieving the movement of attention, leading to the ability to sense whatever it is out there that you wanted to sense. The emotions come into the equation of consciousness as biasing where attention is focused – emotions allow us to ascribe rewarding or penalising values to various things in the outside world. Both are crucial to distinguish us from creatures lower down the animal evolutionary tree. Since *Xenoturbella* has a lot of overlap in its DNA with us, it does not seem to take much genetic difference to get our two fistfuls of porridge under way, and make it conscious.

Why Minds?

Indeed why? Well, I have just pointed out some reasons – to be able to act more effectively in hostile surroundings or in social contacts, or in almost any event where reasoning, thinking or use of past memories is of importance. That is what the conscious part of the mind does for you, as I noted in the previous chapter. You could go to a club to 'get out of your mind' but suppose that once inside a fire starts, and the fire alarm sounds and smoke and flames are seen. Then you need your mind to stay alive. Those completely out of it will soon be dead.

So minds are good things to have – provided your mind is not too frayed at the edges. There are lots of ways that can happen. I have already noted a variety of them. Let me explore them further to show you how much a dependable mind-user's manual is needed. At the same time, we will see there are important aspects of these other mind-user's manuals that need to be included in our own. They will allow a more balanced view of human life that may even allow us to begin to fuse religious experience with a scientific view.

CHAPTER FOUR

WRAPPED IN RELIGION

The Need for Religion

All religions provide answers to the deep questions of our existence. Is there a force or power beyond us which is helping or guiding our lives? What is the purpose of life? Is there life after death? Do we have an immortal soul? How should we best live together equably? These and many other deep questions are answered by most of the world's religions with assurance. The god-based religions answer the first question – is there a superior force controlling the whole universe? – very strongly: god is the begetter and assurance of continuation of the world in which we live. This god is all-powerful, and requires constant appeasement for the wrongs we sinful or forgetful beings constantly commit. These main world religions (Christianity, Judaism, Islam, Hinduism and Buddhism) are still powerful attractors to those needing the quick fix of ready answers about the nature of existence.

The Christian and Muslim religions both worship one god, but with different human mediators expounding his requirements: Jesus (in the New Testament) or Mohammed (in the Koran). Christians proclaim Jesus Christ as the Son of God, who with the Holy Ghost and God the Father forms a triumvirate of Gods, which Christians fuse as one (in spite of the severe criticism from Muslims about God having a son – for Muslims God is to be placed above all that family sort of thing). The Hebrew religion has the same God as the Christians but does not accept Jesus as the Messiah (or a prophet, as in Islam). The Hindu believes in a God, the Atman, who can be directly contacted from within, the holy book being the magnificent Bhagavad-Gita. All of these religions believe in the existence of some kind of immortal soul, with the Christian and Islamic faiths having the soul separated from the dying body to be released into Heaven or Hell according to the level of goodness of the person during their life on earth, and the Hindu soul being reincarnated, with an upgrade or a downgrade as to the address of the new body according to how well you did in your previous lives (as karma). The Buddhist faith believes in a less precisely defined universe, but one based on the mind as predominant, although no soul is in obvious presence in the Buddhist technology of life/death, even though reincarnation with a karma-based upgrade/downgrade system is part of the baggage taken over by Buddhism from Hinduism.

The second question that I raised at the start of the chapter – what is the purpose of life? – is based on the need to live life according to the criteria of the god or gods. The main thrust of life's purpose is thus to pass tests imposed by god so as to attain an eternal life, one lived after death in an ideal manner in 'heaven' or in a better life in this world in the case of reincarnating religions. Thus, religious people achieve a good feeling of never 'dying' but also having an increasingly better 'life' by adhering suitably strongly to their faith. For Christian and Muslim this means keeping away from a sinful life and sinful acts so that on the Day of Judgement they are judged good enough to be let into heaven. The doctrine of reincarnation through a karma-based upgrade in Hinduism and Buddhism makes a similar demand to live a 'good' life so as to get the desired upgrade.

Religions are needed by people because life can be lonely without the presence of a guardian. After becoming adult, with parents no longer in control and guiding you through life's difficulties, a god as the supreme arbiter and guide can be a source of great solace. This explains in an obvious manner one of the great strengths of religion. It also grants you eternal life (and who wants to be snuffed out at death?), as well as giving you codes of behaviour to follow when decisions may be difficult, such as the Ten Commandments of the Hebrew bible. Above all, it gives you a purpose in life as a pawn in your god's great game.

This brings us to the different sources of belief present in today's society. Believers are those who believe because (a) they were brought up in the faith and see nothing better to succour them in life's dance toward death, or (b) the famous X, Y or Z believed (possibly as the founding fathers, but in any case as really good guys), and they all lived the good life, or (c) they had direct religious experience themselves.

The first two types of faith are best called 'blind' faith, with no validity or invalidity to be attached to the faith other than residing in the blind acceptance of 'holy' examples in the sacred scriptures that have excited and sustained the faith through the ages. The truth of the religion then depends on the validity of the original sacred experiences of the founder or founders. It is to these examples we must turn, as we must for the third sort of faith, experienced at the present time by the believer (who then contributes similar evidence as the religious founders).

The Experience of Many

Worldwide, there are about 2 billion Christians, 1.2 billion Muslims, 500 million Buddhists and 750 million Hindus, as well as tens of millions believing in other similar religions (Judaism, Sikhism, Taoism, Confucianism, etc.). Including other religions (such as Jainism), religion wins over non-religion for the 9 billion people on earth, with at least 5 billion believers all-told. This predominance of the faithful is expected to continue into the future when we consider the proselytising nature of many of these religions, as well as the indoctrination of children brought up in families following the various faiths.

One especially important supportive feature that religion provides all believers is an answer to the question as to the nature of one's experience: what is the nature of the mind? The religious answer in general is that mind is part of a soul or universal mind, identified with the Mind of God or some such. This particular mind-explaining aspect of religion is a crucial component. For if the mind is purely material, then contact between god and mankind will be very difficult. Only if the laws of physics are changed by the god for a short time in the brain could such contact between our material minds and an immaterial god be made.

All religions have an assumption that knowledge of god can be obtained in one way or another through suitable devotional acts: prayer, meditation, trance, dance (as in the whirling Dervishes) and so on. But sooner or later there must be someone who can get through to god on their brain mobile. No response then no god. Response implies that god exists, and is talking to you. It may be that only special people can be qualified to get through – the Pope or the local shaman, or the Grand Mullah, or whoever. In some religions anyone who devotes themselves sufficiently to making the contact can finally get through. But someone must. Otherwise there is no evidence at all on which the faith of others could be based.

Of course, that contact with god must be infrequent enough, if mind is material, that the laws of physics are not disturbed too often. If everyone could get though all the time, the physical laws would look very elastic. Just by praying, the results of a physics experiment could be altered. Even the walls of Jericho could be rent asunder, as has been claimed. Proposals along those lines (that faith can move proverbial mountains) have been made, but have never been substantiated by any carefully controlled scientific experiment.

So god can only be contacted very infrequently, and with difficulty, and possibly only if you are suitably qualified. This makes the scientific investigation of religions very difficult. But even if we accept that it is difficult to detect the Hand of God scientifically, we should still attempt to determine of what such contact might consist. Is there really any information that is supposedly coming from the mind of god that should be taken seriously? If there were then it certainly should be in any mind-user's manual.

The Factual Basis of Religion

What are the facts about religions? As I noted earlier, there is an enormous amount that is hearsay. That includes all the sacred scriptures: the Bible, the Koran, the Torah, the Bhagavad-Gita, the Sayings of Buddha, and much more. Even if we could take these writings verbatim, it would not help us to recreate the experiences of general believers who claim to have directly contacted their god in that faith.

More generally, we could look for some commonality across the various religions as an indication of some special process of communication claimed to be with god, or of evidence of the existence of a person's soul. It is the experiences of religious mystics across religions that are most relevant here, since they have struggled and disciplined themselves to achieve this clear view of their souls and thence their communication with their god.

It is in this deep human experience reported by mystics that many people feel that proof has been provided that the soul exists, and through it communication with god achieved. That experience cannot be gainsaid. It comes from numerous accounts of religious experiences of saints and mystics over the past three millennia. These accounts are across many religions – certainly for the major religions of Buddhism, Hinduism, Christianity, Judaism and Islam.

An amazing result then emerges. Across this enormous disparity of beliefs and cultures, and across very different geographic locations on earth, there is described a state of great similarity and claimed to be of great value to the person having the experience. It is attainable only by considerable effort, according to past and most present practitioners. I want to underline that the accounts are so very similar. They describe a state which I will call 'pure consciousness' (one discussed considerably in recent years in the more general context of Eastern practices). This state is seemingly at the basis of mystical religious experiences. It gave (and gives) people a sense of the presence of their god if they were so brought up. For those with no faith in god it is still an enormously significant experience. And those who could not attain it have looked up to those who claimed they could. Indeed, in many cases those who reached the ultimate depths of their inner world through attaining the state of pure consciousness have become the saints or gurus of the world at large.

The remarkable feature of pure consciousness is that it corresponds to the complete absence of any content of consciousness. But the subject is still conscious. That is why the state is sometimes termed 'consciousness attending to itself'. It could also be termed pure attention. In the writings of mystics across all the world's religions, and over the centuries, it is equated in many cases as 'the place where god dwells', although its nature is very strongly suggested to be impossible to describe.

Let me give some examples from the writings of well-known mystics. In Christianity, the great mystic St Teresa of Avila (who has been carefully and reverentially studied by the Archbishop of Canterbury, the premier Anglican in the UK) wrote:

> ... this secret union takes place in the deepest centres of the soul, which must be where God himself dwells, and I do not think there is any need of a door by which to enter it ... This instantaneous communication of God to the soul is so great a secret and so sublime a favour, and such delight is felt by the soul, that I do not know with what to compare it, beyond saying that the Lord is pleased to manifest to the soul at that moment the glory that is in Heaven, in a more sublime manner than is possible through any vision or spiritual consolation.

Another great Christian mystic, John of the Cross, stated about the union of the soul with God:

> In thus allowing God to work in it, the soul ... is at once illumined and transformed in God ...

Brother Lawrence, another Christian mystic, writes yet again of this mystical union:

> When I apply myself to prayer, I feel all my spirit and all my soul lift itself up and without any care or effort of mine, and it continues as it were suspended and firmly fixed in God, as in its centre and place of rest.

Meister Eckhart, the famed thirteenth-century Christian mystic, wrote:

> If a person wanted to withdraw into himself with all his powers, internal and external, then he will find himself in a state in which there are no images and no desires in him, and he will therefore stand without any activity, internal or external.

He further wrote, explaining the conversion experience of St Paul on the road to Damascus:

> The more completely you are able to draw in your own powers to a unity and forget all those things and their images you have absorbed, and the

further you get from creatures and their images, the nearer you are to this and to receive it. If only you could suddenly be unaware of all things, then you could pass into oblivion of your own body, as St Paul supposedly did.

Similar forms of union with god through meditation on the soul are also to be seen in other religions, such as from Abhinavagupta in Hindu literature:

Once consciousness has been successfully doubled back on itself, this power begins to operate and leads [the aspirant] towards the Ultimate [and] who is able to unite with the Goddess.

In the Sufi Muslim tradition, Muhyiddin Ibn 'Arabi similarly writes, in his *Wisdom of the Prophets*:

Supreme Union is the mutual interpenetration of Divinity and man.

Yet through all of these writings there is the theme of 'annihilation' or 'stillness' as a crucial part of this union with god, as it is a feature in pure consciousness. To quote from Muhyiddin Ibn 'Arabi, in this state:

God is mysteriously present in man and man is obliterated by God.

In *The Sufi Path of Love: The Spiritual Teachings of Rumi*, Rumi writes:

Union with God is self-annihilation ...

This theme of absence of awareness in the presence of God is very strong in the writings of numerous Christian mystics, as seen in the earlier quotations. Angela of Foligno wrote, for example:

When I am in that darkness I do not remember anything about anything human, or the God-man, or anything which has form. Nevertheless I see all and I see nothing. As what I have spoken of withdraws and stays with me, I see the God-man.

Similarly, John of the Cross wrote:

wherein the soul becomes naught else than an altar whereon God is adored in praise and love and God alone is on it.

In Orthodox Christianity, the Abbot Vasilius recounted his experience:

The soul can attain to the secrecy which is in God, where the mystery of unity beyond understanding and speech is celebrated, and only when it has gone not only beyond the categories of vice and ignorance ...

Another Christian mystic, John Climacus, stated:

Come to union with the most blessed stillness and I will teach you the workings and the behaviour of the spiritual powers.

Consider further Marguerite Porete, a fourteenth-century mystic. She wrote a book entitled 'The mirror of simple annihilated souls and those who only remain in will and desire of love'. This book was condemned by the French Inquisition as being heretical. Porete was asked to recant her views, but refused to do so, so she was condemned to death. She was subsequently burned at the stake on 1 June 1310. She was undoubtedly of the highest religious piety. However, her writing would have disturbed the religious authorities, in spite of coming from the depth of true experience. Consider one of her writings:

For God is none other than the One of whom one can understand nothing perfectly.

This is completely in unison with the writings of other religious mystics who had accessed the centre of their being when in prayer and meditation. She not only indicated that God was at the centre of her experience, but that to achieve that state she had to repress all her knowledge and sensation. She writes yet further:

Thus it is better that the Soul be in the sweet country of understanding nothing.

She would seem, yet again, to be recounting her experience of pure consciousness, as did the other mystics. Why burn her at the stake? I can only assume that the rawness of her reports could not be stomached, devoid as they were of the usual pictures of Jesus and Mary, etc., that were required of her, if she claimed to be so close to the godhead. She was dangerous – suppose others followed her lead? Off to the stake with her! And indeed, she wrote what could be regarded as even more dangerous material, close to leading into the death of God, when she said, surely again from her own raw experience of pure consciousness:

God is incomprehensible except to himself.

Poor Marguerite. She was true to her experience, so she had to die for it, by a hideous death.

We come back to Teresa of Avila for a conclusion, from what is only a small fraction of the relevant writings from the mystics of the past two millennia:

... in this temple of God, in this Mansion of His, he and the Soul alone

have fruition of each other in the deepest silence ... The faculties, I think,
are not lost here, it is merely that they do not work but seem dazed.

This justifies the claims that the mystics of the world's religions were all
experiencing what they termed a 'union with God' at the centre of their
soul, on entering into the state of pure consciousness. That is the state of
so-called 'annihilation', or 'stillness' as it is termed in the Eastern
traditions of Hindu or Buddhist, and called Samadhi or Nirvana. Many
Buddhist (and Taoist) texts substantiate this view that this highest state of
consciousness – interpreted by some as experience of their soul and
hence of God – is consciousness absent of all ideas, feelings and
sensations. It appears to be universally experienced. It is the soul at work.

We must take care how to move on from our realisation of the existence
of this unique state of consciousness, for there are several questions it
raises. First, does this unique content-less consciousness state really
exist? It sounds so remarkable that if it does then it should be better
known. Second, if it does exist, does the soul actually exist? Third, is this
state one of such great value to attain that I should recommend it to you
all as part of this manual?

As to existence, as noted above, there is considerable experience of
the state of pure consciousness in Buddhism and Taoism. Moreover,
scientific tests indicate that in this state, unique physiological states of
the body arise, so that those undergoing it have extremely reduced heart
rate and other physiological parameters. The state can also be clearly
differentiated from any of the stages of sleep, for example. Furthermore, a
unique combination of brain regions is observed to be involved in
achieving and keeping the subject in the state. These results lend
credence to the objective existence of the state as a distinct experiential
one for a subject.

As to the second question, the implied existence of the soul, the pure
consciousness state can be called one of many things, including 'soul'.
However, it would be incorrect to claim it possesses the crucial property
of soul, that of persistence after death. I made some negative comments on
this claim in the previous chapter, relating to the absence of any evidence
for the passing of information from those who have died to those of us
now alive. On the basis of this I would propose that we should treat the
state of pure consciousness as one created by rerouting brain control
systems so as to cut off all content. I will discuss in Part III how the
attention control system of the brain might achieve that drastic
reconnection.

Finally, is pure consciousness worth it? To those who have achieved it:
yes. But then they may be driven by religious or other motives arising

from needs not present in many of us. In particular one would need to be driven to seclude oneself for years of meditation to attain the state. There would be many years of experience in the world lost by such meditation. Which great creators – scientists, artists, writers – have emerged in the past from such practice? Very few, if any, have been produced, as far as I know – as might be expected, since if all one's time must be spent meditating to annihilate one's senses there would be little time left to develop creative skills, and especially scientific skills.

At the same time, there is a more general point to be made. The great Zen Buddhist monk Hui-neng, who lived from 637 to 713 AD, argued strongly against trying to attain pure consciousness. He said that a man with an empty consciousness was no better than a 'block of wood or a lump of stone'. Hui-neng's teaching was that instead of trying to purify or empty the mind, one must simply let go of the mind, so that the thoughts and impressions are not interfered with.

So an extreme diet of meditation, leading to pure consciousness, is not necessarily the right way. It may lead to an altered state of consciousness, but not necessarily one that can be of use for effective interaction in the world. You would be a dropout if you followed that route.

CHAPTER FIVE

DRUGGED TO DEATH

The Trip to Elsewhere

In the last century the drug scene erupted onto society with a vengeance. Much before then there were avid recreational users of drugs, as attested by the writer de Quincey's autobiography *Confessions of an Opium Eater*, and somewhat later the book by Aldous Huxley, *The Doors of Perception*. It was claimed by Huxley that a new universe inside our heads could be penetrated by taking various mind-expanding drugs. All sorts of reports about distortions in perception began to be recounted by those who had taken one or other (or all) of the ever-increasing list of these so-called recreational drugs.

But it was not until Timothy Leary came on the scene in the USA that the range of drugs was expanded enormously by the discovery of Native Americans' extensive use and knowledge of a whole range of psychoactive substances. Leary was undoubtedly the catalyst of the modern drug scene. He first took the natural hallucinogen psilocybin in 1950 on a trip to Mexico, and then moved on to LSD in 1962, when he had what he said was 'the most shattering experience of my life'. He became a strong advocate of everyone taking LSD, encouraging people to 'turn on, tune in, drop out'. He was fired a little later from a prestigious position at Harvard University for his anti-establishment drug position, but continued taking LSD and many other drugs, helping spread the word about the benefits of drugs especially by getting a variety of well-known Beat poets enthusiastic about them. He fired up the Beat poets Allen Ginsberg, Jack Kerouac, William Burroughs and Abbie Hoffmann to mind expansion of this sort, and to write many verses about this new wonder-world.

The later years of Timothy Leary were not such an easy trip – he was convicted of possession of marijuana in the USA in 1965, and sentenced to the stiff prison sentence of 30 years, but released on appeal. He was soon re-arrested and imprisoned for 10 years this time, but escaped from prison and fled to Algeria, and then Switzerland. He was finally tracked down by drug agents in Afghanistan, and returned to prison for 3 years. He was then paroled in 1976, it is said due to his collaboration with US drug authorities. He then turned to space science and virtual reality before he died in 1997. So ended the creator of the modern drug scene. His accomplishment was to persuade millions of people to 'blow their minds', for some only once in a lifetime, for others every week, if not every day in extreme cases.

Timothy Leary and Aldous Huxley claimed that there is a new world inside our heads, to be visited by a good trip on LSD or by the increasing numbers of commercially synthesised hallucinogens that have since become available. The main mantra of their mind-user's manual of 'turn on, tune in, drop out' is OK except for the last part. Who wants to drop out altogether? That happens to those who get really hooked on drugs. They can end up having their personalities so destroyed by drugs that they no longer function properly in their own social network. They are in danger of disappearing into drug squalor, even moving towards death from overdose or disease.

The Club Drug Scene

This use of drugs to extend experience continues unabated today. Drugs play a central part in the club scene today across the world. Typical UK clubbers follow a well-studied developmental pattern. They start with alcohol at the age of 14, going on to cannabis, and then typically leading to LSD and speed. By then they are regular clubbers, moving to Ecstasy as the drug of choice, though some take ketamine and/or liquid ecstasy. Most recently cocaine has become an important mover, with people from many walks of life using it to speed their brains to ever greater excitement. Even squirrels have been taking it after digging up drug stashes in back gardens in Brixton, South London, for example. 'Squirrel cokekins', as they are called, are to be seen staggering around after imbibing such a stash. In humans, almost a third of 16- to 24-year-olds have admitted to taking drugs. Young minds are being reconnected in a clubbers' paradise by a big E or ketamine, or by getting hooked on coke or crack. The acknowledged loss of control when under drugs, and possible permanent brain damage, are the crucial issues here.

Consider ketamine, for example. As a recent report on drug use in the US states ('Patterns of club drug use in the US, 2004' by Dr J. C. Maxwell, Center for Excellence in Drug Epidemiology, University of Texas, Austin, Texas):

Ketamine users try to 'fall into' a so-called K-Hole, described as involving physical immobilization and social detachment lasting for up to an hour.

The experiences are characterized by distortions of space – a small room looking the size of a football field – and an indistinct awareness of time, with a few minutes seeming like an hour. The K-Hole ends rather quickly, but can be renewed rapidly by another dose of ketamine.

So it is not getting lost in a black hole but in a much more accessible K-Hole that gives people a drastically new experience of the world they inhabit. This is the buzz for ketamine – but it can lead to overdose or unexpected reactions, as reported by entries to hospital emergency departments. Most users of ketamine in the USA also were taking heroin, so it may be difficult to disentangle the long-range effects of one drug from the other.

This story about drugs appears to be no different than the message on meditation. It is part of Leary's mantra to 'turn on, tune in, drop out'. Dropping out certainly will cancel the pain of life – solution arrived at! – as achieved by meditation (which takes considerably longer). But the waters of forgetfulness may arrive sooner than they can know – life is short enough as it is. There is a strong need to help young people develop so that they need not flee the real world by wiping their minds free of it. Even the need to explore new spaces has to be treated with care, since besides the excessive indulgence I already mentioned that there are also permanent neurological changes now being detected in the brain. There are increasing numbers of parents grieving over the loss of their child to one or other of these mind-destroying drugs. Related to this is the apparent increase in incidence in schizophrenia among young cannabis users in the UK, especially among those who are seen as vulnerable.

Drugs and Reward

The relation between drugs and the 'quick route to reward' has been investigated by medical and neuroscientific researchers considerably over the past few years, and the way in which the 'quick reward' is obtained has become increasingly clear. One important route by which reward is signalled in the brain is by a chemical called dopamine. This is used by the brain as a signal or 'tag' of a reward, such as by food or sex. Dopamine release causes the nerve cells in the relevant brain area to fire more strongly, so signalling that something is worth attending to. It also causes learning of the reward values of cues, such as needles, leading to a response to the drug-taker's paraphernalia as well as to increased dependency on such drugs.

The sight of food in a hungry animal brings a rush of dopamine to the prefrontal part of the brain, and especially to the surfaces of the cerebral cortices. These are in two hemispheres, and they form a cover to the nerve cells in the brain stem and mid-brain, sites of automatic control of bodily responses. It is in these cerebral cortices that so much of relevance to the mind occurs and is stored as memory. In particular, it is there, and in adjacent so-called 'limbic' areas next to the cortices (*limbus* = edge or ring), that the memories of past rewarded stimuli are stored.

These 'reward memory regions' are observed activated in animals that have become addicted to drugs such as heroin, when they are exposed to environments in which they have been given heroin earlier. These brain regions appear to be already primed for the acceptance of the drugs, so act as a quick 'turn on' when the drug is injected, without any hard work being needed to attain the reward. It is as if the drug goes directly to the reward centres in the brain. No hard work: just 'turn on, tune in, drop out', as Timothy Leary advocated.

There are numerous other drugs on the scene, many of which cause problems of addiction and of permanent alterations to brain circuits for reward and personality. Various chemical neuro-modulators in the brain, such as serotonin, are found crucially involved. Increased understanding of how these drugs work and how addiction sets in, is occurring through recent neuroscientific advances. But these advances have not changed the message that drugs are dangerous to human use.

Conclusions

The drug scene is clearly an uncertain one for keeping one's mind clear and under your own control. Youngsters will still experiment for a number of different reasons: sheer curiosity, social pressure, boredom, and so on. However, account should be taken by them and their parents of the developing scientific understanding of addiction and its deleterious effects on personality and self-control. Since some people are genetically predisposed to a bad trip from something as lowly as cannabis, even turning into schizophrenic-like states of mind by its use, then they should take care if they can.

CHAPTER SIX

ADRIFT IN THE ASYLUM

Responsible Jack?

Jack is now a year old. He is already able to move around almost freely inside a room. He shuffles along on one leg, the other bent under him to give him balance. He can move around all over the floors of certain rooms. To safeguard the wine bottles and various collections of tapes, discs and DVDs, as well as things stored away in cupboards he can now get into, his mother and father have taught him the meaning of the word 'no'. It means 'Do not go any further in the action you are now starting to take', such as taking a disc from the collection, or putting his hand into a pile of things inside a cupboard.

So Jack is learning to hold back from performing acts not allowed by his parents. He even stops doing those things when I or his grandmother say 'no' sternly to him. It may be the tone of voice that alarms him, but whatever it is, he has learnt to obey in these situations. In other words, he is on his way to having responsibility over his actions. Only when it is clear that he will not take these prohibited steps even if no one is looking at him will his full sense of responsibility correctly be said to have begun.

There are those in society who cannot control their actions, however hard they may be required to try. It is those I consider now. They bring us to the hard question of the nature of free will and how to instil a sense of responsibility and control over one's own actions. I will start by looking at those whose minds have broken down and who thereby cannot be seen as the same people they were when they were taught the word 'no' as an infant.

Cast Adrift from Sanity

Sadly, there are many who lose their minds permanently. About 5% of members of all societies across the world are classified as mentally ill. In the UK this amounts to about a quarter of a million people; in the USA the much greater figure of over 2 million. Across the whole world this comes out as the staggering total of about half a billion people. How is it possible that so many have problems with their minds? How is it that they or their friends cannot prevent their descent into mental hell? More especially, is it possible to guard against it? What can be done to prevent a mental breakdown? Is there a strict mental or physical regimen that could assure mental health throughout a person's life?

There are many varieties of mental ill health: schizophrenia, Alzheimer's disease, autism, dementia, depersonalisation, depression, Parkinson's disease, Huntington's chorea, and many more. Some of them are now being recognised as having a strong genetic component, such as autism and schizophrenia. Others are thought to have a chemical basis, such as Parkinson's disease and Huntington's chorea, one arising from too little and the other from too much dopamine in the brain, but again possibly having a genetic component for predisposition.

Depression is more complex, and although it can be treated by suitable drugs (and more recently by deep electrode stimulation directly into the brain in intractable cases), the result may be explicable in terms of lowering levels of alertness by the treatment rather than getting at any deep-seated cause. In other words, treatments can end up turning people into vegetables. Their minds are damped down so as to only just be turning over, causing no problem to any one – especially since the subject has become no one.

The problems of the mentally ill were dealt with in years past by some more barbaric ways of treatment. Parts of their brain were cut out, for example, leaving them permanently disadvantaged. In particular, frontal lobotomy was very popular for several decades, before it was realised that it was producing even more severe mental problems, with people having to be institutionalised for the rest of their lives.

One (apparently true) story indicates the problems being faced when large parts of the frontal area of the brain were cut away willy-nilly. A woman patient was observed as being excessively anxious throughout her life. She was very house-proud, and was sometimes found cleaning not only the outside walls of her house but even its roof. As she said, she just couldn't help herself over it. To try to give her back some form of control over her life, it was decided to operate on the patient by cutting out a lot of her frontal lobes. That was done. She recovered and went back home. It was then reported that she was still cleaning the walls and roof of her house, as before. But now she sang while she performed these cleansing acts on her house. So she was still out of control. But she seemed happier with it.

Since those days of cutting out people's brains because they cannot cope, there has been considerable reduction in such savage surgical acts. Parts of the memory circuitry may still be removed, as in the patient H.M.

I mentioned earlier, but only when all other methods have been attempted to reduce the severity of the almost completely disabling epileptic fits to which such patients may be subject. In addition is the increasing use of deep electrode brain stimulation to help alleviate such problems as depression as understanding of the brain increases. This is not an irreversible process – the stimulation can be turned off – so does not lead to turning people into vegetables for the rest of their lives. A great advance indeed.

Mental Health in Society

It does not seem easy to prescribe a way of life that will keep any one of us in good mental nick for all our life, especially if you have a genetic predisposition to schizophrenia or Parkinson's, although some things might be able to be done to reduce the danger. An important aspect is one's genetic constitution. That can be determined from family histories. If it were not good – a number of mental breakdowns in one or other branch of the family – then the need for a more careful watch of a person's development would be advocated. Possible mood swings and behavioural problems would need to be investigated carefully and possible ways of reducing stress or helping with emotional problems would be needed from trained advisers. Without such careful monitoring there lies danger. If drug treatment is needed for mental problems, especially if a person became violent, then problems could arise in any society where they may still be allowed to move freely.

This leads to one of the deep problems of drug treatment of mental ill health: how to get patients to take their drugs if they are made to feel so rotten when taking them. If patients are not properly supervised they may flush their drugs down the toilet and go without any drug treatment at all. But this is compounded by the thrust of the authorities to send the mentally ill into the community if possible. The closure of the Victorian-style mental asylums in the UK – the madhouses of old – has reduced the number of live-in mental patients from 90,000 to 30,000. It has helped many of those now back in the community to lead a more normal life. However, the savings made by closing the madhouses of old were not fully transferred to proper community health care for those who appeared able to care for themselves, so could be released into the community. Without proper care of those released – especially health carers to ensure they take their medication appropriately – society in general is at risk from dangerous acts by the psychiatrically ill in their midst.

If the proper care is not there, then tragedies will happen. For example, on Thursday, 2 September 2004 a killing was committed in Richmond Park, an idyllic and extensive green space in southwest London. I described what might be going through the patient's mind at the beginning of Chapter 2: a 50-year-old man was out riding his bicycle when he was stabbed repeatedly by an assailant who was hiding by an oak tree. The killer was a 41-year-old man released a little while before from a hospital in Tooting, south London. He had a history of psychiatric illness and extreme violence. The victim was just in the wrong place at the wrong time. And the killer was not properly cared for in the community by qualified health assistants.

Such dangers are not new and it has been claimed that 40 or so innocent people have so far been killed by those who are out of control due to lack of proper handling of their mental illness. In London alone there were seven innocent victims of random killings in the 18 months up to the end of 2004.

Psychiatry to the Rescue?

Can the professional psychiatrist help? In diagnosis of mental ill health, I would suggest that they do a good job. Batteries of tests have been developed over the decades to tease out the problems – cognitive, emotional, anxieties felt, and so on of patients who have broken down and can no longer function autonomously in society without further help from outside.

The psychiatrist is equivalent to the expert garage mechanic brought in when your car goes wrong. Such an expert has diagnostic tools that they bring in and use to discern what is wrong with your car. And they can be highly efficient, especially if they have had much experience over the years of cars of similar make to your own car. On these grounds, then, the psychiatrist can do a good job.

A garage mechanic is usually effective in curing the fault in your car. Sometimes that may be painful on your pocket, but the car will work again. In a number of cases a psychiatrist can work a similar miracle. Prozac or other drugs may be prescribed and in a short time the depression or the propensity for violent acts is removed.

However, in many cases there is no simple drug prescription which succeeds, but the patient is still allowed to move freely back in society. As I have pointed out above some cases are allowed back into society who are either not being properly medicated or supervised over taking the drugs.

Mental Breakdown and Responsibility

One feature of great importance in living in society is that of taking responsibility for our own actions. All infants must realise such responsibility as soon as they become autonomous. Infants already begin to do so at the age of about one year. They can begin to learn the meaning of the word 'no' applied to certain of their actions. It is this process that is important at that early stage. Rewards are also happily accepted and are necessary as a crucial way to build up a feeling of self-worth in a child. However, when they get older people can still lose their mental equilibrium even if they have been properly brought up, for some of the reasons I have mentioned earlier: subtle genetic defects, difficult environments, brain damage, ingestion of banned substances, or a mixture of several of these factors.

I pointed out earlier how some such people are allowed to move relatively freely in society, although they are in fact a danger to others without a careful routine of treatment by suitable medication. But are these people responsible for their actions? Or are they so out of control that it may be that some form of responsibility for the heinous actions such as murder they can commit should fall on those qualified to act as their carers but who do not do so?

This is a very difficult area to investigate. Some years ago I began to research possible patterns of brain damage among criminals jailed for very dangerous crimes, involving bodily harm to others. I was advised by medical experts that there was a higher incidence of abnormal brain patterns (as seen by EEG) in prisoners than in the population at large. In particular, there were abnormally many brains with near-epileptic discharges. Could this be a signal of underlying brain damage, thereby indicating the reduced responsibility of the criminal put away for many years?

Similar brain abnormalities must also be present in those in society causing them to kill their fellow man or woman, as in the case in Richmond Park or other cases. If a suitable level of medication prevents such murderous activity then there must be something wrong with the normal chemistry of their brains. Criminals put away for crimes such as grievous bodily harm and other acts of violence could instead have more specific brain damage problems, where some brain areas had become damaged by a head injury, possibly some years before.

A case in point was one prisoner who had violently assaulted his mother, breaking her nose in the process. He told me that he had been standing talking to her when 'A red curtain came down and when it lifted I found my mother lying bleeding at my feet'. He had committed robbery with violence just previously, and was sentenced for that to some years in prison. While there he was given a brain scan and found to have a damaged area caused when he was considerably younger, due to a blow to the head. That blow could have been the cause of his violent propensity. The damaged brain tissue was removed, and after a number of appeals he was released.

I raised this and similar cases with a US High Court Judge. His answer was that these cases were indeed the thin end of the wedge on the problem of human free will. If the brain is so powerful a determiner of behaviour, does not the final responsibility for behaviour reside there? And if so, what has happened to the responsibility of anyone for their acts? They can always say, 'It was my brain that led me on to commit that act' – whatever the act is. So free will is therefore a complete illusion. Not prison but brain surgery would seem to be the correct way forward in these cases.

It is certainly not always as simple as that in cases of robbery with violence or many other offences warranting a prison sentence. For many involved in such activity, they exist in what may be called a criminal sub-culture, in which criminality is the norm. Such a way of life will most likely be supported by vast areas of a person's brain, and only by removal of an enormous amount of brain would there be a discernible change. Reprogramming such people is clearly very difficult (although it appears essential to achieve a change of the criminal behaviour).

I cannot continue this discussion at this point, since I have not presented to you all the necessary facts of the case about the mind. The nature of free will and of human responsibility depend very much on what the mind really is: purely an epiphenomenon (hovering uselessly above our heads, as some would claim), or an all-controlling system (coordinating the complex set of activities of the brain to make it as efficient as possible), or something in between (at some times able to take charge, at others being rather incapable of guiding a human in the most appropriate way for society at large). As you might expect, I will go for the last version, but have some work to do before I can convince you how it might work in a manner properly based on science. So we will move to that in the next part of the book, when I get down to the brass tacks of the mind and brain.

CHAPTER SEVEN

FOOLED BY FEELINGS

The Emotional Bath

Emotion infuses our very being. Without it our lives would be cold and meaningless. Imagine yourself with all the feelings you have in response to lovely music, good food and drink, a charming companion, all suddenly removed from you. Your world would be so grey and uninteresting that you would not know how to deal with it.

Emotions are roused when goals that are being attempted are achieved (leading to elation, happiness, joy) or prevented (frustration, anger). They can involve unconscious bodily responses (increased heart rate or sweaty palms of the hands) and the resulting conscious experience related to these physical components. Very strong and sometimes inappropriate emotions can also be caused by brain damage due to tumour.

Consider the butcher who, ferociously and without any warning, suddenly attacked his wife and daughter with the tools of his trade. Luckily, his family were able to protect themselves until the police arrived to subdue him. His brain was investigated and he was found to have a tumour on his amygdala (the almond-shaped lump of grey matter at the base of the brain, crucially involved in emotional values of stimuli). A successful operation for removal of this tumour enabled him to soon re-emerge as the loving father he previously had been before its emergence.

We see therefore that emotions have a strong basis in brain activity. They also play an important role in interrupting ongoing brain activity. In humans, emotions have a number of ways in which they can bring about control, such as interrupting ongoing brain activity or causing that activity to deteriorate. Emotions may also pre-empt cognitive mechanisms so as to lead to single-mindedness and irrational actions, as in the case of the butcher I just mentioned. This precedence of emotions is achieved over attention and planning, and is connected to the most emotionally salient concerns (involved with trying to achieve important goals and the possible consequences) a person may have. Macbeth's fascination with the imagined dagger – 'Is this a dagger which I see before me, the handle toward my hand? Come, let me clutch thee' – just before murdering

Duncan is an example of the inner working of concerns against each other before his first desperate act on his road of no return.

In the brain emotions are controlled by the so-called limbic system, where the Latin word *limbus* means 'ring', as I mentioned earlier. The limbic system forms a ring round the edge of the cortex of each hemisphere. I mention the limbic system because it is composed of clumps of neurons – called nuclei – which are also observable in many animals down to reptiles and lizards, or even below. So emotions have played a crucial role in animal survival over the aeons. The more primitive the brain of the animal, the more primitive the sorts of emotions and the fewer the ways in which emotions can help the animal survive better in its niche.

From their archaic beginnings so low down the evolutionary tree, it is expected that emotions are very important in effective survival. The primary emotions of anger, sadness, joy and so on all play a very important part in spurring us on to achieve greatness. Anger can be aroused when a goal is prevented from being achieved due to unclear or unacceptable causes. The anger in a person drives them to strive even more against the odds to achieve their just deserts. Joy enables them to function more effectively – to think more clearly and plan more effectively, and with greater energy. Sadness is used to withdraw a person from a competitive world so as to try to accept what was previously unacceptable to them, such as the loss of a loved one.

The self-conscious emotions are more important in society. Embarrassment, guilt, shyness, pride are all important for complex social interactions. They are used by humans, as the most social animal ever, to enable internalisation of the messages from others, and to signal to others acts of contrition for incorrect acts or of a wished-for position in the pecking order. Some think that the human brain developed so far beyond that of other animals to help make these social interactions more effective.

Out of Control

If the brain controls the emotions, it can also cause the emotions to speed out of control, as many attested cases have shown for humans in the past. This can especially happen if there is damage to certain parts of the limbic system mentioned earlier as being the site for the creation of emotions. 'Blind rage' is a well-known epithet. It occurs, for example in cases of road rage, where a suspected slight by another driver leads the slighted driver to pursue and sometimes even kill the other driver. Recently, a car driver ran down a pedestrian he suspected had shouted that the driver was gay, although the pedestrian had just shouted 'not to drive that way' (since the driver was speeding in a built-up area).

Activation of certain underlying brain structures causes emotional states. The detailed nature of this control has been probed by electrical brain stimulation of humans and animals. A dramatic demonstration of this control was achieved by the neurosurgeon José Delgado in the late 1960s. He placed an electrode, controlled by a radio transmitter, in the aggression centre of the brain of a bull. After the bull's recovery from the operation, he and the bull met in a bullfighting arena. As the animal charged at him in the arena, he stood his ground and calmly clicked on the current in the transmitter. The bull stopped dead in its tracks, with no more aggression in its mind – a beautiful demonstration of the control nature of the brain, and of how electric current can set it off to cause extreme acts of aggression or stop these acts completely.

The Interaction of Emotions and Cognition

If the emotions can cause such extreme changes in response and planning, they must be able to modify cognitive process – thinking and planning – in a very effective way. How could this occur? To answer this important question, many experiments have been done to see what happens if emotions take over completely or if instead subjects concentrate hard to prevent that take-over.

One experiment was very clear about the mechanisms involved. Male subjects were asked to look at pornographic videos as they lay in the bore of an fMRI scanning magnet, allowing experimenters to detect activity going on in separate parts of their brains. The subjects were asked to watch the videos and either (a) enjoy them or (b) not get emotionally excited at all. In the first condition their limbic system (remember that is the region of the brain involved with emotions, including the amygdala) was all lit up. But the region involved with cognition (the so-called dorsal or higher part of the cortex near the top of the head towards the front) was subdued in activity. On the other hand, in the second condition, when they were not supposed to take notice of the erotic happenings in the video, their limbic region was subdued by their dorsal regions, which became far more active.

In other words, there are regions in the brain (the limbic regions) that are involved with processing emotionally strong material, while cognition goes on upstairs in the dorsal parts of the cerebral hemispheres; these two regions involve mutual inhibition. This explains why emotions can sometimes take over cognition in the mind. On the other hand, cognition can subdue emotion if thinking and planning are strongly motivated. These are well-known features: 'ice-cold intellect' corresponds to cognitive processing that excludes feeling, while 'blind emotions' are just the reverse.

Lessons for the Mind-User's Manual

Emotions must be present and developed in a person to be effective in their life. But they cannot be allowed to get out of hand. Especially there must be careful guidance of infants through the 'terrible twos' when they begin to pit their will against those of their parents. To allow them too much latitude is dangerous, since they will not then develop an internal self-control system to prevent their emotions from taking control and untold havoc then ensuing. However, for their parents (or carers) to be too harsh on the infant could also damage them for the rest of their life. This requires a careful balance between the growth of the infant's own emotional feelings and the need to guide the infant to respond to the needs of those around him or her.

These features are only very general ones arrived at from general features of emotional development. However, they are made more precise by the results of brain imaging on adults, which show the strong battle between feeling and thinking. Assuming an infant has no problem with the wires in the brain that carry the competing signals between the two sides in this war, then the balance of power between the two competing forces must be developed so as to end up finely balanced by the time the infant becomes an adult.

CHAPTER EIGHT

THE MIND-USER'S MANUAL PREREQUISITES

The Checklist

I have now surveyed an important set of features of the mind and of some other mind-users' manuals, and pointed out that none of them will really do except the one based on science. The bottom line in all of these other manuals is their lack of proper scientific evidence for the claims made in them. This is in spite of their containing important messages about the nature of the world, such as the experience of pure consciousness or stillness. It is an amazingly universal feature of human experience, but the rest of the special pleading of these manuals is unproven.

This leads us to the serious problem of moving forward using the latest results from science to build a proper mind-user's manual as we go. What must the checklist contain, so that as we tick off the various items we progress towards a user's manual that will properly be based on the actual machine inside the human brain?

Item 1. Based on Science

I have emphasised this criterion often so far. It means that we take all of the scientific knowledge about the brain as part of the overall knowledge base for our user's manual. Important components of this knowledge are results from non-invasive brain imaging as well as understanding coming from brain injuries (what faculties get lost or otherwise go wrong) and also from mental ill health. Also, we can use not only results on humans but also relevant results arising from observations of animals – their intelligence and the related structure and functionality of parts of their brains, for example. This is a vast database, but I will try only to use those parts that are absolutely essential.

There are some who claim that science is the new religion. It is followed as slavishly as the religions, which completely permeate the lives of their fanatic devotees. But that claim is completely false as far as the nature of science is concerned. As I have repeatedly pointed out, scientific advance is based on the repeatability of claims put forward by various scientists about certain phenomena. Thus, the most successful equations ever devised by a scientist were recently voted on as those of James Clerk Maxwell, which he worked out and published in 1846 while at King's College London. He devised these equations to unify electricity and magnetism, so giving birth to the science of electromagnetism. It was soon realised that these equations explained the behaviour of light. The developments, on their basis, of radio and later of radar systems, were enormously powerful repeatable demonstrations of the validity of the equations. Undoubtedly these equations have been tested again and again in a vast variety of circumstances. They have always been found to be correct.

Similar testing has been made, for example, of Einstein's equations of special relativity that he postulated in 1905. These equations predicted how the energy of a particle changed as its speed was increased, especially close to the speed of light (186,000 miles per second). While this is an enormous speed, it can be nearly reached inside particle accelerators constructed since the 1930s. Very light atomic particles, such as the electron or proton, can be accelerated to these enormous speeds, where the effects of the equations can be tested. Accelerators were ultimately designed using the equations, and led to the amazingly effective exploration of the inside of the electron and proton themselves, leading to the discovery of the family of quarks. Without the equations, and their continued verifiability, no such advances could have been made.

Thus science has advanced by a powerful partnership between experiment and theory. New ideas – as in the explanation of the nature of the emission of heat from hot bodies – led, for example, to new experiments that either justified or denied the validity of the new ideas and theories. But the new theories can only replace the old if the new experiments are repeatable. The fiasco of cold fusion indicates how the relevant experiments must be repeatable. If they are not then they cannot be used to support any new scientific theory. That is why, for example, paranormal phenomena have been so hard to track down – they are involved with highly unrepeatable results. Ghosts, mental telepathy, spoon bending, messages from the dead, and so on have all been found to be based on fraudulent or unrepeatable phenomena. As such they cannot form a basis for an advance in theories designed to explain them.

Item 2. Based on Inner Experience

Consciousness and mind crucially involve our inner sense of self. Thus it cannot solely be by investigation of external events that our theory of mind must advance. Inner report must be included.

This leads to the old chestnut: how can science ever be used scientifically to investigate what goes on inside a person's head *inside their own mind*? But psychological tests have constantly used this report, and without it many experiments could not be usefully performed. If a subject has to report whether or not he or she recognises or just detects some stimulus, then inner report is crucial. A similar feature occurs for a vast range of experiments on emotions.

I have been engaged for several years on the EC Project called ERMIS that I mentioned earlier. This involved a number of partners across Europe constructing a machine system that is able to recognise the emotional state of a subject from his or her speech and facial expressions. To do that, training data was collected, in which subjects were nudged into different emotional states, and their speech and facial expressions recorded in the process. But to provide 'ground truth' other people were then asked to recognise the emotions of these subjects. But these assessments were themselves reports of inner states evoked in the viewers by the subjects as they go through various emotional states. We therefore could not have built an emotional recognition system without depending on such inner report.

Item 3. Able to Explain the Religious 'Stillness' Experience

I described in Chapter 3 general features of religious experience and its remarkable commonality expressed in the existence of the pure consciousness experience (PCE) or that of stillness. I noted there how PCE was to be regarded as the ground truth – the experiential basis of mystics – for many apparently disparate religions. Moreover, PCE was a state that appeared again and again in the writings of mystics as the crucial gateway to the experience of god. The PCE can therefore be regarded as the main stem of resource growth of all religions. But it is a state of the mind. It should therefore be take seriously in any mind-user's manual. I will use it as an added component of the inner report to test any theory of mind I propose.

Item 4. Explaining Altered States of Consciousness

Not only is there the remarkable state of PCE but many other states of being exist, some natural (sleep, dreams, etc.), others arising in states of mental ill health (such as depersonalisation), others still only being fostered by drugs or alcohol. In spite of some of these states leading to severe breakdowns, or possibly because of that, these states are of great relevance to any model of the mind. If that model cannot account for this great variety of states in ever-increasing detail then the model must be rejected and a better one created able to face up to the real world of the mind. It is also important to be able to explain these altered states as part of the natural world, to dispel the mysticism that has been built up around the experience of these so-called 'inner spaces' by the likes of Aldous Huxley and Timothy Leary.

Item 5. Self-Improvement Possibilities

A mind-user's manual should be able to provide some operating instructions. This means that it should give advice on how best to use your mind. There are many self-help books on the market, and these have provided some help to those feeling disadvantaged, ever since the time of Norman Vincent Peale, with his *Power of Positive Thinking*, and even before by various mind improvement schemes. In spite of my having no panacea to improve the mind just like that, it should be possible to deduce, from a scientifically based understanding of the mind, how it can be used most effectively. So I will try to develop some simple approaches to using the mind in various situations.

Item 6. Implications for Mental Health Problems

In the same way that advice on using the mind should be forthcoming for the normal mind, as importantly there should be advice on the abnormal mind. Structural damage to the brain will cause some obvious effects, but more subtle features of a disease such as schizophrenia should also be in the remit of the discussion. Any understanding of consciousness worth its salt should thus be able to have implications for this and other mental diseases. For both items 5 and 6, there may be a considerable way to go before simple and effective suggestions can be developed. But that does not mean that I should not attempt to show the sort of understandings that can arise from the approach I am advocating.

How to Begin

I have made my list of six items to guide us in our work ahead. There could be more such items, but the ones I have suggested have a suitable generality not to tie us down too specifically in the hard task ahead of us: for me to explain how I think the mind works, and for you to understand and hopefully resonate with my explanation of what is the deepest problem facing us as humans. It may be that a full answer of how our minds work is a long time ahead. Yet I will try to convince you that bringing a scientific attitude and the present results of science to bear on the problem will lead us toward what I suggest is a reasonable and even understandable solution. Much detail will still have to be worked out, but general principles are becoming clear.

Having presented, then, my list of six criteria, how do we use them? They will still support many possible views on consciousness and the mind, so we must add something more. It is a more global view as to what the brain is for, and most especially to answer the question:

What is consciousness for?

I am not going to give a specific answer to that question until the next part, but I want to suggest an answer which will guide us as how best to proceed given the mass of data that we now have available based on items 1–6. My general answer to the above question is simple:

Consciousness is for highest-level control of all actions.

In other words, consciousness functions as the highest level control system in the brain, which itself controls, and is affected by, the body. But that is not enough. We need to apply more precise theoretical tools to the enterprise. In particular, we need to begin to explain the vast array of brain areas involved in consciousness in the brain. These come in a confusing set of shapes and sizes, and especially of functions. It is these aspects of the brain and mind we must now plunge into, for without some way of getting our hands on the brain at work I just will not have any right to claim 'this is the correct theory of mind'.

PART II

CONSCIOUSNESS TAKES CONTROL

Clothed and in his right mind

Mark 5 : 15

In this Part, difficult sections, which can be skipped initially but can be read at a second reading, are put in boxes, separate from the main flow of the text.

CHAPTER NINE

CONSCIOUSNESS TO THE RESCUE

A Beginning for Consciousness

Consciousness is the most subtle and mysterious entity in the universe. It is as if a magic wand were waved over each infant brain as it entered the world to bring it into this amazing conscious state. But while these sentiments express our awe in the face of its subtlety, that will not help us to probe its nature in a scientific manner. I mentioned certain guidelines at the end of Part I that I suggested were of value in helping reach a satisfactory solution to the difficult question of the mechanism of consciousness creation in a person's brain:

1. Use a scientific approach (the only way to make testable progress).
2. Accept the reality of inner experience, as of an 'owner' of that experience (something common to us all).
3. Relate to the common religious experience of stillness or pure consciousness (observed and well documented across all the world's main religions).
4. Take account of other altered states of consciousness (various states of sleep, under drugs, and so on).
5. Consider possible mental improvements (so acting as a standard user's manual).
6. Relate the resulting explanation of consciousness to help explain and if possible alleviate mental health problems.

To have a good scientific basis for an answer to the question of consciousness in the brain, I will need to expand considerably on the 'mind-kit' in the brain, which I briefly introduced in Chapter 3. Without such a suitably detailed mind-kit of adult consciousness, we cannot expect to be able to understand infant consciousness, since an infant develops its consciousness very rapidly up to the same level as that of an adult. At one year infants can direct attention very effectively to a scene around them. Their eyes can carefully search a page, to enable them to pick out an animal, such as a koatimundi, in a very complicated jungle picture and point unerringly to it. They can indicate their wants very strongly. And after having had a book read to them, infants can increasingly often sit down with the book and 'read' it through again and again to themselves, pointing at some pictures, all the time muttering to themselves in – I hesitate to call them words – but sounds that obviously mean a lot to the infant. An infant is a more effective survival machine at this young age than when he or she first appeared on the scene.

There is clearly a beginning of consciousness in a developing infant. At some stage – in the foetus or at the very early infant stage – consciousness begins to emerge. At an early enough foetal stage there can be no consciousness. When it is composed of a single fertilised cell there is no consciousness, nor when it consists of only two, four or eight cells; when the foetus is composed of sixteen or thirty-two cells there is still no consciousness. It has no brain at these stages, just an aggregation of cells. When the brain has begun to develop, but not yet differentiate into its component parts, there is still no consciousness. But sometime during differentiation and maturation of the brain, be it at week twenty-four or thirty, or even later, some time after birth, we expect there to be consciousness. Some time during this enormous growth and maturation, the beginnings of consciousness will emerge from the ever-more complex neural circuits being created in the developing brain. We do not know how this occurs. To call it a miracle is both an understatement – we certainly do not understand it presently – and an overstatement – there is no proof that we cannot understand it in due course, through careful scientific probing. So we have an important challenge facing us: how does consciousness begin in the infant? To answer this, it is crucial to probe most carefully into consciousness itself. How do we do that?

Paying Attention to Attention: The Rescue Begins

Let me return to what I just wrote about developing infants: 'their eyes can carefully search a page'; in other words, they attend very carefully to the various parts of the page, moving the focal point of their visual attention to each of the animal-like objects on the page until they find the one they have already stored in their memory. Their eyes scan the page, taking the focus of visual attention with the eyes. It would seem that at least an infant's attention system is working effectively in these search patterns.

Infants are blossoming into consciousness in front of their parents' eyes all over the world. It is a miracle going on anew in every family. The infants revel in their conscious powers. They work hard to make their consciousness blossom – constantly looking for fresh vistas and new challenges to conquer, though only able to step a small way forward each time from their own still limited and circumscribed experience. In Part I, I gave a rather bleak view of the way some adults handle their minds. Consciousness is a miraculous phenomenon – as its flowering in any infant should bring home to us all so strongly. Why not nurture it and develop it to the highest possible level? Instead, once we adults have achieved our own consciousness some of us treat it with disdain, suppressing its richness by trying to get round the way it controls our whole experience. We trick it through drugs, alcohol or meditation – even to the extent of withdrawing completely from our consciousness of the external world by being 'blind' drunk', by getting 'drugged to the eyeballs', or by withdrawing into the stillness passing for union with god, all of which are death to consciousness. We are on this earth for too short a time to spend time and effort making ourselves unconscious for longer than we need.

Instead of being negative, I will take a leaf from the infants' book and be positive and creative about consciousness. To be able to properly justify such an attitude I will need to show what consciousness is good for – what it does to help us. I can only do that, yet again, if I have a good model of consciousness, so I need to develop a simple account of the scientific understanding of consciousness in terms of the precursor 'ownership' signal I mentioned earlier. This is the real heart of the book, giving a unique view on this miracle we call mind. I hope the ideas presented will be of use to developing infants when they are old enough to learn what it means, and certainly to all adults. We will all be able to use this model of our own minds to help us develop as effectively as possible. Infants soon intuitively work to learn to control the things in their environment. The most important thing in this environment is the infant's own mind. The infant can be helped to improve that with more effectiveness if we, and later the infant, know what consciousness is for.

In terms of my 'mind-kit' – a scientifically based ownership model of our minds – we can then look afresh, but more scientifically, at the most important features of a variety of forms of normal experience. It will even be possible, in terms of this model, to approach the very different experience of stillness or pure consciousness, which I emphasised earlier as being the bedrock of all religious experience. We will further be able to discuss the changes of experience brought about by stroke or by other causes of brain deficit. Again, scientific evidence will be brought to play, using simple arguments, to consider the nature of such altered experience. Dramatic cases of loss of behavioural control, such as in tumours of the amygdala (the maddened butcher I mentioned earlier) or loss of the prefrontal cortex (as in Phineas Gage, with his loss of social control), or loss of the sense of self in Alzheimer's and in schizophrenia, will also be explored. I want to emphasise that we have in front of us the possibility of being able to tie down and explain scientifically the whole range of human experience, in terms of brain activity. This is the basic feature of this manual that is not present in the approaches and manuals of others. It is truly a first.

Is it Worth the Trouble?

But why worry so much about consciousness? I mentioned earlier recent claims that it is not worth it after all: consciousness, it is claimed, actually gets in the way of the serious processing that the 'unconscious' brain is able to achieve. Some vociferously claim we should follow the routes to unconsciousness I have been denigrating earlier.

What is the evidence for downgrading consciousness? Some is scientific, and though it will not cause me to alter my experience-based keenness on consciousness, I feel we need to look at it since it holds some lessons for us, especially when we turn to the deeper questions like free will, creativity, and so on.

To show how useful are advanced cognitive powers, let me consider a very unusual experiment that was conducted by John Fabre, the French naturalist. The experiment used a group of animals called processionary caterpillars, a type of caterpillar that blindly follows the one in front of it, as in a procession. The experiment consisted of several of these caterpillars, a flowerpot filled to the rim with dirt, and pine needles. The caterpillars formed a complete circle around the rim of the flowerpot, with the first one touching the back of the last one. Some pine needles, the essential food of the processionary caterpillar, were placed in the centre of the circle. The caterpillars began their procession around the flowerpot, one following the other in a circle. This went on hour after hour, day after day, for an entire week. In the end, every one of the caterpillars dropped dead of starvation. The one thing that could have saved them – their food – was only six inches away, but without purposeful thought or action of a cognitive nature the caterpillars continued with their unthinking instinctive routine that eventually drove them to their deaths. Consciousness would have kept them alive.

Next consider the results from a set of experiments carried out by the American scientist Benjamin Libet and his physician colleagues performed on patients back in the early 1970s. I mentioned them briefly in the first part of the book. The patients suffered from intractable movement problems, and were scheduled for operations to open their skulls and have parts of the brain removed which were causing them severe and otherwise untreatable movement difficulties. While the operation was being carried out, Libet and his colleagues (with the patients' consent) applied a low electrical current to the exposed touch area of their cortex, to see what level of current was required, and how long it took to achieve a conscious experience of the back of their hand being touched (although no actual touch was being applied). Amazingly, the emergence of the conscious touch experience was very slow – up to half a second before it occurred from the time of onset of the electrical current to their brains.

This slowness amazed Libet and his colleagues and it has since amazed the scientific world. The experimental results were very controversial, even being denied by some scientists as actually having been obtained correctly. Although now the furore has died down and the results are accepted by the majority, the problem of understanding such a result is still with us.

A further result of Libet and his colleagues was as amazing: that the consciousness of a movement is delayed by fractions of a second after the actual movement has begun to be prepared in the brain (as shown by careful measurements of the relevant brain waves).

Some have interpreted the results as simply implying that consciousness is only able to be used to veto a movement in preparation, being too slow to cause its initiation. In other words, consciousness may have a control value, but that is limited only to after the event has been planned in the mind (say, of making a response like lifting your finger). Others take it to imply that consciousness is an epiphenomenon, created solely by brain activity, and therefore having no purpose at all. The movement of your finger is carried out unconsciously, and only comes into consciousness after all the really important action has taken place. Finally, others take it to mean that consciousness not only has no real causal powers, but may even get in the way. This more negative interpretation is supported by further features of consciousness that have been discovered since then.

The most crucial evidence against the usefulness of consciousness is that it filters out irrelevant material from view. Such material may be of great importance to prevent accidents. For example, I was walking along my road recently when a car came past me going very fast. Without stopping, it careered onto a major road without the driver noticing any other traffic. However, a car was coming down the major road, having right of way and so not expecting such an intruder, and had to brake very hard, with a sharp squeal of brakes and tyres, to avoid hitting the first car. In the first car was a driver quite unaware of very important information – the presence of the second car, with right of way. Consciousness had not worked for the dangerous first driver, who was concentrating too much on the wrong thing – a mobile phone – and was not allowing awareness of other more important things to get his attention. He was not using consciousness for his own survival nor that of the imperilled driver of the second car. Of course the awareness of the sudden emergence of the first car by the second car driver allowed the second driver to take suitable evasive action. So was consciousness at fault or was it the ultimate saviour? The question needs rephrasing, since there were incorrect priorities set by the first driver that caused this near-accident. Note the priorities: mobile phone first, other car users second, whereas it should have been other car users first, mobile phone calls second. It was not attention or consciousness per se that was at fault, but the higher-level goals to direct consciousness that were set by the user in the first car.

Another phenomenon that shows how consciousness can make you blind to things you should really take notice of is that of change blindness. This occurs when someone is looking at a scene and some parts of the scene suddenly change. For example, a plane may suddenly appear in the middle of the sky – but it may be totally missed by the person looking at the scene.

An amazing example of change blindness can occur of a person talking to someone else standing opposite them. While they are conversing, a man comes along carrying a door, for example, and moves between the two speakers. The speakers do not see each other for a few seconds as the door goes between them. However, while the door is going past, the second speaker (who is in on the act) is replaced by someone else entirely. In many cases when this test has been carried out the first speaker carries on speaking but completely misses the sudden change in identity of the person to whom they have been speaking. How blind and inefficient we can be!

A similar test of how strong attention and consciousness can be in preventing distraction to other items is termed 'inattentional blindness'. I experienced this myself some years ago at a meeting on Consciousness in Tucson, Arizona. I was sitting with others in a lecture on consciousness in vision, and the lecturer tested us on our powers of attention by asking us to count the number of times a basket ball was being passed successfully between students in a group shown on a video. The video lasted for some minutes. Most of us were able to be effective in correctly counting the catches. But then the lecturer asked, 'Who saw the gorilla walk between the students?'. Very few answered that they had done so. The video was replayed, and we all clearly saw the gorilla (a student dressed up in a convincing gorilla suit) as it walked between the students, stopped and turned to the camera, beat on its breast, then sauntered off the stage. So that was inattentional blindness – and a very effective demonstration of it to me!

A more careful study of how strongly attention can push out distracting stimuli from awareness is the phenomenon of the attentional blink, mentioned in Part I. This involves a subject looking at a rapid stream of stimuli – pictures, words or letters, for example – in which two special stimuli have been specified to the subject before the test by the experimenters as being important to detect. The first and second targets may be a white X and then a white letter (to be recognised), or two particular words. The stimuli arrive fast and furious – one every tenth of a second or so. If the timing of the second target is delayed after the first target to about one quarter to one third of a second after the first target has been successfully detected, the second target is then very hard to be aware of. It is in that brief period after the first target that the attentional blink occurs, as if attention had blinked its 'eye' shut, so not allowing awareness of any more stimuli at that time.

The attentional blink is very attractive to me as a past physicist. It is analogous to the physicists' trick of looking into the inside of matter by throwing a very fast moving stream of atoms, protons or neutrons at matter. The target is thereby broken up into smaller constituents, as was found in the 1950s and 1960s in the discovery of the elementary particles – called mesons – accompanying the proton and neutron as partners in the strong nuclear force, and later of partners to the electron involved in the weak and electromagnetic forces. So trying to break attention down by firing a very rapid stream of stimuli at a subject was right up my street. There have been hundreds of scientific papers published on the attentional blink since it was first observed. The results have shown some very important features of consciousness and attention, to which I will return later. I claim it even supports my 'ownership' thesis of consciousness. In any case, this breaking up of attention is crucial to understand this important human faculty.

Inattention and its Consequences

In the USA there is a vast toll on life and health by inattention as a cause of car accidents: in 1999 40,000 people were killed and 3.2 million injured in car accidents, the majority caused by inattention or fatigue. Similar statistics have been reported in other parts of the world. Loss of attention and consciousness of your driving environment turns you into a danger at the wheel.

Mental diseases also cause enormous suffering through changes in conscious experience. About 1% of all people suffer schizophrenia. This corresponds to 2 million people in the US, and half a million in the UK. Schizophrenia is a disorder of experience, as indicated by writings on the disease. In particular, it involves cases in which attention to the self is too strong – it is called 'hyperattention' – and causes considerable distress:

> *Such hyperattentional dysfunction might represent the primary cognitive abnormality seen in schizophrenia* (noted by the schizophrenia specialist psychiatrists Sarter and Bruno in 1999).

> *The patient does not feel being fully existing or alive, fully awake or alert, or fully present and affected* (as noted by another specialist psychiatrist, Josef Parnas, in 2000).

As these comments indicate, in schizophrenia the sense of self as object seems tragically to be damaged. Other components of experience can also be distorted. For example, the body image of schizophrenics can be distorted, even as far as suspecting that a part of their body has been removed – such as their thyroid gland, their womb or their genitals.

Another mental illness with terrifying consequences is Alzheimer's disease. There are 4.5 million sufferers in the USA, and it is predicted, since Alzheimer's is especially a disease of the old, that this will increase to 16 million by 2050 due to the ageing of the population. In Alzheimer's the memory disintegrates, then so do experience and personality, until only very primitive responses can be made. In the end the brain degenerates so much that it can no longer support crucial functions and the patient dies.

A typical case, as seen conjecturally from the sufferer's experience, is that of Mary: a reconstruction of her experience was given recently:

> *Often, Mary was afraid, a nameless, shapeless fear. Her impaired mind could not put a name or an explanation to her fear. People came, memories came, and then they slipped away. She could not tell what was reality and what was memory of people past. Dressing became an insurmountable ordeal ... Mary gradually lost the ability to make sense out of what her eyes and ears told her. She worried about her things: a chair, and the china that had belonged to her mother. They all seem to have disappeared – where had they gone?*

So the breakdown of attention and memory and the related loss of consciousness can lead to terrible results. The misdirecting presence of consciousness can be a burden, causing lack of attention to events threatening our survival. But without it, working at its highest level of efficiency, we are not able to make sense of the complex world we inhabit, and especially of our complex social surroundings. So we must hang on to our miraculous consciousness as much as possible. But what precisely are we exhorted to hold so dear?

What is Consciousness?

Consciousness is the natural phenomenon closest to each of us, but presently one of the most difficult to understand. I have already described in Part I numerous but differing approaches to it. How can we – the whole human race – have got it so wrong, since only one of these different explanations can be true? They differ immensely, and fight each other strongly for the right to be regarded as the true understanding. The lesson of this epic ongoing battle is that our experience of our own minds is not one full of clarity and light – in fact, it can less euphemistically be said that our ignorance of our minds is appalling, even though we experience our consciousness infinitely closely. I see this as due to a number of factors:

1. A high proportion of brain processing goes on outside consciousness (I reported it to be about 90% earlier), and this unconscious activity only enters consciousness when the processing has become salient and developed enough. Thus mental precursors to our conscious thoughts are hidden from us.
2. There are numerous states of consciousness, as noted earlier, so we should not expect that we can easily give a simple and unified definition or explanation that covers all these cases.
3. Even in normal conscious experience there are a number of divisions of consciousness: direct sensory experiences (as when smelling a rose or looking at a beautiful scene), remembering something from the past (the meal you had last night or for me my last year's trip to Santorini), thinking hard about writing a book (as I am doing now), or being in a strong emotional state (such as extreme anger or sorrow).

Some degree of structure is introduced into conscious experience by the divisions in ordinary conscious experience arising above. There are more general features that should be mentioned, especially the intentional aspect of consciousness, which is the fact that consciousness arises when one is conscious of something. This 'thinginess' of consciousness has been emphasised strongly in Western philosophy of mind since the time of the Austrian philosopher Brentano, even to the extent of claiming that 'consciousness' only means 'consciousness of something'. Yet there is the basic feature of the 'self', in particular the feeling of ownership of one's experience, which is not properly catered for if one only emphasises the content of consciousness to the detriment of the entity – yourself – experiencing that consciousness. Without 'you' as the centre of experience there can be no experience of consciousness itself.

To probe the nature of consciousness in more detail by looking for that inner self is difficult, since it requires care in being able to interpret what is noticed. Many different features have been brought back from such introspective foraging into our inner mental world. Some agreement has been reached on common features that are detectable. In particular, specific features can be detected that have been termed variously presence, transparency, ineffability, uniqueness, binding, inner perspective, and numerous others.

Presence is the experience of 'being there' as an entity. It involves the persistence, latency and seamlessness of consciousness. It also involves that which is present and has the experiences, which I call the 'owner'. It is this component which needs careful exploration, since if an owner is thought to have conscious experience of some kind, we are back to an infinite sequence of owners, with each owning the experience of the one before it. So the owner is more subtle and difficult to track down.

Transparency arises since we can look through our experiences to see the 'object' beyond, and not see our own processing getting in the way. Such an experience may be warped, as in schizophrenia, but in general we do not have the machinery of our processing – the activity in the 90% of the brain which is unconscious – brought into our awareness. It would be highly inefficient if that happened, since our thinking would then be slowed down and swamped by all the activities going on in our brains.

The property of *ineffability* arises from the intrinsic, inexplicable nature of each of our conscious experiences. Since we cannot be aware of the unconscious activity out of which our consciousness arises, this emergence seems to be a miracle. It is as if consciousness occurs on no apparent basis at all – as if it is completely non-material (so helping support the idea of a non-material mind and an eternal soul). However, remember that appearances can be very deceptive.

Uniqueness is clear from the fact that one only has one conscious experience at a time, although this can break down, for example, in cases of multiple personality disorder (if it exists, which is still controversial). However, this breakdown is abnormal, and justifies considering uniqueness as a standard property.

The term *binding* is used to describe the way that different features of objects – their shape, colour, motion, and so on – all fuse effortlessly in our final conscious experience of the objects. Breakdown of such binding can occur due to brain damage, and again justifies its recognition as a standard feature.

The various features mentioned above I partly explained by the style of processing (in neural network terms) used by the brain in my 1999 *Race for Consciousness* book. But I did not explain there the nature of the inner perspective. It is the crucial feature that is not at all simple to explain in information processing terms, as I noted above about the subtlety of the owner. It is the hard problem of consciousness, as noted succinctly in 1996 by the American philosopher David Chalmers. It arises as a problem, I would claim, from the absence of any concept of the 'inner self' from the modern Western cognitive approaches to consciousness.

The Nature of the Inner Self

The inner self is very elusive. The Scottish philosopher David Hume only observed perceptions, not anyone experiencing them, when he tried to introspect his inner self. 'All I ever see is a bundle of perceptions,' he wrote in describing the results of his attempts to see his inner self.

So how does awareness then arise if there is no inner self? This is the 'hard' problem facing Western cognitive science which I just mentioned. It has been suggested by its practitioners that awareness arises by a process of self-monitoring, some sort of 'perception perceiving itself', so to speak. This self-monitoring approach to awareness has many devotees. But they are wrong. Awareness just cannot be a kind of 'inner perception': this has been shown by many philosophers over the previous century, related to the names of Kant, Husserl, Frank, Henry, Shoemaker, Zahavi, and many others. In particular, it has been shown conclusively that such inner perception would lead to an infinite regress of selves looking at selves looking at ... and so on, in order that the selves involved can have the information that they are indeed looking at themselves.

Since this is a crucial point, let me expand on it.

The Structure of Consciousness

To begin with, let me go over some old ground to get to the much deeper question of how the self could not be constructed. First of all, we must realise that your self-awareness could not arise by you observing your 'I' through noticing some property, and infallibly seeing it as identical to yourself. For to identify a self as equal to yourself by this property, you need to know that you observe it with immunity to error. This immunity aspect is crucial to the nature of 'I'. As the philosopher Ludwig Wittgenstein pointed out, if you tell me 'I am certain I am in pain', I cannot then ask you 'Are you sure it is you who is in pain?'. You are immune to error in identifying yourself as 'I', the owner of your own experiences. Otherwise who is that 'I' who says 'I am in pain'?

Coming back to the problem of the grounds for your self-identification, they cannot be solely by an identification of some property with yourself. For how do you know that the 'yourself' that you claim to be able to recognise as you is due to possessing this property? Specifically, where is the immunity to error of identification of you as seen in this entity?

To guarantee that it is indeed you there in the entity, you would have to have a further identification process, based on a further observation of a property guaranteeing the 'you' claimed through the property really to be your immune-to-error self. But this second property would have to be of a very peculiar sort. If I recognise myself in the mirror then I may be wrong that it is me I see – it could be someone else passing in front of me or done by a magician so that the image in the mirror is not me, although I think it is. There are many examples of people being fooled by their supposed self-image or by their apparently broken limb, when after all the image is of an object belonging to someone else. Even if all possible such identifications were made it still would not ensure that they all were not faked. But such identifications are all one can go on in this self-monitoring approach. None are certain as being certainly of you. Thus we can conclude that your self-knowledge – your feeling of being an 'I' – cannot be based on identification with any property you can observe about your self. A more detailed discussion of this aspect of self is given in Box 1.

BOX I: Further Considerations on the Self

Suppose that self-awareness were achieved by a reflection on some perception. The perception must therefore be grasped by an act of reflection, as being identical to the reflection. Thus the reflection is identical to the perception, and so they both belong to the same stream of consciousness. A difficulty arises, however: how does the reflection (which is assumed to lack self-awareness) know the perception and the reflection belong to the same stream? This needs a further act of reflection. But this act of reflection would need an infinite sequence of such acts of reflection, each achieving proof that the previous one belonged to the same stream of consciousness. One way to avoid this infinite regress is to assume that the reflection was already self-aware. But this is a circular argument, since then the reflection already has the property of self-awareness which we are trying to create!

This same criticism also applies to higher-order thought theories of consciousness, in which consciousness arises by an unconscious thought being thought about by a so-called higher-order thought, in that way having the power of consciousness miraculously bestowed in it. Again, an infinite regress is needed to give knowledge that it is oneself that is being thought about from higher up.

Self-monitoring theories of self-awareness will not do. But we are now in a predicament that is as follows: the contents of consciousness are not all that there is to consciousness. There must be more than purely the smell of the roses, the sounds of the Grieg piano concerto or the taste of the delicious meals in Paris. There is a 'you' having that experience. How do we proceed to discover the extra ingredient – the X-factor of consciousness to give that inner feel? How do we find that part of us that is having these experiences?

I have already said in Part I that there is an inner self, but as I have just pointed out, that inner self cannot be just composed of a set of self-monitoring acts, or the set of properties one knows about oneself. It must be content free. Therefore it has no properties of any standard form. Such a subtle centre or core of being is called by some the 'pre-reflective self', since it cannot be observed by any self-monitoring or reflective process. It is the experiencer that cannot itself be experienced – for if it could, then who is the experiencer experiencing that experience?

To make real progress in explaining consciousness, any theory worth its salt must throw light on how this inner perspective arises. What must be the nature of the pre-reflective self I have just mentioned? To answer that, we should probe how the pre-reflective self (which, let me emphasise, is that component of the self more primitive than that observable by reflecting on one's properties in an 'external' manner, as if they belong to someone else) gets created so as to give a 'centre' to conscious experiences. It is to the pre-reflective self that such consciousness belongs. It is the inner self, functioning at a pre-linguistic level (as in an infant of 6 months, say, or a primate), that in some manner 'experiences' the contents of its consciousness. This extra pre-reflective self allows there indeed to be consciousness – called qualia by philosophers. These qualia possess the content – the colour or smell of the rose – but also involve some entity having the relevant experience. That experience is not, however, of a fully-fledged inner person or a so-called 'homunculus'.

Instead, experience has to be stripped down to the most primitive form possible. It has no content – no smell, no redness of the rose, or whatever. Otherwise an infinite series of such homunculi suddenly emerge, howling like banshees, the experience of each only explicable in terms of that of the next one, who needs a further homunculus to experience, and so on. So the experience of the owner can only be that of its ownership of the contents of its phenomenal experience, whatever those contents are. Nothing else could be present in the owner's experience, since otherwise the infinite regress is needed to explain how a conscious experience of that further content could arise. We would never get to the end of consciousness if we go down that route.

If awareness is not a kind of 'self'-perception, as some philosophers mistakenly tell us, then the basic question of self-awareness is this: 'How is consciousness aware of itself: how does it experience itself?', as Dan Zahavi would ask. It thus comes down to the question of how it would be possible to create a perceptual experience that is only given to me: an experience for which uniquely I am the *owner*.

We are thereby led directly to the question of how to find ownership in the brain. What would be its signature? Does it have a tag, as in shops which use electronic tags to prevent anyone going outside with their goods if they have not legitimately been paid for? We need to find your ownership tag in your brain for the content of your consciousness. If we cannot find an owner in any human beings at all, then we should be concerned that the problems that have been raised about ownership – the hard problem of consciousness, according to the philosopher David Chalmers – would not have any scientific basis: there would be no brain system supporting its deepest component. Our inner self would be invisible to science. But we are not at that point yet – the brain is very subtle, and has surprises to throw at us.

Consciousness Needs Attention

The problem of ownership of experience I have just raised is a very difficult one. One way to solve a difficult problem is to go off and solve a different problem. This would only help to solve the first problem if the second problem were able to help solve the first one, as well as being easier. One aspect of consciousness I have already emphasised is its closeness to attention. Without attention to a stimulus we appear to be unaware of it. This is clear in blindness, in which there is a lack of ability to be conscious as well as a complete lack of attention. There are other situations in which people have damaged attention systems, resulting in a deficit of awareness, as in the condition known as neglect. This usually arises from the result of a stroke causing damage (usually to the right hemisphere of the brain), leading to a tragic inability to direct attention focus. A neglect patient will not be able to notice items in their left field of view. They may even claim that the leg in bed with them is not theirs but belongs to someone else.

Another case of loss of attention control resulting in loss of awareness is the attentional blink, mentioned earlier: the loss of ability to move attention from the first target to the second in a rapidly presented stimulus stream leads to loss of awareness of the second target, this being worst at about 300 milliseconds after the first target. Inattentional blindness has also been mentioned earlier, being the inability to detect unattended change in the environment.

As noted by the scientist Kimron Shapiro and his colleagues, who are experimenting closely with the attentional blink (and gave it its name), 'The further function of attention is to allow selected perceptual information a foothold in consciousness'. So we must look further into attention to understand consciousness.

CHAPTER TEN

PAYING ATTENTION

The Nature of Attention

The brain has a limited capacity for processing its information up to the highest level. It takes a lot of brain tissue to make a complex decision about a complicated action on a complex object, even without consciousness being involved. But if you were to attempt to make a number of movements all at once with different parts of your body, on different objects, you would soon come a cropper. We marvel, for example, at the circus juggler, able to throw several balls into the air at once and catch and throw them up again sequentially, so they seem to remain permanently in the air. Unless you have practised for a considerable time, as has the juggler, you will not be able to achieve this dexterous feat. The detailed mechanisms behind this marvellous trick are not yet fully known, but must correspond to developing an ability to track several balls in the air at once, at least as far as knowing their general position and the need to respond to them. At the same time, the juggler will have trained himself to make automatic the necessary sequence of fast throwing and catching movements of the successive balls. Over-learning a sequence of movements so as to make them automatic and thereby able to be performed outside attention clearly lessens the processing load on the brain. It can work on which is the next ball to catch and throw up again, and then the next, and so on. Oh, effortless skill! But oh, so much hard training! It certainly does not happen on the first try!

We thus need to make a choice of the allocation of our brain's processing resources. There must be selection of which components we attend to of the incoming flow of information from the sensors – from the eyes, ears, mouth, nose and touch sensors of the body surface. A limited number of components of this incoming stream have to be extracted, amplified and processed. This will be at the expense of all of the other components, which will be temporarily or altogether neglected. The brain will then be able to handle properly the selected components, and make an efficient response. The mechanism that achieves this limitation to what is to be processed up to awareness is that of attention. It acts as a filter on incoming stimuli, shutting off all others that are to be ignored while the attended one is being processed. These unattended stimuli will not be lost entirely, as shown by the fact that most of us can walk and talk at the same time (except for some well-known but very likely apocryphal Presidents of the USA). If we focus our attention on our companion during a walk we can still walk in an automatic manner. But if we are walking over very rough ground we will then have to attend more carefully to where we put our feet, so the conversation may become a bit disjointed. That corresponds to our attending now to the conversation and now to where we put our feet. The same applies to driving a car, especially as noted in the distraction caused by a mobile phone call.

The study of attention has a long history. It was already noted by the Greek philosopher Aristotle that 'Of two movements, the stronger always tends to extrude the latter'. That attention can be directed was also known in antiquity. The philosopher Lucretius wrote, in the first century BC, that one can possess 'attentive ears and minds'. The division of attention into that directed voluntarily compared to it being externally driven was also known early. The automatic 'tug of attention', as compared to its willed direction, was noted by St Augustine as long ago as about AD 400, and discussed later by the French philosopher-scientist René Descartes. Many thinkers on attention have remarked that it enhances sensory sensitivity (as noted by the Greek philosophers, by Lucretius and later by Descartes), and the ability to move attention covertly was also commented on long ago by Aristotle. Here the form of attention movement not involving shifting your eyes' point of focus is called 'covert', since it is not observable. Again, Aristotle pointed out that attention was basic to unifying consciousness.

At the turn of the previous century, the American psychologist William James (brother of the great novelist Henry James, with William James also possessing great literary skill) was much concerned with attention, and he wrote about it with great depth and understanding. About that time a severe difficulty was discovered in attentively analysing one's own inner experience. This problem arose from the failure of introspection studies, carried out by different subjects, to agree on the detailed nature of their reported experiences. This 'hole' in our possible way of understanding the mind – from the 'inside', so to say – paved the way for behaviourism, which claimed that there was nothing happening inside an animal's head, including that of a human. Only external behaviour was a suitable object of study. Only some decades later, in the later part of the twentieth century, did it become possible to renew a scientific study of mind and attention seriously. Very soon attention was recognised (again) as crucial to consciousness. Even more recently, consciousness has, in its own right, seen to be deserving of more detailed scientific study as a crucial component of information processing in the brain. Its introduction into artificial software 'agents', for example, is now being seriously attempted. The European Commission is even considering serious funding of projects to build a 'conscious machine'.

One of the best definitions of attention to date can be found in William James's remarkable trail-blazing book *The Principles of Psychology*, written in 1890. He noted of attention: 'It is the taking possession by the mind, in clear and vivid form, of one out of what seem several simultaneously possible objects or trains of thought. Focalization, concentration, of consciousness are of its essence. It implies withdrawal from some things in order to deal effectively with others'. James thereby hit the attention nail on the head beautifully.

Depending on the type of information and, furthermore, on the criteria for the selection, one can identify different types of attention, as both psychological and neuroscientific evidence confirm. When information is visual, then attention is termed visual, which is subsequently classified as spatial, if the location of the visual object is the criterion, or object based, if the object's features are the criterion for search. Similarly, when information concerns motor actions, such attention to action is termed motor. Other classes of attention can be identified as well, such as attention to particular instants in time (time attention) or attention to ideas, to touch, taste, and indeed to each of the senses (or in a conjoined fashion to more than one sense at once).

The Brain at Work

Considerable knowledge has been gained about the human visual system and its various pathways employed in the brain, and a reasonably good understanding of visual attention has been able to be developed building on this knowledge. I will turn to how the brain supports attention as a way of understanding its detailed modus operandi that is crucial towards understanding consciousness. The resulting discussion will depend on an understanding of the brain's overall structure, which I will explain as we need it.

Only early visual processing stages in the brain are explained in reasonable detail, and their contribution to visual attention well accounted for, whereas the later stages of processing and, in particular, the integration of these later stages with higher cognitive processes, are still somewhat ambiguous and vague with regard to their contribution to the overall function of the relevant parts of the brain. It is, nevertheless, these later stages that are most relevant to the control of information processing by attention in the brain, so I will only briefly describe the early stages of attention control and focus more on the later ones shortly.

Attention is most often defined, for example in the visual modality, as the process of selection of a part of a visual scene for further more careful inspection. This selection process involves partial or complete exclusion of the rest of the scene. Unattended inputs fail to reach awareness, as shown by experiments in which a subject is completely unaware of the sudden appearance of an object at an unattended point – as in the phenomenon of inattentional blindness that I mentioned earlier. In a very similar way attention can also be paid to inputs in other modalities, or to actions.

Let me concentrate on vision, which occurs in the brain by visual information flowing up a hierarchy of brain areas starting in the primary visual cortex (after entering the brain at the thalamus at the top of the brain stem) and moving slightly downwards (ventrally) to where object representations are stored (denoted by 'what it is'), as shown in Figure 1. Besides this object route of information flow in the brain there is a parallel route through the upper (dorsal) part of the brain where spatial and motion information is stored (denoted by 'where it is' in Figure 1). This information flow is described more fully in Box 2.

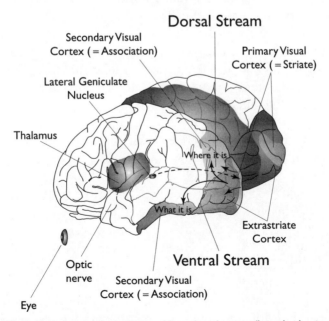

Figure I The visual processing streams (dorsal and ventral) in the brain

BOX 2: Visual Processing in the Brain

Upon presentation of visual stimuli to the eyes and activation of the photoreceptors in the retina, signals generated by the latter pass to the back of the retina, where intense signal processing and information compression take place by means of the enhancement of line edges and related reduction of the total input. From the retina, this dimensionally reduced information goes through a part of the relay station termed the thalamus (in particular, to the region of the thalamus called the lateral geniculate nucleus, as shown in Figure 1), where the activity representing the stimulus is further reorganised so that the temporal aspects of the visual information are emphasised. The activity is then relayed to the visual cortex at the back of the cortex.

After processing through the thalamus, visual information enters the first and lowest area of processing in the cerebral cortex, which is the sheet of grey matter hanging over the whole of the thalamus and over other sub-cortical nuclei. This first cortical area is called the primary visual cortex. Here a topographic map of the visual stimulus is compiled by means of the rough space-conserving organisation of the connections from the retina to primary visual cortical nerve cells: each such cell represents a site on the retina, and thus a site in the outside visual world. However, there are many more primary visual cortical cells than input connections from the retina: the primary visual cortex analyses the input stimulus into short oriented lines or edges that compose the stimulus, as well as into moving and colour components. Beyond this first visual area, there is a split of the stimulus traffic into two separate streams, each processing a different aspect of the visual information and shown in Figure 1. One stream, described as a lower 'what' pathway (the downward-curved arrow marked 'ventral stream' in Figure 1), is sensitive to increasingly complex object shapes and features contained in the visual stimuli (such as the shape, form, etc. of the object) as one proceeds more towards the lower frontal part of the brain. The other stream, described as the upper 'where' pathway (the upward curving arrow marked 'dorsal stream' in Figure 1), is sensitive to spatial information (i.e. the location or motion of an object). Both of these areas are said to consist of what are called secondary visual cortex.

The lower pathway consists of a number of different cortical areas which perform different functions: first coding the visual scene in terms of small edges of specific orientations, then pairs of these edges and textures, and then more complex parts of figures, and finally complete figures. These object representations are in what is called the temporal lobe (see Figure 2), whereas the visual areas are in what is called the occipital lobe (see the lobes of the brain in Figure 2). The upper pathway includes various spatial- and motion-coding areas in what is called the parietal lobe.

Figure 2 shows the lobes of the brain, a way of portioning out the vast expanse of cortex into distinct regions. We have already met the visual cortex – termed the occipital lobe in Figure 2 – which is for early vision. We have also met the temporal lobe of Figure 2, which is for object coding (the 'what it is' area of Figure 1) and the parietal lobe of Figure 2 for motion and spatial layout coding (the 'where it is' site in Figure 1). There is finally the frontal lobe displayed in Figure 2. This lobe is highly expanded in humans as compared to other primates, and rightly so since it functions as the highest executive in the information processing performed by the brain. It is that area of cortex by which we humans are supreme among living things in such executive powers as planning, thinking, imagining and so on. Its anterior portion, not involved directly in motor response, is termed the prefrontal cortex: it is there where executive control is thought to reside (as known from loss of that control in people like Phineas Gage who lose important parts of their prefrontal

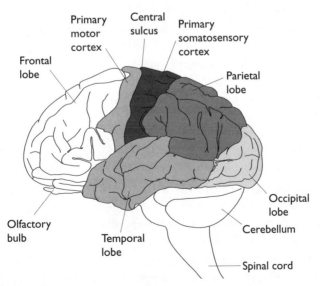

Figure 2 The lobes of the brain (as discussed in the text)

cortices). Where these lobes are in the brain is shown schematically in Figure 2.

Let me remind you that the brain is composed of billions upon billions of nerve cells (one hundred billion in humans), each of these cells being very small (no more than about one-tenth of a millimetre or less in length). This ensemble of cells is mainly embedded into the surface, or so-called 'cortex', of the brain. To fit in more cells a larger surface area of this cortex has been achieved by making it corrugated, with folds – each called a gyrus – and deep ravines, each called a sulcus. These myriad nerve cells are connected to each other, with one cell connecting to upward of a hundred thousand others. The connections, termed axons, carry pulses of electricity, moving at about a metre per second, from one cell to the next. So in the cortex and with a similar arrangement in the rest of the brain, there is a constant shuttling to and fro of these pulses of electrical activity. Each nerve cell only sends out a pulse of electricity when it receives a sufficient level of incoming pulses. There is thus a constant flow of information between nerve cells (essentially describing 'who is activating me' from the given cell), as described in Part I. Enormous complexity of the connection between nerve cells is possible with a hundred billion cells and tens of thousands of inputs into any one cell. That complexity means it is possible to envisage the brain supporting the creation of the symphonies of Beethoven or the plays of Shakespeare or invention of the powerful theories of the universe by Albert Einstein – and even supporting the miracle of consciousness needed in the act of creation of these works of genius.

Information is processed in a somewhat hierarchical manner in the brain. The initial visual input to the retina goes to the primary visual cortex, as I mentioned earlier, and described in more detail in Box 2. It then climbs up a hierarchy of visual areas, in the two possible ventral/what or dorsal/where pathways, which I also mentioned earlier, and as displayed in Figure 1. This process of 'climbing up' means 'becoming more complex': the lowest level areas break up a scene into bars of different orientations, while higher level areas are concerned about more complex shapes appearing in the visual scene. These two hierarchies – the 'what' (for objects) and the 'where' (for space) – lead at later stages to fusion of sensitivity across several modalities, so that both the touch sensation and the shape of an object will be coded in what is termed 'multi-modal' cortex. These fused codes for stimuli are thought to be at the highest level of coding for sensory representations in the brain.

Attention acts on the two visual streams (and those in other modalities) in a beautifully elegant manner. It begins to explain why I earlier called the brain a 'mean lean attention machine'.

Attention as Control

Let me suppose that you are searching for a face in a crowd of people coming toward you off a train. The mode of action of attention in the brain in this case is through the relative amplification of the neural activity for the attended face for which you are searching and associated inhibition of any distracting elements in the visual neural representations in the early cortical sites I mentioned above – these distracters being other people's faces, bookstores, cafes, train timetables, and so on. The activity in your brain, representing the face you are searching for, would thereby be amplified by your attention if the face actually appeared, while that of all other faces and the other distracters would have reduced neural activity. In this way you would be able to be more efficient in your search. For example, if you make a mistake and think someone else is the person you are searching for, as you approach them you realise, as you attend more intently on that face alone, that it is not the face of the person you are meeting. You avoid having to be aware of all the faces of the strangers in the crowd as they come rushing towards and past you. Most of these faces are so different from the face for which you search that the task is no problem. Only closely similar faces are more problematic. The processing load has thereby been drastically reduced.

Such is attention. It makes search efficient. It also helps you single out a specific face so you can check it out carefully before you make the embarrassing mistake of going up to the wrong person and saying 'hello' or even embracing them. The way attention achieves its ends – of picking out what you have set up as your 'goal' – is, I claim, most elegant. It does so by setting up a signal in a specific site, now known to be in your parietal lobe. It is this 'attention control' signal that does the job. It penetrates back to the earlier cortical areas, like the temporal lobe, or to earlier parts of the visual cortex. Attention then changes the signals in these various areas, to amplify those corresponding to your face target signal and inhibit those for any others present. What could be more efficient? Boosting the wanted incoming signals and reducing those not wanted. No embracing of complete strangers!

Such attention-based boosting/reducing modulations of early cortical activity have now been observed by many neuroscientific experiments, both at single-cell level and at that of aggregates of many cells in monkeys. In humans (in whom it is more difficult to experiment on at single-cell level, due to having to open up the brain), brain imaging methods have allowed observation of similar boosting/reduction across the whole brain.

The new brain imaging machines that can achieve this are remarkable in their power, and are now being developed to probe ever more sensitively into how the brain functions in all its subtle and glorious ways. Nothing can be hidden, especially from batteries of different types of brain imaging machines. The whole brain of a person can thus be observed in its gloriously subtle activity when the person is shown various stimuli or does various tasks, without at any time the brain being penetrated by a surgeon's scalpel. Non-invasive brain imaging can also show brain tumours and other serious medical conditions rapidly and without invasion of the patient's brain, allowing for amazing advances in our understanding of the brain at work. People can even be caught out in lies or in self-created 'memories', which they claim to be true.

Brain imaging machines come in two main types and four main forms. The two types correspond to detecting any increased flow of blood arising from increased nerve cell activity, and alternately to observing more directly the electrical or magnetic activity across the brain due to nerve cells producing electric fields and concomitant magnetic fields as part of their interaction with each other. The first form, detecting blood flow, is measured by two different techniques: by positron-emission tomography (PET) machines, or by functional magnetic resonance imaging (fMRI). The second form, of electric or magnetic field measurement, is by electro-encephalography (EEG), or by magneto-encephalography (MEG).

In total these methods allow detection of brain activity occurring in various separate parts of the brain without having to invade it by cutting open the skull and sticking in an electrode. This non-invasive approach has provided a new window on the brain and so has been enormously exploited over the past few decades, with ever increasing sensitivity as to what activity is where and when. How these brain imaging machines achieve this remarkable feat is explained in more detail in Box 3.

BOX 3: Brain Imaging Machines

Positron emission tomography (PET) is based on the observation of two photons (a photon is the 'particle' of light) both arising from the radioactive decay of a suitably short-lived radioactive (positron-emitting) atom. A subject ingests the radioactively decaying material producing such photons, which are then distributed throughout their body and brain. Sensitive detectors around the subject can detect the two photons emitted; there will be more from areas in the subject's brain that require more blood due to neural activity than from less-active areas. Mapping these active areas when a subject is performing some psychological task allows detection of the site of the brain areas active during performance of the task.

Magnetic resonance imaging (MRI) is based on the blood-oxygen-level-dependent (BOLD) signal emitted by blood flow to active neural tissue in the brain when in the presence of a strong magnetic field. All the material of the body and brain is composed of a high proportion of water. The strong magnetic field of the external magnet aligns the spins of the hydrogen nuclei in the water, like spinning tops all lining up on parade. Zapping the subject with short bursts of radio waves knocks these spins out of line, as if they had all broken ranks; as they get back into line they wobble or 'precess', as does a spinning top. This precession generates an oscillating magnetic field which can be picked up by a suitably sensitive magnetic sensor, and used to map the tissues under investigation. In particular, a specific signal is given out when there is an increase of blood flow brought about by nerve cell activity, arising from the need for more oxygen to be brought to the active brain area. The resulting BOLD signal is specifically used in what is termed functional magnetic resonance imaging (fMRI). Here the BOLD signal is measured from the brains of subjects performing psychological tests (such as searching for a specific target amongst distracters, doing arithmetic problems and so on) while lying inside the bore of a strong magnet producing the necessary strong magnetic field.

Electroencephalography (EEG) is based on the measurement of the low-level electric field component on the scalp arising from the electrical activity of neural tissue in the brain. This electrical activity is at a very low level, but sensitive equipment can detect the effects of underlying changes in nerve cell activity in different areas, picked up on metal electrodes stuck suitably closely to a subject's scalp, as a psychological task is being performed by the subject. This can be made even clearer by averaging over many repetitions of the same task. When upwards of 128 electrodes (or even 256 in recent experiments) are attached to the scalp, and careful shielding used, clear spatially different signals and fast responses (within a millisecond) are able to be detected over the scalp.

Finally, magneto-encephalography (MEG) is based on the very low-level magnetic field around the brain associated to the electric field measured by EEG. It is necessary to have numerous detectors, which also need to be at a very low temperature so as to be super-conducting, and to work in a magnetically shielded room, in order to detect the small currents which the brain's magnetic field generates. The advantage of MEG over EEG is that the former can detect more accurately the deeper nerve cell activity than the latter. Both possess the same high-speed responsiveness (sensitive down to one millisecond).

For overall comparison between the four sorts of brain imaging machine, the blood-flow based machines (fMRI and PET) have greater spatial accuracy (down to a millimetre or so) compared to the loss of spatial accuracy, especially for deep sources of nerve cell activity, from MEG or EEG measurements. However, both these latter techniques provide far better temporal sensitivity than the former, with sensitivity to changes over one millisecond as compared to a second (for fMRI) or many seconds (for PET). Increased use of several of these measuring systems simultaneously (or at least on the same subjects, with the same paradigms) is now occurring.

Using these new machines, the signals of attention have been discovered to occur in a network of areas spread over various parts of the cortex, both in posterior visual sites and in parietal and frontal sites. For example, in 1999 a team of brain scientists led by the American John Reynolds tested the effect of adding a second stimulus to an earlier one being observed by a macaque. They showed that the effect on single cells in secondary visual cortex of directing attention to one of a pair of stimuli drove the response of the cell towards that elicited by the attended stimulus alone. They concluded that, 'This finding is consistent with the idea that attention biases competitive interactions among neurons, causing them to respond primarily to the attended stimulus'. Scientists at the Queen's Square brain research centre at London's University College have used the latest data analysis techniques for MRI (so-called 'structural equation modelling') to analyse the changes over time of activities in different brain areas from three subjects paying different levels of attention to visual motion. They showed that the data could best be explained by the existence of the increase of the strength of the connection between a motion-sensitive area and the posterior parietal cortex brought about by attention. They further demonstrated that this modulation is partly driven by the prefrontal cortex.

We thus know increasingly more about how attention control signals act on nerve-cell activity at earlier levels of the brain hierarchy, as well as involving a broad network of areas including higher levels of the brain. The lower-level areas act mainly in a passive manner to the ministrations of the attention signals in the brain. I have already mentioned the existence in the brain of these attention control signals – the signals that cause modulation of the responses of lower-level nerve cells that would otherwise respond to many inputs. We now have to start tracking down where and hopefully how these control signals of attention are produced. It is in these areas that we must begin to understand how attention is created, and to design a model of that process.

The answer to the conundrum – where and how attention control signals are created in the brain – is now being uncovered by the non-invasive brain imaging methods detailed in Box 3. The brain is giving up its deepest secrets to the inquisitive eyes of brain scientists. Numerous experiments have now been performed using brain imaging techniques to show that there exists in the brain a complex network of cortical modules involved in controlling attention. This network has been noted to be very similar for attention controlled by external rapidly appearing inputs (so-called exogenous attention) and the top-down or endogenous form controlled by internal goals. However, there are also 'saliency' maps in lower cortical areas that may help guide where attention is to be directed by these rapid inputs. This would allow a breakthrough of a very salient stimulus – say, a very strong or alarming one, such as a fire alarm, or an explosion – into attention.

In order to understand how this might work, consider that, as before, you are searching for a face in a crowd. In the process you will have set up an image of the desired face in your brain. That image will then help you create an attention control signal to amplify any incoming signal close enough to that face. Such an image – a template or goal – is termed 'endogenous', it having been set up by you inside your brain. On the other hand, if a bright light suddenly shines in the station, your attention will be attracted to it, and it can now be termed an 'exogenous' goal (where the goal has been set by signals originating most crucially from outside).

From many brain experiments carried out over the past decade, the most important cortical components of the attention control network are recognised as being in three sites: in the parietal lobes for perceptual processing and the creation of an attention control signal to modulate earlier, lower-level activity; in what is termed the anterior cingulate cortex (in the middle of the brain at the top of the head) for guidance of the direction of attention through emotional memories; and in the prefrontal cortex for rules and templates for guiding responses. A recent review concluded that 'Attention-related activity in frontal and parietal areas does not reflect attention modulation of visually evoked response, rather it reflects the attention operations themselves'. Also, the American brain scientists Corbetta and Shulman, in a more recent wide-ranging review of attention, concluded: 'One system, which includes part of the intra-parietal cortex and superior frontal cortex, is involved in preparing and applying goal-directed (top-down) selection for stimuli and responses'.

I have now given you an outline of how attention works in the brain: there exists a higher-level attention control system which generates the attention modulation signals that affect the lower-level primary and secondary visual cortices. In a similar manner we expect similar higher-level control networks that control attention in other senses: audition, touch, and so on. I summarise this control nature of attention in the brain by a model consisting of two modules, one whose activity is controlled by attention, the other which generates this crucial attention control signal to achieve its control. Such a model is shown in Figure 3.

The right-most module in Figure 3 denotes the regions of the brain that are controlled by attention. They consist of lower regions – especially in occipital and temporal lobes and in motor cortex – in which input or response activities are modulated by attention; these areas do not function so as to control attention in any strong manner. It is the left module in Figure 3 that generates the attention control signal to modulate the activity in these lower areas. There are also other areas, such as the limbic area, which code for the emotional value of an input; these regions can also affect where attention is directed. Such breakthrough into attention of emotionally valued stimuli is clearly of survival value. Thus, if there is a juicy peach to which you have not been attending, it is obviously valuable for you to attend to it if you are hungry for such succulent fruit. It needs to break through your attention system and draw your attention towards the peach. Similarly, if there is someone looking at you in a

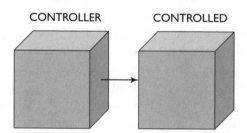

CONTROLLER   CONTROLLED

Figure 3 A control model of attention. The controlled region consists of visual cortical areas (or similar areas in other senses, even including motor areas for attention to actions). The controller network creates and sends out a signal (shown by an arrow) to the lower-level controlled areas of cortex to amplify the desired activities and to reduce those corresponding to distracters. The controller region consists of areas in the parietal lobes and prefrontal cortices

threatening manner, it is valuable for you to tend to attend to that person rather than to other things around you.

More generally and to recap, under attention the controlled areas have neural activity which is altered by the attention control signals. These control signals are generated by what is called a controller in Figure 3, which creates the attention control signals itself. This generator of such control signals is composed of what are termed 'higher' areas, especially the prefrontal and parietal lobes. It is those we must understand better to begin a serious probe into attention and thence to consciousness.

CHAPTER ELEVEN

ATTENTION AS CONTROL

Control for Attention

As we saw in the previous chapter, attention in the brain functions by means of signals created in a separate higher-order control region in the brain sent to modulate the neural activity in the controlled, lower-order regions. The creation of such modulation is itself expected to involve a non-trivial level of internal complexity. The control signals have to solve various problems, such as helping goals be more effective in searching and detecting a face or other object in a complex scene, or in making complex motor actions. Moreover, there has to be suitable learning so as to design an attention control signal able to achieve control modulation purely for the incoming desired face you wish to detect and not for any of the distracter faces teeming around in the station. Similar control problems have been studied for many years by control engineers, so it could be worth our while to consider their solutions to control. It is not that we expect the attention system of the brain was itself constructed or analysed by a control engineer (the intelligent control designer?), but evolutionary pressures could be expected to produce at least as efficient a system as that achieved by any engineer. So we should naturally turn to engineering control ideas to help us understand how to construct an efficient attention control system for handling the information processing in the brain.

We have seen that attention involves complicated networks of connected brain regions. Such complexity is to be expected when we realise the nature of the tasks the attention control system must solve for some – how to bluff a whole nation into believing a 45-minute warning of setting off weapons of mass destruction by an 'evil' dictator, how to persuade people to believe in things about their minds or the world in which they live that have no basis at all in fact – I hope I do not need to go on.

Engineering Control

To explore this complexity, let me remind you what engineering control is about. It is concerned with how to control an operating plant in a factory or an engine in a car or aeroplane. Control ideas have played a very important role in the development of ever more advanced engineering systems over the past two hundred or so years. Thus James Watt (in whose name the unit of electric power is defined) invented the 'centrifugal governor' in 1788, by adapting it from a control 'governor' used in windmills to control the speed of steam engines (to which he also made many more improvements). It has been said of Watt that he ushered in the industrial age, changing what had been 90% rural to 90% industrial employment.

In the governor shown in Figure 4, the rotating balls on the left-hand side of the figure are pushed upwards and outwards by centrifugal force as the speed of the steam engine axle increases. This then progressively closes the steam valve on the right of the figure, causing the engine to slow down; similarly, as the engine slows the balls fall and the steam valve is automatically opened further, so allowing more steam and hence greater speed. This and other improvements allowed steam engines to be controlled in an automatic and safe manner so as to function as efficiently as possible. They led to a great family of devices for automatic control.

A later, very important, contribution of control to society was in the development of powered flight. The Wright brothers made their first successful test flight on 17 December 1903 in their famous powered plane at Kitty Hawk. By 1904 their plane Flyer II was able to make a fully controllable stable flight for substantial periods of time. The Wright brothers achieved such stable flying – the first in the world and without peremptory landing long before their desired final point of the flight – by means of using stable navigational control. They controlled how the plane

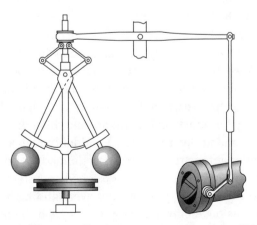

Figure 4 A version of the centrifugal governor used by James Watt to control the speed of a steam engine

lifted into the air using their process called 'wing warping', which used a wire running through the wings that could be pulled by the pilot to turn left or right. They later developed more sophisticated control methods for navigation.

Since then engineering control has expanded in both applications and in sophistication. More general control involves a plant that may make steel, for example, or some other manufactured commodity. The plant control signal will be required to produce the steel of a suitably desired composition, requiring control of the temperature at which it is made. On the other hand, an engine controller may be designed to keep the speed of a machine propelled by the engine from being too high or too low. There will therefore be a module (in software or hardware) that stores the desired state of the plant or of the engine being controlled, such as the upper and lower limits of the temperature of the steel during its manufacturing process. The goal may be used to give more or less heat to the steel in the plant, or more or less power to the engine to speed up or slow down the machine it is powering. If the goal is not being met, as determined by measurements on the steel or the plant, then a control signal, registering the error, must be generated to turn on more heat or power (or turn it down). This creator of control is naturally termed the plant control generator – it is the 'governor' of Watt's steam engine controller. Finally, there must be the 'plant' – be it the steel processing plant or the engine itself – that must be acted on by the control signal. The plant itself can be a very complex system, so the control tasks faced by control engineers are not at all trivial.

I remember the first time I was brought face to face with the power of control systems. I was travelling to Helsinki in cabin class, and was sitting at the front of the plane, with an empty aisle seat next to me. As we were about mid-flight the captain came and sat beside me. After a little conversation, I asked him who was flying the plane. 'Oh, it's on automatic,' he replied, smilingly. 'What about when you land?' I asked him, trying to keep the anxiety out of my voice. 'Most of the time it's landed automatically, but we have to keep our hand in, so we do land every now and again – especially when it is rough,' he replied. We continued talking for most of the flight, and then he returned to the cockpit before it landed, 'just in case'. I suddenly realised that we could even now be under automatic control as we landed – very smoothly, as it happened. How magnificent to have designed a system able to control such a complex task as flying a plane, and even landing it smoothly. Such control applications have moved a long way beyond the pioneering James Watt and his governor and the Wright brothers. Very impressive!

There are therefore a variety of distinct functional components in

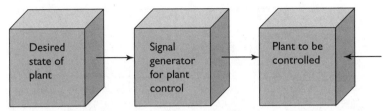

Figure 5 Basic engineering control system. This is composed of three basic modules: a goal module, to hold the desired state of the plant, a control signal generator module to generate the necessary control signal, as guided by the goal module, and the plant being controlled. The input on the right-hand side of the figure corresponds to the raw material of the plant, such as steel, whose temperature is to be controlled by the control signal entering the left-hand side of the plant, such as the flow of heat to the steel in the plant

engineering control models, able to begin to handle difficult problems like landing a plane, which could help us understand how the brain might move attention to serve certain goals by controlling the nerve cell activity at lower levels. To begin to look at attention in control system terms, we can divide the region creating the attention movement control signal into two main parts: the goal system and the attention movement generation system to achieve the goal (Figure 5). There is as well the plant being controlled, be it steel manufacturing or other manufacturing machinery, a steam engine, an aeroplane, a ship, a car, a space craft, among many others.

Application of Control Ideas to Attention

The division of labour involved in attention control, and the large set of brain areas involved in various attention tasks, as noted earlier, implies that some form of engineering control approach could be helpful to understand how the brain achieves the overall process of attention.

In order to apply engineering control ideas to attention, we note the existence of brain sites involved in attention with the following features:

- They amplify or decrease sensory input (in sensory cortices).
- They create control signals for this amplification/inhibition (in parietal and prefrontal cortices).
- Other possible functions could also be performed by brain modules involved in attention, such as in error detection, predicting the new state of the controlled system or feedback from it, etc.

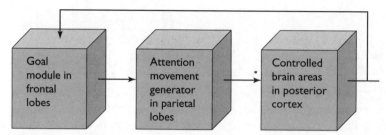

Figure 6 Simple ballistic control model for attention. The arrows indicate the suggested flow of information in the brain between the relevant modules, whose sites in the brain are as indicated in the boxes (and described in the text): input arrives in the different possible modalities from the eyes, ears, etc. into the brain, as shown by the arrow on the right-hand side. Some is processed up to a relatively high level in lower cortical areas, while there is a fast route to the frontal lobes to help breakthrough of attention to salient stimuli. The goals in frontal lobes are used to guide the attention control signal in parietal lobes to achieve the desired amplification/inhibition in lower-level cortices by suitable feedback

From the above I extend the simple engineering control model of Figure 5 to attention in Figure 6.

The model of attention I have shown in Figure 6 is the simplest possible. It is properly called a 'feed-forward control' or 'ballistic' model, as is that in Figure 5. In ballistic control a goal is set up in the goals module which biases the attention movement generator to move attention around the posterior cortical sites where objects and spatial information are represented, to help select that activity specified by the goal. In control theory, feed-forward control is regarded as the basic, simplest form of control. It involves what is properly called 'ballistic' movement control, since once the goal has been set up it drives the attention focus ballistically to what has been required by the goal.

Ballistic control is now known to be used by the brain in making motor actions. If you want to point to something or direct your fingers to touch a particular object, as I am doing in typing this chapter on my laptop, then you and I will use ballistic control to achieve our aims. I set up in my mind (in my frontal lobes) the particular letter key I want to press, and away goes the motor attention command signal to make the correct action; this signal is then translated into various muscle movements further down the motor hierarchy in my brain. In the end I make the movement and pass on to the next desired key.

Let me briefly describe to you some evidence that supports the simplest ballistic, feed-forward control model for attention of Figure 6.

Support for Ballistic Attention Control

There are at least two sorts of evidence for the presence of the three components (goals, attention movement signal generator, and lower-level areas of modulated attention) of the ballistic model of Figure 6 for attention movement control. First, there is the observation of the separation of sites in the brain involved in the movement of attention and those involved in attention achieving modulation; this evidence has already been described.

Second, there is evidence from brain-damaged people of the effects of their brain damage on their attention control and resulting modification of their experience. Given the observations of the different sites involved in ballistic control of attention, as described by Figure 6, there should be agreement between the resulting deficits in the movement of the focus of attention, as observed in brain-damaged patients, as compared to the powers possessed by the normal brain in controlling attention and detected by brain imaging machines. This extra consistency is a check on the validity of the results from the separate normal and deficit brains, like the checking of addition of columns of figures by also taking row additions and then adding all the rows together and comparing with the addition of all the column sums. All the evidence from these damaged brains completely supports what I am saying on the separation of powers as shown by the ballistic attention movement control model of Figure 6.

In the normal brain a number of experiments have been performed using brain imaging techniques, and, as remarked, already have led to strong evidence for the existence of the three main components of the ballistic model of Figure 6:

• Attentionally controlled regions of cortex (the 'plant' in control terms): this consists of posterior cortical sites in the brain in which input processing up to feature level (oriented bars or angles between them or even curves embedded in complex figures) occurs, and in which selected activity is to be amplified, the distracting activity inhibited for later higher-level processing. The brain sites involve various feature maps, such as for colour and shape in a cortical area termed V4, or for motion sensitivity in another cortical area called V5. In general, these modules are in primary and higher-level visual cortices. We also include as the controlled areas those parts of cortex involved with object representations, sited in the temporal lobes. Both of these assignments to parts of cortex are strongly supported by brain imaging and single-cell recordings. Overwhelming evidence for amplification/reduction of attended/unattended inputs has already been mentioned: it has been observed at all levels, from that of the single nerve cell up to the global brain networks active in attention.

This implies that all of anyone's brain can be considered a plant for information processing. Indeed, the phrase 'the machinery of mind' is most apt to describe the nature of your brain. I know it is a soulless description of the mind to regard its machinery as plant-like, but I use this term deliberately to make it clearer that there is no obvious soul, from this point of view, in the brain. I therefore have a very hard task to create a soul from such soulless matter. I am proceeding by deconstructing that overall plant (the whole brain) to find out how its machinery works in control terms. Moreover, the soul certainly does not reside in lower-level cortices, so the epithet 'plant' can more easily be applied to these definitely soulless regions of cortex.

Thus the important control strategy of attention filtering has allowed me to decompose your brain into a smaller 'plant' of neural machinery in your posterior cortices, and a controlling network of cortical areas in other lobes, as I have already mentioned. I thereby removed the epithet 'plant' from these higher-order control regions of the brain. I hope it will cease looking so soulless soon. I will continue by decomposing the other parts of the brain, other than the attention-controlled, soulless plant. Then there may be a better chance for the soul to emerge from its hiding place. Moving on, we come to the:

- Attention movement signal generator: an area of cortex which produces the desired relative amplification/inhibition of the input signal in the lower-level cortices to attain higher-level processing. There is evidence from brain imaging during covert movements of attention that control signals are generated in the parietal lobe, although the exact siting is still controversial. This support for the parietal lobes comes from many brain imaging studies, as well as from neglect studies in humans. There is evidence that spatial attention movement is controlled by the upper part of the parietal lobe, while the movement of the focus of attention to objects and their features is controlled by a different mid-brain parietal/temporal area. This split may arise from the dorsal/ventral pathway split mentioned earlier, with dorsal cortical sites being activated more rapidly by the motion/spatial-sensitive stream of neural activity than by the object-oriented ventral ones, so giving a spatial bias to the initial control of attention movement.

- Goals: this area of cortex has been observed to hold, for up to many seconds if needed, the neural activity representing movements required to be made on receipt of a given 'go' signal, such as to move attention to a particular place when a fixation light is extinguished. The goal area is sited in what is termed the dorso-lateral prefrontal cortex (on the convex frontal part of the cortex, where 'dorsal' denotes upwards and 'lateral' is to the side of the brain). To support this claim, for example, the second of a pair of sequential saccades (rapid eye movements) cannot be made accurately if a certain part of prefrontal cortex has been damaged, although there is no deficit in making single saccades. This indicates that this site is needed for holding a memory of the place to which the second saccade should go to while the first saccade is being made.

Is Ballistic Control Enough for the Brain?

I presented a control model of attention movement control as that of ballistic control and shown in Figure 6. A goal is chosen, as set up from outside the control system in general, and held on the goal site. It is used to bias the specific attention control signal created by the attention control signal generator. This attention movement signal is then fed back to lower-level posterior-sited cortex, without any correction being able to be made to the movement. Such ballistic control clearly encompasses a considerable amount of data on attention movement control in the brain, as a similar approach to motor response does for motor control. But it is well known that some form of feedback control is also used for motor control by the brain, as it is in flying a plane and in many other more sophisticated methods of control. Errors made in the initial motor program can then be corrected in mid-flight by the more sophisticated methods, if errors were made in the ballistic system or if the environment has changed rapidly.

It is expected that the inflexible pressures of survival will press heavily on an inefficient control system, such as one that is too inflexible in the face of its own errors or rapid changes in the environment. That has occurred for motor control in the brain. It takes note of what it is doing in its control signal while it imposes this control. It is not just ballistic, but importantly uses feedback in the control system. So we should expect a similar upgrade of attention control to have occurred in the brain brought about by the aeons of evolutionary pressure to be more effective. Feedback control achieves this by speeding up the control response if internal or external errors occur. So we must move forward to consider how feedback control may speed up attention. As a result, we will discover a possible mechanism at the heart, I suggest, of the creation of the experience of the inner self and so of consciousness itself. How marvellous that the brain could give up its innermost secret by paying careful attention to itself!

CHAPTER TWELVE

SPEEDING UP TO CONSCIOUSNESS

The Attention Control Copy Signal

If you are driving your car along a winding road you need to attend very carefully to the curving right side of the road (or left side, depending on the traffic rules), following correctly the curves of the road, stopping at traffic signals, etc. In acting in this manner you would need to use your ballistic attention control system, which I described in Chapter 11, in order to move the focus of your attention. I showed the structure of the model in Figure 6. To recap: it consisted of three regions, the first containing neural activity representing the attended scene, sited in your visual cortex. In the case of driving your car along a difficult road, your visual cortex would be filled with activity brought about by what you are seeing of the road, the hedges or fences on either side of the road, and possible road signs warning of even sharper curves to come, other cars and so on. Besides this activity, there were two further networks of modules in Figure 6. First, there was the generator of the attention movement control signal, which sent this attention control signal to your posterior visual cortex to modify its operation by amplifying activity representing the target you desired to attend to, most especially the side of the road you are driving on. At the same time, this attention signal would inhibit the neural activity from distracters, such as other cars passing you in the opposite direction (unless one suddenly veered off and came towards your car, when your attention would undoubtedly be broken into by the more salient input, very likely through circuitry also involving your prefrontal cortex as well as some lower-level visual cortical contributions). Second, there was your goal module, which contained the desired state, either as a given constant state in the case of a straight road, or more generally as a sequence of states – those of the curving road ahead of you – to be followed by your attention, and thence by your motor response of turning the wheel. Such time variations would arise, for example, if you were driving your car along a very curving road, with it bending and twisting so much so as to make your driving a very hard task requiring all your attention.

But these three regions – the input stimulus activation (the 'attention-controlled cortex' in your brain, including both the attended and distracter regions for objects), the goal activity as the target to which you wish to attend, and the attention movement signal generator to focus your attention on the target component of your brain activity caused by your visual input and singling out the target item for more detailed processing – are only the simplest form of engineering control system to move the focus of your attention around. Several further modules are used in general engineering control applications, and are also known to be used in motor control by the brain. When added to the ballistic control model, they achieve a more robust control system, able to handle situations in which errors of execution can be prevented very rapidly or uncertain response systems can be taken account. Considering how important attention is to your survival, I will now explain how these further components could be used by your brain to speed up the movement of the focus of your attention.

A crucial way to extend the ballistic model of control of the previous chapter is by feedback control. So far the goal or target you have set up (either from earlier guidance as top-down or from a rapid external signal drawing your attention bottom-up) has driven the signal guiding the focus of attention in posterior cortex in a blind fashion, taking no account of how well the goal is being achieved. Feedback, if introduced, can be used to help correct for errors in this movement process while the movement is being carried out.

The feedback can be either external or internal. In the former, external signals, arising from various sensors sensitive to changes brought about by an action, send signals to the action control system to indicate what has happened in the external world, and in particular whether or not the goal has been achieved. In the internal case, copies of the action control signal are used to generate expectations about how effective the action will be in attaining the required goal. If it is predicted that there will be an error, early corrections can then be made to modify the action and thereby make a more efficient stab at the goal. Both of these extensions, using the external or internal signals indicating goal achievement, need the addition of extra modules in the control apparatus.

Let me consider a thermostat. This is a device to keep the temperature of a room at a set level. It does so by measuring the temperature of the room, and comparing this with the desired temperature. If the actual temperature is below that required, the heat is turned on by the thermostat signalling to the boiler, and the room heats up again. If the temperature is above that desired, then the heat is turned off, and the room cools down. However, the temperature may fluctuate considerably about the desired temperature if there are constant openings and closings of doors, for example. To avoid this, a predictor associated with the door opening could be introduced. This would receive a copy of the signal indicating the opening of the door and send a signal requiring more heat to be turned on to counteract the blast of cold air from outside. In this way, there could be an early turning on of the heating system when it was predicted that shortly the open door would cause the room temperature to lower.

One additional control component is thus the predictor – called a 'forward' model in engineering control theory – basically because it looks forward into the future. This is what I introduced into the thermostat to make it work faster in response to demands for more heat. In the case of attention control, the prediction model generates an estimate of the state of the posterior cortex about to be brought about by the attention movement control signal. The predictor model produces as output an estimate of the attended state at the next time step. In the case that sensory feedback is delayed in response to a change of the focus of attention in the posterior cortex, this estimated or predicted state is of crucial importance in the creation of fast control. Such delay occurs, for instance, in motor control with respect to feedback from a limb, which can be some hundreds of milliseconds in duration. You could be dead by then!

In order to calculate an estimate of the state of any plant, it is necessary to have two items: first, the estimated state at a previous time step (assumed to have been created earlier by the predictor model), and second, an internal copy of the action producing the next state. Such a copy will allow the predictor model to work out how the movement control signal will change the current state, whose estimate we possess. For the thermostat this copy was of the command to open the door to let in cold air. This copy of the movement control signal has been called the 'efference copy' of the original control signal.

At this juncture I agree that this is an unusual new word I have introduced you to, and for some time I debated with myself about deleting 'efference copy', and reducing the whole book to words that are in common parlance. But then I looked up 'efference' in various dictionaries, to check that it was still in use in the general language of our times. I found the following definition:

Efferent = '*conveying outward or away, as to efferent nerve, a nerve carrying impulses away from the nervous system*' (Chambers Dictionary).

Numerous other dictionaries give similar definitions, all associated with the carrying away from a central region of some quantity or other, being a copy of some item used elsewhere than where the efference copy flows or is taken to.

The term 'efference copy' fits exactly what I wish to describe, it being a copy of a signal being sent out by the attention movement signal generator, the original attention signal itself speeding away from the generator to effect its work of filtering out distracters and amplifying the activity related to the attended stimulus in posterior cortex in the brain.

The efference copy of a control signal is very useful in engineering control to speed up the control action, so that incorrect control responses are able to be corrected before they can cause any serious damage. Such a signal is an important component in control mechanisms, especially for achieving fast control. The efficiency of the mechanism will depend naturally enough on other components of the control system, such as the accuracy of the forward model and of any other components. These will have to be learnt by suitable training methods in the case of complex systems, for which a specific forward model, for example, may be unknown, and has to be created from observations of the action of the plant.

Speeding Motor Control

The efference copy of motor actions is present in many of the actions we take. We all know that if we move our heads the world does not move with us – it remains quite stationary. This stability of the outside world under self-movement is explained by use of an efference copy signal of the movement control signal I have earlier described, to cancel out possible movement of external objects across the retina. This cancellation can be fooled if, for example, you move your eyeball passively (i.e. gently, with your finger): the world does then move. Try it. In that case there is no corresponding efference copy of a motor control signal to cancel the movement of objects across the retina since you have not sent out any motor control signal to move your eyes (the movement signal to make your finger move your eye is a very different sort of signal than an eye movement signal, and cannot be used in a similar manner to cancel external movement of inputs across the retina).

People who have lost muscle control of eye movement may send out the signal to move their eyes, but there is no subsequent movement. There is, however, an experienced movement of the external world. But this movement is in the opposite direction to that desired, indicating there has been use of an efference copy to move the world inside the person's brain in the opposite direction to that desired. However, there was no actual eye movement, so the efference copy compensation mechanism has nothing to compensate, so over-compensates in this case: the world moves in opposition.

That type of evidence for the existence of the efference copy in motor control in the brain is still only indirect. There is now clear evidence that such a signal actually exists in terms of a neural signal for eye movement flowing through the brain up to prefrontal sites. The signal is not used for direct eye control, as shown by the continuing capability of eye movement production when the efference copy is removed by cutting the connections carrying it to other brain areas. However, more complex movements – requiring the holding of memory of a first saccade, for example, before making a second one – are not able to be made properly when damage occurs to the efference copy: this copy is therefore crucial in solving complex tasks.

In support of the need for the use of efference copy in motor control is the fact that there may be a considerable time delay before feedback becomes available to the movement control signal generator; this delay may be upwards of several hundred milliseconds, as I mentioned earlier. The basic idea is that for rapid and effective control, a forward model of the state of a given plant (such as the position of a limb) has been created and used so that actions can be made on the musculature (the plant in this case) without having to wait for sensory feedback to correct movement errors. Such a forward model, as described earlier, maps the current state estimate and the action just taken onto an expected new state. Action signal generation, producing a new action based on the newly estimated internal state, is then used.

These more sophisticated control approaches, using forward models, depend on the efference copy mentioned above. They stem from the so-called and important 're-afference principle'. In this the effects of self-motion are removed from signals being fed back from sensory receptors, the so-called re-afference signals, where afference is the opposite to efference, with signals coming in from the periphery instead of going out to it in the case of efference. Subtraction of the efference copy from the afferent signal thereby removes any expected feedback component from the sensory signal. This re-afference principle was advocated independently by the German scientists von Holst and Mittaelstadt and the American scientist Roger Sperry in the 1950s. The image of a moving external world as arising from self-motion is thereby prevented by brain circuits based on this re-afference principle: the important property of stability of perception is maintained. Such a process is clearly very important in animals such as head-bobbing birds, where sensory processing is needed to continue through the head-bobbing phase. Otherwise the position of, say, a piece of food, would move as the head bobs forward, and the bird would be unable to feed – bad survival value. For humans, the subtraction of effects of self-movement clearly occur in stabilising the world when you move your eyes, as well as in the world movement when you cause you eyes to move by gently poking them with your fingers.

The discovery of such a process for motor control in living systems has made the re-afference principle very attractive as a control component and so it has been tested carefully. Roger Sperry, for example, permanently rotated one eye of a frog, and found it could no longer compensate for self-motion, so that the frog kept moving round and round to steady its external world without ever being able to do so. More recently, inability to tickle oneself has been recognised as involving a suitable re-afference signal (available as a copy of the tickling motor command) cancelling otherwise 'foreign' sensory signals of being touched by another. When you are tickled by someone else there is no efference copy of the tickling command available.

The efference copy of the tickling movement signal has been proposed as a signal of the movement having been made by the animal itself (where even chimpanzees and rats are known to display signals of laughter on being tickled, besides us humans). The cancellation of the tickling sensation has been suggested as being achieved by removing the predicted sensory inflow from the actual sensory inflow, which arises from the surface of the tickled region of the body. It was found by the experimentalists that if the self-tickling movement is delayed by suitable mechanical means beyond about 300 milliseconds, then the ability to tickle oneself now arises. In other words, self-tickling movements no longer become one's own, able to be predicted by using an efference copy of the motor command to do the tickle movements, if their associated efference copy is too separate in time from the actual tickling sensory feedback itself. You can only predict so far ahead in time. No chance of winning the lottery or at horses with such a short predictor!

Another control module, of relevance in engineering control, motor control and attention control, is that used to give an estimate or prediction of what feedback is to be expected from the plant after a given control signal has been applied to it. This feedback acts as an observation made on the plant, and can thereby be used to update the state estimate from the forward model, to keep it as close to reality as possible. However, the predictor of the feedback allows various changes to the control signal to be made very rapidly, before the plant feedback is available.

Finally, there is a so-called error or monitor module, valuable in training the various control modules, as well as crucial for correcting errors that may have arisen in the attention movement control signal. The output of the monitor module is calculated as the difference between the desired and the actual, or between the desired and the estimated, state values of the plant; the monitor output is the relevant error signal. The overall system is shown in Figure 7.

To summarise the processes occurring in the network of Figure 7, the control signal generator sends its movement signal to the 'plant' (such as the arm, with the control signal being to move the arm to a specific place or object), as well as sending an efference copy of itself to a forward model for modifying the estimate of the state of the arm (its position in space, for example). This new predicted position of the arm can be used to produce an error signal from the monitor. This error signal is based on a comparison between the desired arm state (from the goal module), and that predicted after the new action (from the forward model, updated by the efference copy from the control generator module acting as a proxy for the actual control signal) or actual arm response (by the sensory feedback signal, from the new position of the arm).

The presence of this more sophisticated brain control model for motor actions (compared to that in Figure 5) is supported by tests of a variety of subjects on a range of controlled movements. For example, a group of

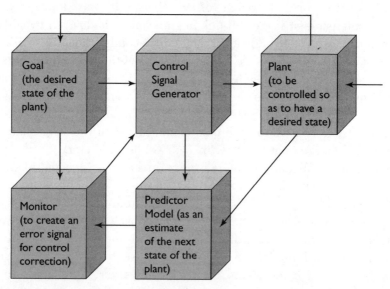

Figure 7 Feedback control model, as used in many areas of engineering control, as well as in explaining motor control by the brain. In motor control the plant is the motor muscular apparatus (such as the arm), and goals are desired actions to be taken

American scientists required a set of subjects to make movements of a hand-held pointer to a target of variable size. As the size of the target box decreases so, it was found, does the time to point to the inside of the box (it getting harder as the box gets smaller). In a similar manner, there was a corresponding increase in the time each subject took to make similar imagined movements. The detailed nature of the slowing observed in the case of subjects with motor cortex or parietal lobe deficit led to the conclusion that there is a forward model sited in the motor cortex while there is a motor control monitor involving the parietal lobe. Other sites are also expected to be involved, especially the cerebellum (sometimes called the 'little brain', and crucially involved in motor control; it is shown in Figure 2 underneath the back of the brain), suggested as being able to modify the output of movement control signal generators, as well as containing a forward model of the motor apparatus.

Further recent results also strongly support the existence of a forward model in motor control. One set of experiments analysed eye movements related to the unseen movement of a subject's hand towards a given target. It was found that each saccade was to a spot that the hand would move to about 200 milliseconds later. The overall eye movement was in terms of several saccades made during the smooth hand movement. So a predictor was at work allowing the eye to move ahead of the arm, using an efference copy of the arm's motor signal to send the eye ahead. Perturbation of the hand was followed by a brief inhibition of the saccades for about 100 milliseconds, with a following saccade to regain the predictive capability of the eye, about 100 milliseconds later. So the eye movement can work, it would seem, with a 100-millisecond look-ahead time – a real speed-up indeed: the eyes clearly have it in this instance!

Speeding Attention Control

Let me now apply the feedback control model of Figure 7 to attention. The use of the efference copy signal will allow attention movement to be speeded up, as it did for engineering control and more specifically for motor control in the brain. Shortly we will recognise the efference copy signal of attention movement as a crucial component of consciousness. But first let us consider it purely as a mechanism for attaining a more efficient and faster movement of the focus of attention.

Numerous past models of attention have used some sort of control framework, however much it was varied to suit the task. We here take the control model of Figure 7 seriously, since it provides a very general framework for the nature of control of any sort. At the same time there is a puzzle in neuroscience about the numerous areas being observed active in attention control. So this generality and flexibility of the engineering control approach, exemplified in how that architecture could apply to attention in Figure 7, may allow us to explain in more detail the different functions being performed by these numerous areas of the brain.

The model of Figure 8 incorporates various effects more fully by explicit treatment of the goal module. Goals can be generated internally – as in 'I want to meet that particular person off the train' – or externally when, for example, there is a sudden loud voice sounding through the station as an important announcement is made, drawing the attention of most people to it. This external driving of the focus of attention is achieved in the model of Figure 8 by the fast, direct input to the goals module from the input, as has been observed experimentally. The internal goal, after it has been created, is assumed to be held in what is called a 'working memory' module in the frontal lobes until it has been attained, again something observed both by brain imaging and at a single-cell level in monkeys. A more detailed version of the control model of Figure 8 is shown in Figure 9, with the nature of the connections made more explicit, and is discussed in more detail in Box 4.

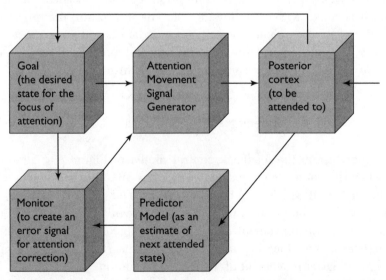

Figure 8 The extended attention motor control model of the brain. Here there is identity of the modules of Figure 7 to those in Figure 8, but now they are relabelled to be related to the various functional components of attention movement, as well as being able to be sited in various brain sites

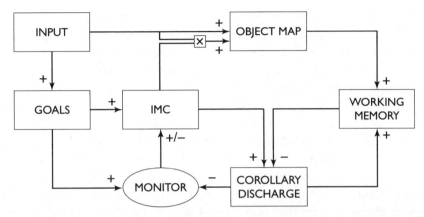

Figure 9 The more detailed feedback control model for attention. IMC = attention movement signal generator (where IMC denotes 'inverse model controller', the technical term in engineering control theory for the movement signal generator module); the + or − signs indicate excitation or inhibition exerted by the connection to the given module to which the arrow points; remember that the term 'collorary discharge' (with its own buffer module in the figure) is to be identified with 'efference copy' (which means the same as corollary discharge). The corollary discharge site (its buffer to hold activity for later use) is shown to be connected in an excitatory fashion to the sensory buffer (working memory) site, although inhibitory connections to other components are also needed to prevent distracters from emerging into reportability. Once the threshold of reportability has been reached, an inhibitory signal is sent out from the working memory site to cancel related activity on the IMC and the corollary discharge buffer, so they can start to process new inputs to reportability. The error monitor sends an error signal to the IMC to boost attention, so corresponding to attention being a scarce resource, not able to be shared easily among different tasks if errors are occurring in a given attention task (say, due to distracters, as in the attentional blink). There is now evidence arising (especially from recent data on the attentional blink) of the existence of both the various sites in Figure 9 as well as their proposed connections

BOX 4: A more detailed model of the attention movement control signal

I show in Figure 9 a version of the control model of Figure 8, but now with the nature of the connections between the various component control modules made more specific. This is elaborated on in the caption to Figure 9.

At the same time we have also taken specific account in Figure 8 of the other modules that I mentioned earlier: the monitor and forward modules; these have not been introduced previously into models of attention. Thus goal activity (generated either internally or externally, as I have just described) is compared in the monitor module with that arising from a forward model in the module marked corollary discharge (identical to efference copy). The resulting output of the error module is the level of error in attaining the desired goal. This error can be used to modify the attention movement control signal generator to amplify the attention control signal to make it stronger and to fight off distracters. In other words, this error boosting mechanism provides attention to a desired target with a boost, so making it more dedicated to attaining its goal to be attended to. This thereby provides a neural model of the origin of the scarce nature of attention (where scarceness is equated with not being able to attend to more than one thing at once if it is difficult enough to do so).

I emphasise again that my approach, by its generality of having at its disposal the whole gallimaufry of engineering control, gives a unified but flexible framework from which to take maximal account of the underlying control nature of attention as observed by psychological analysis and brain imaging experiments. It includes the most important of previous approaches to modelling attention. To support and make more precise the engineering control approach, we must now search for evidence in the brain for the various components of the model of Figure 8, both for endogenous and exogenous goals. There is positive evidence for the existence of each of the further modules, as shown in neuroscientific detail in Box 5.

BOX 5: Evidence for the elements of attention feedback control

I presented evidence in the previous chapter for the existence of the relevant ballistic control modules for attention (those in Figure 6). Thus we have already discussed evidence for the existence of the goal module (in prefrontal cortices), attention movement signal generator module (in parietal lobes) and attended plant modules (as posterior cortical areas). Considering the remaining components of Figure 8 separately, we arrive at the following conclusions:

- Monitor module: it provides a measure of the error occurring during an attention movement, obtained by comparing the actual to the desired attention target. Evidence has been cited earlier for the monitor involved with motor action control being in the parietal lobes. The same site is also expected to be involved in the movement of attention, from evidence already quoted as well as from the coming together there of inputs from many bodily sites (these being needed for effective determination of errors in attention as well as in action control). There may also be error signals arising from the cingulate, a region in the middle of the frontal lobes where the two halves of the brain are closest together. A number of experiments have shown that the cingulate is involved in conflict resolution and error correction; even a separation of these two functions has been suggested in different parts of the cingulate.

- Forward model: this updates the estimate of the attended state of the plant. We note that a crucial difference has now crept in: attention singles out only a part of the activity in lower posterior cortex, corresponding to the stimulus desired to be attended to. Thus it is estimation of the 'attended state' that is crucially to be achieved by the forward model; all the rest of the lower (and distracting) neural activity is not to be considered. Here we see the powerful filter action of attention, a feature already noted as long ago as the fourth century BC by Aristotle. Moreover, this filtering of activity supports the crucial character of attention as a gateway to consciousness. The latter is only expected to arise once the attended state estimate is available: attention yet again appears as the gateway to consciousness.

Visual attention is known to be involved in eye-movement preparation, as indicated by what has been called the 'premotor' theory of attention. In this, attention is regarded as a precursor to movement, but with similar properties except for muscular response. There is considerable support for such an approach. Also, forward model activity is observed in the updating of receptive fields (the region in space whose illumination causes a cell to respond), even before a saccade occurs, as has been shown to occur in what are termed frontal eye fields and a region in the mid-brain termed the superior colliculus, as well as in the parietal lobes. Even stronger evidence has recently been obtained for the existence of a forward model for the direction of a saccade: saccades are shown to precede unseen arm movements by about 200 milliseconds, and this could only occur by means of a predictor of the direction of movement.

Thus there is support for the existence of a forward model, possibly sited in the frontal eye fields (along with sub-cortical components), together with possible contributions from the parietal and other regions. The siting of the monitor partly in the parietal lobes leaves the forward model to be expected to have some frontal basis in the frontal eye fields, as supported by the underlying frontal recurrent architecture (involving sub-cortical loops of activity circulating around) needed for dynamic sequence learning and generation and the good connectivity of parietal lobes and the frontal eye field in the prefrontal cortex).

- Attention copy signal (efference copy or corollary discharge): this provides a copy of the attention movement control signal sent from the attention movement signal generator to be used in updating the error on the monitor and in allowing modification of the estimate of the attended state by the forward model. The existence of this attention copy signal is crucial to our approach to consciousness (as I will develop shortly). What is the evidence for its existence in attention movement control?

The presence of a copy of the eye movement and motor action control signal is well recorded, as I have mentioned earlier. This copy also plays an important role in self-actions, such as not allowing one to tickle oneself, as I described earlier. The corresponding situation is not so clear for attention. However, the tight coupling between attention movement and saccade preparation that I have already mentioned (such as contained in the premotor theory of attention) is relevant to help understand recordings from frontal eye field and lateral intra-parietal area cells that possess relevant pre-saccadic responses, occurring up to 70 milliseconds before a saccade. Single-cell recordings in the frontal eye field imply, from these predictive responses, the presence of a copy of the signal of the intention to make a saccade. Attention and saccades are coupled strongly together, as noted above, which implies that this pre-saccadic activity could be generated by a copy of the attention movement control signal.

This evidence supports the existence of a copy of the attention movement control signal in various sites (including the lateral intra-parietal area and superior colliculus). It also supports the proposal that the frontal eye fields are involved in updating the posterior attended state estimator noted above.

Points I wish to emphasise in association with the attention movement control model of Figure 8 are:

- The model applies to other sensory modalities, such as audition and touch.
- There will be competition/combination between different sensory

modalities in the overall model, with a multi-modal parietal region devoted to handling the overall competitive process needed to correctly share attention (and observed by brain imaging experiments).

- There exists separate control of attention to object features (colour, shape, etc.) and to space, although there seems to be some evidence that spatial attention is primary, and used to guide temporally later feature- or object-based attention control (although this is still controversial).
- There must be extended learning (especially in childhood), possibly through learning of the feedback error, using the monitor signal, to lead to effective modulation of the attention movement signal generator of posterior cortical input activity.
- Sub-cortical sites will be involved in input representations, and in the setting up of goals, as well as in the monitor and forward models.
- Sub-cortical activation, through acetylcholine, together with other neuro-modulators, such as noradrenalin, is also to be expected to be crucial in the spread of attention control.
- There will also be use of the reward 'juice' of the neuro-modulator dopamine in learning (in numerous sub-cortical and cortical sites), as is well documented.

There is also the question of how the executive control, known to be exerted by the prefrontal cortex (as was lost in the case of Phineas Gage, when he lost a good part of his prefrontal cortex in a mining accident), is

Table I Cortical modules involved in the control architecture of attention movement, as related to the modules in Figure 8, and as discussed in the text

Name of module	Brain site of module	Function of module
Plant	Posterior cortex	Processes the stimulus input
Attention movement generator	Parietal lobes	Create the attention movement control signal to move the focus of attention
Goals	Prefrontal cortex	Hold the desired target stimulus which is to be attended
Working memory	Parietal and temporal lobes	Holds activity for a short time: acts as estimator of the attended state
Attention copy	Parietal and temporal lobes	Holds a copy of the attention movement control signal, as an estimate of the predicted attended state
Monitor	Cingulate cortex	Creates an error signal from the difference of the goal and attended state estimates

achieved by means of attention across different modalities. It has been suggested that the parietal lobe is able to support especially extended competitive interactions by means of its strong inhibition between nearby cells. This could be brought about by strong activation of small inhibitory neurons there, these being especially sensitive to the acetylcholine flooding through that region as part of the attention activity. Thus overall control may be fought out mainly in the parietal lobes.

I conclude this discussion of the manner in which attention can be speeded up by presenting a table of the relevant modules to achieve this (Table 1).

Working Memory

We have now reached the point where we have gained a suitably deep understanding of attention that it can form a framework for our attack on consciousness. More could certainly be added to the model of attention I have developed so far, for example filling in more details of the architecture of Figure 8 (partly done in Figure 9 and Box 5), but this is not the place to delve much further into attention control in the brain. To proceed with deriving an understanding of consciousness from the model of attention I have presented to you so far, I have to specify one more aspect of the activity in the model of Figure 8 for attention to include a crucial feature that has been understood ever more completely by psychologists since the mid-1960s and by brain imagers more recently.

The essential component I have missed so far is termed 'working memory'. It has two parts: a short-term memory component and an executive component. The first of these corresponds to activity held 'in your mind' for several seconds, such as a telephone number, while you dial the number. It is then forgotten. If it had not been deposited into long-term memory it would then be lost and you would have to look it up again if you needed to repeat the phone call at a later time. The second – the executive – corresponds to the control system in your brain that makes the decision to make the phone call, or to rehearse the phone number in your head if you could not get through the first time. Other executive actions could be decisions needing to be taken at the highest level, such as, for me, that between immediately going out to get a coffee versus continuing to work on this page of my book.

The first component of the working memory system – the buffer – is to be regarded as a 'slave' system, which holds activity that is sent to it for a fixed period of a few seconds only. It does not take decisions nor initiate rehearsal of its own activity, such as deciding if your phone call needs to be repeated in a few minutes time and you want to hold on to the phone number by rehearsing it.

Various forms of such slave buffer components of the working memory system are known to be present in the brain: for the phonological content of speech input, for visuo-spatial inputs in vision, for objects such as faces or places, and possibly other forms of input.

The importance of such buffer sites is that they can support the holding of concepts for further processing over extended periods of time. This is generally regarded as one of the essential components of thinking and consciousness. It can also be seen as a crucial component of the feedback engineering control model of attention of Figure 8. Usually in engineering control models a forward model is supposed to contain an estimate of the state of the plant. For the forward model of the movement of attention, this will be modified so that it contains an estimate of the attended state of the posterior cortex. But this estimated state needs to be held for a few seconds in order to be able to be used by executive systems to think or decide or whatever about what is being attended to. This interpretation – that the buffer site of working memory is to be identified with the forward models for attention state estimation – fits well with the fact that attention control is being exerted by the overall modules of Figure 8 on the posterior cortical activity. Thus, it is crucially the target goal state of the posterior cortical activity that is of interest. It is that for which the forward model needs to produce an estimate. The other activations in posterior cortex are those of distracters in the external world, and not of further present interest. So it is appropriate that the forward model only concerns itself with the desired attended component of the posterior activity. As I have said before, attention is the brain's ultimate filter.

It is natural to identify this attended state estimate as corresponding to that of the buffer in the relevant modality. Thus the phonological store holds phonological activity extracted under attention from incoming speech for further processing, such as for response or attaining gist over an extended speech input.

Consider someone listening to another person talking at length. The content of this speech must be held over periods of several minutes, or in the case of a lecture or a political address this could extend to up to an hour. In the latter case it is clear that an extended form of memory is needed in addition. However, a buffer is certainly needed to guide the content being laid down in this more permanent memory. As expected, buffer sites appears to have good connections to permanent memory stores, which are sited near the most crucial brain system for long-term memory storage, the hippocampus. This is a set of cell sheets in the middle of the temporal lobe, and sited between the lower parts of the two hemispheres. It is therefore well protected, except from serious brain injury or from the surgeon's scalpel cutting out tissue causing otherwise untreatable epilepsy. Cases where this region has been removed are well known to lead to severe loss of long-term memory; a case of this sort (H.M.) was reported in Part I, and the enormous problem then ensuing for the patient noted.

CHAPTER THIRTEEN

THROUGH ATTENTION TO CONSCIOUSNESS

Working Towards Consciousness

In the previous chapter I introduced buffer working memory sites in the brain, where activity is held for a few seconds while it becomes accessible to further attentive processing (such as planning, thinking, reasoning, etc.). I interpreted these sites as specifying the attended 'picture of the world': they are the buffer sites for holding the result of attention being paid to the world, in terms of the attentionally amplified lower level stimulus activity in the brain attaining these buffer sites. For example, if I attend to the cup of coffee by my right hand then a representation of that cup will be activated on the appropriate buffer site for objects. It will have, associated or bound to it by various neural mechanisms, the activities in lower-level visual cortices representing, in my brain, the lower-level features of which the cup is composed, such as the various parts of its shape (its semicircular handle, its partly spherical body, and so on), the brown coffee in its interior, and other features.

I now bring in consciousness, employing ideas current since William James's important work at the end of the nineteenth century on the need for neural activity to have a suitable duration in order for consciousness to arise of the relevant input. This has been explored and updated in more detail in my 1999 book *The Race for Consciousness*. To summarise: a competition on a working memory buffer (as discussed earlier) between sites with neural activity extended in time, leads to one of these activities winning, suitably guided by past context, the emotional value of the related stimuli, and long-term experience in memory. There is, in particular, in what I called the 'central representation' on the buffer sites in the well-connected parietal lobes, information about the state of the body, of intentions for action and of object character. I proposed that the activity being held for several seconds in that buffer site in the brain is a good candidate for the contents of consciousness. The activity on that buffer site is known to be well coupled to that on lower-level cortical sites, by various mechanisms binding the lower-level features with the object stimulus represented in the temporal lobe, as I just mentioned. Such binding of lower-level features to a higher-level object representation gives depth and meaning to that content. This is not a new proposal, and has been seriously put forward over several decades by numerous psychologist and neuroscientists. I formalise it as:

> *The Contents of Consciousness Principle: these are to be identified with activities on the relevant buffer site, and hence with a representation of the attended state of the external world, with the associated set of neural activities representing the bound lower-level features composing the object being viewed.*

In this manner we relate consciousness to attention. To justify this identification we need to follow various avenues:

1. Experiments show that various relevant buffer sites are co-activated with the experience of consciousness in subjects. These sites are thus to be regarded as the neural correlates of consciousness. There are further sites beyond those solely activated concomitantly with conscious content, as to be expected, since there must be further components of brain activity to support the buffer sites so as to fill out their content with more detailed features (as discussed above). This has been shown by numerous experiments.

2. Experiments show that when the buffer site is not activated then there is no awareness of the associated input stimulus, even though there may be considerable activity that shows this stimulus has caused activity in lower-level cortical areas. In the case of vision these lower-level sites would be involved with the feature components of the stimulus (the colours and edges and component curves and sub-shapes of an object, for example), as well as some object-like higher representations. These latter may not be as strong as those arising if there was awareness of the stimulus itself. But this high-level activity, such as of the semantic category of the object, can still be strong enough to affect later decisions. Thus subliminally (non-consciously) showing the word 'doctor' will cause a slightly later showing of the word 'nurse' to elicit a faster response than other words or non-word strings in a word/non-word decision task. Again, experiments are in support of the occurrence of such priming at a non-conscious level.

3. When a buffer site is destroyed there is no awareness of activity in the associated modality. Thus damage to the right parietal lobe (the site of some buffer sites) will cause neglect, in which there will be no

awareness at all of objects in the opposite side of space or alternately or as well as the opposite side of the patient's body. This feature is compounded with the possibility of damage not only to the relevant buffer site but also to other components of the attention control system, such as the attention movement signal generator. We will return to this question later when we consider defects in experience more fully, but in any case the evidence is consistent with damage to the relevant buffer site causing such a deficit in consciousness.

There are numerous other supports for such identification, but we will leave these and turn to the important problem of consciousness itself.

Introducing Consciousness

In Chapter 11 I presented a control model of attention. It was developed in a general engineering control framework and then applied to particular aspects of motor control by the brain and to visual attention in Chapter 12. I also presented in Chapter 12 strong evidence for the existence of these various attention control sites in the brain. We will therefore use the architecture of Figure 8 as a basis for the further search for consciousness. We would expect that, if our control model of attention is of real worth, it will allow us a glimpse of the way that consciousness might arise as a component of the overall movement of attention. It will be through this movement of attention that awareness of an external object or of an action arises. We must now consider how that could occur.

We must be careful in the expectations we place on attention. In particular, we must realise that while attending to an event is necessary for consciousness of it, attention is not in itself sufficient for consciousness: a blindsighted subject benefits from a prior cue directing his attention to a blindsighted part of his visual field in spite of having no awareness of that cue. There is also controversy over whether, in a very rapid stream of objects, there is total unawareness of the second of the two objects (unavailable for later report) or only short-term awareness but ensuing amnesia of the object – so-called 'attentional blindness'. There is also subliminal attention capture of objects, with coding up to semantic level, as numerous psychological experiments have shown, and which was mentioned at the end of the previous chapter. That attention is always needed for consciousness has been recently controversial; for more detail on this see Box 6.

BOX 6: A Controversy over Consciousness and Attention

In a recent paper it was proposed by the Dutch neuroscientist Victor Lamme that attention and consciousness are distinct. Feedback of neural activity between two regions was claimed by Lamme as the only necessary ingredient to create consciousness. But this claim is destroyed by the large number of feedback systems in the brain which function outside consciousness. A simple example is that of the densely amnesic subject H.M. who had his hippocampus on both sides of his brain removed (to help cure his otherwise intractable epilepsy). Yet H.M. has no apparent defects of conscious processing except for long-term memory deficits. Those who meet H.M. say that he converses very agreeably and sensibly with them, although he will not recognise them at all if he sees them again ten minutes later. The hippocampus has remarkable recurrent connectivity in the special cell sheet called CA3 (right inside the overall recurrence of the hippocampus). CA3 has now been shown to be crucial for the ability to remember a learnt pattern from a fragment of it, since such a facility is lost in transgenic mice (who were unable to create such recurrent connections in CA3 due to their defective genes). Thus, at least the hippocampus is an example of a neural network which creates pattern completion, but it is not needed for ongoing consciousness. There are numerous other sites of feedback activity in the brain with similar characteristics.

The subtleties of the relation of attention to consciousness, mentioned above in association with blindsight, do not change the fact that attention is the closest neuro-physiologically and psychologically well-researched faculty we possess to consciousness. It is *the* gateway to consciousness. We will use it to guide our modelling of consciousness. The attention 'gate' has subtleties about it that will require careful consideration, but these can only be usefully discussed, as I have already pointed out, after an initial, suitably powerful model of attention has been created. I have prepared the ground by developing such a model in the previous chapter. Its essence appears in the model of Figure 8.

I earlier mentioned that the perceptual component of attention involves activity in the parietal lobes, as associated with certain of the control components moving attention that I discussed above. This parietal activity, and related deficits of awareness arising from parietal damage, has led to the parietal lobes being regarded as a crucial region for consciousness creation. Such a conclusion has been supported by recent brain imaging results, such as that when there was awareness of emotionally relevant inputs during extinction and neglect experiments in subjects; the parietal lobes were especially important in those tests, with observation of increasing activity correlated to the awareness of the inputs.

The Creation of Consciousness from Attention

The control model of visual attention discussed in the previous chapter is at last ready to be analysed for its ability to support the additional experience of consciousness of an input being attended. One component of this depends on the 'contents of consciousness principle' I enunciated and gave support for at the beginning of this chapter.

But I must repeat that this neural activity is relevant only for the content of conscious experience. In spite of the good connectedness of the parietal lobes, and the extended duration of its neural activity, there is no obvious reason for inner experience to arise from that activity. Why should it? A robot built with the above internal neural machinery would be expected to be a zombie. Since this position is one at odds with all the models of consciousness produced until now, including my own, presented in my 1999 book *Race for Consciousness*, the matter clearly needs to be discussed at greater length.

What has been missing from all of these earlier models, in spite of the claims of their authors that they are sufficient for consciousness? It is that any neural system, constructed on previously proposed architectures and mechanisms, would have no sense of ownership – of their being an inner self. For example, in many models the neural activity arises from a set of what are called 'attractor neural networks'. In an attractor neural network, activity is continually recurring back and forth between the neurons as it 'relaxes' finally into some state of activity which remains the same, or the activity oscillates back and forth, like a wave oscillating up and down. So this gives neural activity with suitable duration in time. However, there is no mechanism for the existence of an associated 'inner feel' to such activity. There is no mechanism to provide the sense of 'holding' or of 'possession' of it. That, I claim, is what is missing from all of the models proposed so far. It is a fatal flaw, since there is nothing of 'what it is like to be' in those systems. They have content but no breath of conscious experience.

Another important point indicating that something is missing from the continuing buffered activity in parietal lobes to make it the 'content of consciousness' is that continued activity can occur in numbers of other sites in the brain. I have already mentioned that this certainly is the case for activity in the frontal lobes. But yet they can be lost without apparent loss of consciousness, as the case of Phineas Gage shows. So there must be a different sort of activity than mere continued neural activity to grant the full epithet 'conscious' to it. The extra magic component is to do with inner experience, the 'what it is like to be' aspect that still somehow has to be created. So the working memory activity, suitably bound to lower-level feature activity, provides content, but not yet for consciousness.

Our task is thus to insert some form of inner experience involved with ownership of the about-to-be-present content. It is the crucial step. But how could it be achieved? I will have to delve more deeply into the attention control model I developed in the previous chapter. It will not be an easy ride. But to summarise where I am going, let me state the result as succinctly as possible: ownership comes from the attention signal used to create what was earlier called the 'efference copy', but which I now term the attention copy signal. It is the attention movement 'reverse echo', granting some sort of presence to the content represented by buffer working memory activity (which has not yet been created by the workings of the attention control signal). The attention copy signal carries the signature of the presence of the about-to-be experienced content, but a presence that is as ghostly as an echo signal coming back across a valley or in a cave or cavernous room.

Let me expand on that analogy. I am standing in a steep-enough sided valley, and call across it. I hear an echo of my call. It sounds as if there is someone else present, responding to my call by the echo. Someone else is there across the valley. I will use this feeling of presence to create the experience of ownership of consciousness. However, it will be through a pre- or reverse echo that presence is created in the brain: the copy of the attention movement control signal – providing the ownership feeling – arrives before the attended input stimulus. That is what, I propose, creates the pre-reflective self. The content of the pre-reflective self experience is only that of ownership, I claim.

This attention copy signal provides then the sense of 'being there' before anything of content is actually there, so is a reverse echo. An echo arrives after you have shouted, but here the attention copy signal is there before the content arrives. But that reverse timing feature is necessary to guarantee that all will be correct – so immunity to error about 'I' – before any content arrives.

Having given you a brief tour of my consciousness model, let us return more fully to the control model of Figure 8. An input is to be attended to, chosen originally by its emotional attractiveness, either from high-level goals or due to external demand. A suitable attention movement signal is created by the attention movement control generator of Figure 8 to focus attention on the brain activity representing the input, and catch and hold it, at the same time repelling distracters. There is an efference copy signal arising from this signal to move the focus of attention. As I said, I will call this signal the 'attention copy' signal. This attention copy will arrive at its buffer (to help speed up the access of content to its buffer, and to generate an error signal, if appropriate) some hundred or so milliseconds before any signal from the amplified input at its own buffer (where the attention amplification was turned on by the attention control signal arriving at its new focus of the attention in the posterior cortex). Such amplification requires some 100 or so milliseconds to be achieved, as shown by several detailed experiments over the past few years. Thus, the attention copy signal is used to help bring this forward, so speeding up the emergence into consciousness of its content.

We can catalogue the various processes as they occur when attention is being moved from one site to another in the architecture of Figure 8. This flow of information is described in Box 7 as a sequence of processes.

The flow of activity is complex as it sweeps ever further into the brain from its input to visual cortex (from the eye) to the temporal lobe (where objects are recognised) and to dorsal regions (where their spatial positions are extracted). With attention feedback included, the detailed flow is described in some of its complexity in Box 7. This involves the description of the support that attention provides for a target stimulus gaining acess to its buffer working memory site, and so to consciousness as described earlier. It is here that we see the gateway aspect of attention at work, performing its sentry-like role in a way depending on the proper functioning of the modules of neurons to help speed attention on its way, and that I have already introduced in the previous chapter.

BOX 7: Detailed flow of information

1. The attention movement control generator in Figure 8 produces an attention movement control signal, under either external or internal goal guidance.
2. A copy of this attention movement signal is simultaneously generated.
3. This attention copy is sent to its own specialised buffer site, so as to be available for rapid checking of any expected error by the monitor.
4. Simultaneously the attention copy supplies a wake-up signal to the buffer site, as shown by the arrow with a positive (for

excitatory) sign on it from the attention copy buffer to the sensory buffer; simultaneous inhibition of possible distracter activity on the sensory buffer is activated by this attention copy signal.

5. In the meantime the attention movement signal from the attention movement signal generator reaches the posterior cortex (in Figure 8) and amplifies the relevant stimulus activity there representing the goal, and inhibiting that for distracters.

6. The resulting amplified activity accesses the sensory buffer site, and ultimately achieves enough activity to be larger than some threshold, so as to be able to be distributed around the brain to other buffer sites for report. This report signal also turns off the goal activity in the goal module that caused the initial guided attention amplification in the first place, as well as annihilating the attention copy signal on its own buffer. This thereby allows new and fast movements of attention to other stimuli, with least interference from the movement of the focus of attention that had just been made to the previous stimulus, now on its sensory buffer.

7. Before the sensory buffer is accessed, the error signal from the monitor created using the next attended state (using the copy of the attention movement signal to update the predictor model as the attended state estimator), if present, is sent to the attention movement generator of Figure 8 to boost amplification of the goal stimulus activity in the posterior cortex, as well as inhibiting that for distracters represented in the attention movement signal generator module.

To summarise: activity from the environment is processed by a hierarchy of feature detector modules, ending up with activation of a high-level object representation. If this is to be attended, then the object activity is amplified strongly enough, bound to its companion lower-level feature activity, so that it can access the buffer working memory site to give a new attended state. Before this happens a copy of the attention movement signal is used to help speed up this process by preventing any distracters accessing the buffer sites and helping amplify the actual object representation on the buffer site. Once this access is achieved the activity on the buffer site turns off the attention copy to allow rapid access of new attended stimuli.

To justify that amazing claim, I will start by repeating the above analysis interpreting the nature of attended neural activity in terms of possible conscious experience. As I said above, the content of consciousness arises from the stimulus activity in posterior cortex, after suitably strong attention amplification, attaining activation of its representation in its buffer site. The specific content of consciousness is determined both by this sensory buffer activity as well as by the correlated activity in lower cortical sites for the more specific features of the stimulus object or place. Awareness of content follows from the 'contents of consciousness' proposal that I mentioned earlier in this chapter. How inner perspective arises is thus as follows.

There is a gap of time before the amplified stimulus signal arrives strongly enough at its sensory buffer to cancel the attention copy signal waiting on its buffer. This will be so both for the externally based driving of attention by a direct input to the attention movement control signal generator, and in the internally created goal case. During this time gap the attention copy signal will be sitting bubbling away on its own buffer. The basic proposal of the model of Figure 8 is that this briefly buffered signal (possibly together with suitably correlated activity in other sites) provides the conscious experience of ownership and gives the sense of inner perspective. This leads us to the ownership principle for consciousness, expressed below:

The ownership principle: the ownership of conscious experience is created by the attention copy signal being held on its own buffer site for use in speeding up attention and to make it more robust against a variety of errors.

We turn to consider this ownership principle, and related points about ownership and agency, next.

Ownership and Agency: Components of the Self

To explore ownership further, the self has a variety of components, involving subjective as well as objective character. Here we are concerned with subjective aspects of self going under the descriptions of ownership and agency, as recently discussed by the American philosopher Sean Gallagher. He notes that it is important to distinguish between these two concepts. I can consider that I am the agent of a movement of my arm as I move it. On the other hand, if my arm is moved passively by someone else, I can realise that is so, but still know that it is *my* arm that is being moved. Thus, agency and ownership are distinct.

This distinction is especially revealed by the possibility of error, a feature I have mentioned earlier, but will repeat since it is crucial to my discussion. It goes like this: I cannot be in error when I claim that my arm moved. Similarly I cannot be in error that it is I who feels pain. It is not sensible to ask 'Are you sure it is you who feels pain?'. This important feature of conscious experience is what has been termed 'immunity to error through misidentification with respect to the first person pronoun', originally by the American philosopher Sidney Shoemaker in 1968. Such an error, shown through careful experiments, can occur over the attribution of agency. This was done by tests on subjects viewing their gloved hand moving. An experimenter's hand can replace (by suitable image tricks) the subject's own hand without them realising, provided the movements made by the experimenter are not too different from those of the subject. On the other hand it is difficult to conceive of attributing to someone else the inner conscious experience involved with ownership.

It is a reasonable thesis that the most primitive form of self-knowledge is that of the ownership of the movement of attention. This can arise in any animal with the most simple attention control system. It is not even necessary to possess a frontal goal module (possibly due to lack of frontal cortex), since attention could still be moved by sudden external stimuli. As noted earlier, such low-level attention movement control occurs for rapid inputs even in humans: these stimuli gain nearly automatic access to the attention movement controller, as known by many studies of attention shifting. Such externally caused movement can also occur without the need for peripheral feedback. It is therefore much more rapid than the internally created variety.

This mechanism of ownership, proposed here as arising from the copy of the attention movement signal, helps explain the continued consciousness of subjects who have lost all sense of proprioceptive feedback (that for the positions of the limbs from specialised nerve cells in the muscles) by de-afferentation of the relevant sensory input nerves. Such people should have suffered severe deficits in their sense of self if, for example, there was a solely bodily basis for that; they did not. Thus the case of a person who suffered a viral attack that destroyed his proprioceptive system was investigated by the British doctor Jonathan Cole and his French colleague; they reported that the subject, on coming round from the viral infection, found himself as if 'floating' in his hospital bed. Yet they never said he felt any reduction in his 'I'. The 'I' is apparently above all that bodily thing; it needs to be to create a more soul-like aspect to the inner self.

The claim I am now making is that the buffered attention copy signal produces a conscious experience of ownership, breathing the light of inner experience into temporally extended neural activity. It is that which creates the sense of 'I' that is not destroyed by de-afferentation. Any robot thereby equipped would no longer be a zombie: it would have an inner feel of the ownership of the amplified input brought about by the short-lived attention copy signal on its own buffer. The claim is based on the related one, which I earlier called the 'contents of consciousness principle', that the content of consciousness arises from temporally extended activity on a suitably well-connected sensory buffer site. I posited earlier that this created the experience of the content of consciousness in the buffer site of Figure 8 in the earlier contents principle. For the coupled monitor/buffer sites of Figure 8, I now propose that the new item of information arising in the process of moving your attention to a new stimulus is a copy of the signal causing your own movement of attention. It is this item that I claim is the spark of 'how it is like for you to be conscious'.

Thus the crucial feature of the information flow in the architecture of Figure 8 is that the sense of ownership is created by the buffered attention copy signal, it being held for a suitable length of time before being annihilated by the amplified signal representing the attended object arriving at its buffer. I claim that this process grants immunity to error through misidentification of 'I', unless there has been an almost total breakdown of the attention control system. This can be seen for the undamaged system: the sense of ownership engendered by the attention copy signal on its buffer can only be cancelled by the appropriate afferent input amplified by the original attention movement signal itself turning off the 'ownership' attention copy buffer signal.

In other words, the attention copy signal on its own buffer stands like a sentry at the gateway to the sensory buffer, giving initial support only to those trying to enter the gate that are exactly like the goal stimulus activity. But once the amplified posterior cortical stimulus has achieved reportable access to its sensory buffer – it has broken through to awareness – the sentry has its orders changed (by destruction of the sentry's buffered activity by the correct sensory buffer activity). It is now ready to receive a new order (a new attention copy signal from the attention movement generator). But the brief period of holding the previous attention copy on its buffer produced, it was claimed by the 'ownership principle', the experience of ownership in the subject of the about-to-be-experienced content of consciousness, arriving, with its associated and concomitant activities in relevant posterior cortical sites.

Putting it in a different metaphor, the pre-echo of the attention movement signal is its copy. Holding that for a suitable time on a buffer site will lead to a feeling of presence – that of the attention movement signal itself. This pre-echo feeling will engender an experience of 'presence' in relation to the about-to-arrive attended object activity: the experience will therefore be one of ownership of that object activity.

No conscious experience can arise until the attention copy arrives at its buffer. Content-full conscious experience of the amplified input leads to cancellation (or reduction) of this buffered attention copy signal, which can only happen if there is identity of the two attention control signals, that for the amplification and that given by a non-degraded copy of that signal. Since these two signals are identical, then attribution of ownership through the attention copy experienced on its buffer can only be to the correctly amplified input produced by the original attention movement signal. There is, thus, no chance of error in attributing such an experience to oneself.

We note that this semi-identification of the representations of the attention copy buffer and the sensory buffer must occur in a manner in which activations in the former – the attention copy buffer – are not bound to those in lower sites in the same manner in which those in the latter – the attended sensory stimulus activity – presumably are (so as to give consciousness detailed content). Content is not supposed to enter the pre-reflective self created in the model of Figure 8 (which I will call the 'attention copy model'), nor will it by activations on the attention copy buffer if the latter has no binding to lower-level content. How this important 'hiding' of this buffer from the outside world is achieved is presently poorly understood.

There can be damage to this subtle circuitry. For example, it is possible that the attention copy signal could be lost, due to destruction of its buffer, for example by reason of stroke or brain injury, but there was still an amplified input to the sensory buffer. That could also happen by virtue of damage to the axons from the nerve cells creating the attention movement signal. If the monitor was damaged then there would be no error correction, and so the attention system could have severely compromised top-down control. If the attention copy component of the buffer site were lost (so no attention copy signal preserved) there would still be severe problems of attention control, since error values could be incorrect in the short term (due to the loss of the forward model to speed up attention-based response) but be corrected by feedback information. In either case not only the sense of ownership but also any top-down attention control would be damaged, leading to deficits in any resulting experience.

There is still a question to answer about this explanation of conscious experience: is there someone actually reading off the movement of attention? In other words, is there still a homunculus hidden in the works? Do we need a 'reader' to keep track of the persistent neural activity claimed to be at the root of consciousness? If there were such an agent then we would be back on the treadmill of the infinite regress: the homunculus would need another homunculus inside it to cause it to act, and so on. However, the model does not assume that the activity on the attention copy buffer has agentive powers. It has no autonomous action, but is driven completely by the attention movement control generation site. Thereby the homunculus has been deconstructed so completely that it has no 'will'; it is no centre of power. It only responds to incoming neural activity and then interacts in a suitable manner to grant immunity to error of misidentification of the first person pronoun mentioned earlier so as to grant solely ownership, not agency. The origin of movement, drive or will is from guidance by the goal modules in the prefrontal cortex, themselves being driven, for example, by emotional value in limbic sites.

The deconstruction of the homunculus is thereby complete, with only its most vestigial powers being left: only the experience of 'what it is like to be'. No content. No autonomous agent present. In spite of this deconstruction, there is continuity of experience, given by short- and long-term memory representations. Short-term memory grants continuity over the short term – of orders of seconds – while long-term memory provides a more permanent store of 'self' descriptors that form the basis for personality (provided they are not lost, as in the case of H.M. I mentioned earlier).

Finally, we consider features of consciousness left out so far: how are co-occurring events in different modalities, say in touch and hearing, brought into a unified consciousness when attention is drawn to them? Further, how is spontaneous conscious thought brought about?

The first of these questions can begin to be answered in terms of results arising from brain imaging of multi-modal attention processing, by the American neuroscientist Downar and his colleagues recently. They found that besides areas of cortex involved in the control of attention in separate modalities there are sites observed that are common to all of them. Thus, we can suppose there are higher-order control sites for multi-modal attention movement, especially buffer sites for the copy of the attention movement controlled by these sites: by the attention copy model these multi-modal buffer sites would bring about co-occurring conscious experience across modalities. Alternatively, there may be apparent co-occurrent conscious experience that arises from a rapid switch from one modality to another, too fast for the switch to be noticed in experience. Only detailed experiments could distinguish these two (or other) alternatives.

The second question, of spontaneous conscious experience, can be explained in terms of internally generated neural activity. This could arise in an associative manner from previous activity or by noise in the brain bringing about completely new neural activity. Such novel activity would bring attention to bear on it, and hence arise in consciousness, by the attention copy model. This virgin activity would use previous chains or schemata (stored sequences of experiences in long-term memory) to allow for more rapid development, attended from thought to thought, and by the attention copy model arising into consciousness, especially if the thought was goal directed. Moreover, already present memory representations would be used to give sense and direction to the thought stream. In this manner we see that the attention copy model can rise to further challenges about experience

Support for the Attention Copy Model

There is support for this model from various forms of deficits and from other sources. For example, in anosognosia, the denial that one has a deficit brought about by some types of brain damage dissociates into various forms. These forms were analysed by a group of Italian psychologists recently, who separated them into impairments for upper and lower limbs, and those for cognitive loss. They concluded that the only suitable model for such dissociations involved the loss of 'the functioning of monitoring modules (possibly located in the parietal lobes)'.

Further support for the presence of some form of monitor at the basis of phenomenological experience comes from brain imaging experiments using 'introspective' types of paradigm, where a subject has to internally monitor their sensory experience. One such is the motion after-effect. This effect arises if a person looks for some seconds say at water falling down a cliff face. If they then look to one side of the face, it appears as if there is motion upwards, against the cliff face. This experience gradually dies away with time. The subject had to press a button when their motion after-effect experience ended.

Results of fMRI brain imaging of such subjects showed two networks of active cortical areas, one involving posterior sites, the other those more anterior. The posterior sites appeared mainly involved as motion processing filters, as in the motion sensitive area MT. The more anterior sites appeared to act as templates set up for testing the experience of illusions such as in the motion after-effect, being active mainly during the motion illusion period. A crucial site in the posterior network was an area in the inferior parietal lobes, suggested as acting as the site of the creation of the perceptual experience of the motion after-effect.

A similarly important parietal site was detected during binocular rivalry switching (where two different images are presented to the separate eyes, and a subject experiences a switch between the percepts of the two stimuli). In this task, the subjects made no motor response, the fMRI time series being used to detect similar temporal structure across a variety of areas. Other attention-shifting paradigms have also supported a crucial role for parietal sites (as well as related modules in the attention network mentioned earlier). There is also support from transcranial magnetic stimulation (involving application of a strong local magnetic field to the cortex, halting activity while the field is on) for the key role of parietal lobes in conjunction search, since application of transcranial stimulation about 100 milliseconds after stimulus onset causes a significant delay in response time in the paradigm.

Important evidence showing the existence and use of a copy of the attention movement control signal has been presented very recently (2005) by two French scientists, Claire Sergent and Stanislas Dehaene, during a careful study of the attentional blink using EEG measurements on subjects' brains. They found that for trials in which a subject was aware of the second target there was a shortening of the signal of awareness of the first target that they identified as arising from interaction of activity on the site for creation of awareness of the first target (its sensory buffer site) and the attention movement precursor signal (the so-called N2 signal) for the second target. This is exactly as would be predicted by the model of Figure 8, as arises from a copy of the attention movement control signal (whose signature is the N2 signal) being sent to the site of creation of awareness. The N2/attention copy signal is therefore not involved in attention amplification on lower cortex but explicitly interacts with very high-level activity just arriving in consciousness.

Finally, we note that there will be different attention copy buffers in different modalities, as well as those involved with attention to multi-modal sensory stimuli. The manner in which these produce a unified experience of ownership is presently unclear, although total unification may not be expected in all situations, as found experimentally by the Cambridge psychologist Tony Marcel. He discovered, working with subjects exposed to degraded stimuli, that phenomenal experience of these degraded stimuli can be different in different modalities. Such independence of information indicates that some form of interaction will be going on between the buffers for different modalities. This could be achieved by some form of binding (such as through synchronisation of neural activity) to be present to achieve the usual experience of a single owner, although it will be helped by the overlap of buffered activities in the different ownership sites, as well as by use of long-term memory of the reflective self (lost in cases of severe hippocampus damage). Details of this interaction need further experimental evidence to be obtained, especially on the N2 brain signal, and this is ongoing in brain science.

I have presented preliminary evidence that there exists a set of monitors in the parietal lobes for attention paid to various modalities. As importantly, evidence was presented for there being an attention copy signal of the movement of attention being sent to various sites (not only to posterior cortical sites for attention amplification). This copy signal is a key requirement for the model presented here, and the Sergent-Dehaene evidence adds to the evidence for its existence presented in the previous sections. This attention copy is generated as output from the attention movement control signal generator, proposed to be sited in the parietal lobes. For example, such a copy is observed as pre-saccadic eye movement activity in frontal eye fields, supplementary eye fields and some specific parietal cells. The well-observed sensory buffer sites are also placed in parietal lobes. We therefore consider there to be sufficient foundation for the consciousness model of attention copy based on the architecture of Figure 8, for it to be used as the basis of further analysis. We next turn to extend the consciousness model of Figure 8 to self-consciousness, where frontal sites do play a crucial role.

The Experience of Self

Self has a number of aspects. The first aspect of concern in this section is that of agency, which is more advanced than the most primitive of all, that of ownership, and which I have just been discussing. Agency has been analysed empirically, for example, through the fact that there is loss of the sense of agency in schizophrenics suffering from delusions of control. For them there is degradation of signals from the site of attending to and thereby preparing a particular motor action or of language production in a suitable motor area in the brain. This approach through agency has led to numerous important insights into the disease. However, it does not deal directly with consciousness itself but only with internal monitoring of motor actions (which can occur unconsciously). For example, one does not think about having a thought in order to have it: agency is not enough for consciousness. But experience of agency is important. Let me consider more directly, in terms of the model of the previous section, how consciousness of self at the level of agency or intention could arise.

One possibility is that the experience of agency arises as that of the movement of motor attention. In other words, it is the experience of motor attention ownership. This could arise from an extension of Figure 8 by inclusion of working memory structures of motor attention control and its attention copy, in a similar way that we extended Figure 6 to Figure 8 to create the pre-reflective self through the attention copy signal. Agency would then be created by buffering a copy of the motor attention control signal (on the motor equivalent of a sensory attention copy buffer) with later receipt of the motor feedback signal on the motor equivalent of the sensory buffer.

The existence of a motor attention buffer is shown by a recent publication. In the paradigm employed by the experimentalists, movements were made by subjects to a target light in front of them, which was moved rapidly a short distance to left or right at 25 milliseconds after the start of their movement. The subject had either to reach to the final position of the target as rapidly as possible or to reach in the opposite direction. The subject then repeated their movement shortly after the movement had been completed, to show how much 'motor awareness' of it they possessed (so assumedly from activity held on an appropriate buffer working memory site). Rapid errors (those errors towards the moved target) were both made and experienced by the subject, as were the voluntary corrections made later. Both these movement modifications indicated that the motor attention working memory was activated, the early movement being identifiable as under exogenous control, the later one being endogenously controlled, assumedly by a frontal goal module.

This experiment shows the existence of a separate motor awareness system, which we identify with that supposedly predominant in the left hemisphere according to the British neuroscientist Matthew Rushworth. In all, we can consider motor agency as arising from activation in an attention motor control buffer equivalent to the buffer for sensory awareness. But the nature of any possible 'motor consciousness' is much more murky; there is clearly considerable further work to perform before the nature of motor attention/intention and of motor awareness becomes well founded.

Limitations

We next need to consider what fundamental limitation any scientific model of consciousness possesses by virtue of the nature of consciousness itself. In the same way that a model of the weather is not the weather itself – it does not rain or have hot sun beating down by means of the equations of flow of moist air or whatever – so the attention copy model cannot 'be' conscious. It can only try to capture the bare principles of the experience. At best we can only capture the essential features of conscious experience – its two components of ownership and of content. The various experiential components can only be shown to be present, in principle, in the attention copy model, not actually be experienced themselves by you, the reader.

These points are relatively obvious, but the further question then arises as to how the attention copy model could help guide the construction of machine-like consciousness. This is a very important question, since it could be claimed that there is no way of probing the inner experience of such a machine, built on attention copy model principles. For how would we ever be able to have the so-called inner experience of the machine, however it is constructed? But in spite of our inability to give a complete definition, we do not, for example, stop having children because we cannot justify that they are in fact, or will become, conscious. We know, by close contact, that they are so. We may sadly find, after birth, that such consciousness is limited due to a birth or developmental defect. But that does not mean we cannot intuit this consciousness, even of a more limited form, in others.

There is a similar argument with machines. With constantly increasing computing power, there is both the possibility and the need for such an experiment to be made: to construct a system on attention copy lines. Would it then be conscious?

The most persuasive approach would be to construct a system composed of 'active' neurons, with membrane potential continuously active, and spike activity being transferred between such neurons in a similar manner to that in our own brains. A system so constructed, with attention capabilities along the attention copy model lines, would be a good candidate for a conscious system. To discuss how to prove such awareness (beyond the above-mentioned intuition) requires a detailed discussion of the set of required 'probing' experiments (as in the Turing test). However, in a nutshell, the main thrust would be that all possible experiments that could be performed on the system would lead to observation of two types:

1. responses expected by a conscious system, including verbal report of apparently autonomous origin;
2. inner activity (probed by suitable 'electrodes') that corresponds to that observed in similar regions in our own brains.

That is how we tell that our children are conscious, especially if they appear to have some defect in their conscious experience, so must be studied closely (even in brain imaging machines). It should be the same for any attention copy-based conscious machine.

Thus, there is no reason, in principle, why the attention copy model could not be used to develop a machine that could be investigated for possible conscious-like activity. We will return to this later in Part IV for a more complete discussion.

The Ownership Conjecture

In this chapter I have explored the attention control model of the previous chapters by analysing the interpretation of the further control signals involved beyond a ballistic attention control model. The attention copy signal, held on its buffer, is proposed here to provide the experience of ownership of the about-to-be-experienced content of the input to which attention is being paid. It is this inner experience that, it is claimed, provides the experience of 'what it is like to be' and bridges the 'explanatory gap'. It does so without appealing to non-material or non-brain-like elements.

The approach I have developed is based on two 'principles of consciousness' that relate the underlying neural activity in particular brain regions with the associated experience of consciousness. The first of these, the content principle, states that the content of conscious experience arises from activity in certain sensory buffer sites, coupled to brain activities coding for detailed features of the stimuli making up that content. This principle is based on a broad range of experimental evidence, and has been assumed by an increasing number of those working on consciousness. The second principle is new; it is the 'ownership principle'. It was derived from a detailed model of how the focus of attention is controlled in the brain, using an engineering control framework. The components of this attention movement control model are in the main justified by a broad range of results from neuroscience, from those using brain imaging to results involving single nerve cell activity in various brain regions and under a range of experimental conditions.

The ownership principle can still only be regarded presently as a conjecture. It is founded on a lot of experimental support. But the copy of the attention movement control signal, at the basis of the principle, is still to be fully tracked down. There is evidence for it as an early signal at about 200 milliseconds (the N2 signal) after a stimulus has caused initial activity in the brain. My interpretation of this early signal, that it is identical with the attention copy signal creating the experience of ownership, has been supported especially by experimental and modelling results on the attentional blink, as well as by a broad range of neuroscientific results. Thus the ownership principle has good scientific grounds for acceptance. It will lead to a new approach to the full panoply of conscious experience, with enormous implications for humanity in the future.

CHAPTER FOURTEEN

RELATIONS

Relations to Past Ideas on Consciousness

There are three distinct strands of attempts to explain the mind from a scientific point of view. A presently very influential one is that of Western cognitive science, based on recent discussions of, among many others, the American neuroscientist Antonio Damasio, the American philosopher Daniel Dennett, and the two neuroscientists Frances Crick and Christophe Koch. A second strand is more philosophical, and involves more direct attempts to explore inner experience per se, rather than its effects on behaviour and brain. This involves Western phenomenology and Eastern mysticism. There is also a whole slew of other recent scientific models of consciousness which are relevant to the scientific attack on the mind.

Western Cognitive Science

According to Western cognitive science, there is no 'ghost in the machine', as the Oxford philosopher Gilbert Ryle emphasised in his influential book *Concept of Mind* published in 1949. By this phrase is meant that there are not two distinct worlds, one an inner, mental one, the other that of the observable bodily functions, including the activities of the brain in all its subtlety. However, the claims and theories of the various approaches to consciousness advocated with great heat and strength by various advocates all stem from the doctrine that there is nothing other than 'intentionality' (as the philosopher Brentano put it): all is content in consciousness; there is nothing else. In other words, there can only be 'consciousness of'. There cannot just be 'consciousness'. Even earlier the British empiricist philosopher David Hume wrote that he could find 'nothing other than a bundle of perceptions' when he tried to catch his 'inner self'. It is only that bundle of perceptions that has been considered by Western cognitive science and neuroscience. Anything else would seem, in the writings of such researchers, to smack of dualism. Discussion for them must therefore be limited only to the contents of consciousness.

This approach leads to the basic and deep problem: how can a sense of self, answering the question of 'what it is like to be', arise? Such a possibility is either ignored or its relevance denied very strongly, as by the American philosopher Daniel Dennett. Those Western philosophers who have realised that there is a missing element have attempted to fill it with independent, dualistic-like 'stuff', such as information, as did the American philosopher David Chalmers. If they accept the real challenge of consciousness they realise that there still exists an 'explanatory gap' between mind and brain, or there is lack of inner experience, as expressed by the question 'what is it like to be a bat?' raised by the American philosopher Thomas Nagel. These problems are present since Western thought is still strongly shackled by complete denial of all but content in consciousness. So such protagonists can only add an extra element to those of the material world, and become dualists in all but name. All the other researchers in that gallimaufry of the 'consciousness explained' camp cannot bite the bullet of the self; they are either left to claim that there is no inner self at all or are left floundering as to what is still missing and complain of 'hard problems' and 'explanatory gaps'.

The attention copy model tries to bridge this explanatory gap by introducing the attention copy signal, suggested as creating the experience of ownership. It is in this manner that the heresy of dualism is avoided by the model, since the inner self is clothed in neural activity, and is not some other non-material 'stuff'. At the same time, the attention copy model supplies an answer to the difficult question facing Western phenomenologists (Husserl, Sartre, Merleau-Ponty, Henri, Zahavi) as to how the pre-reflective inner self could be content-free yet have interaction with the contentful outer world of experience. That apparently insoluble problem is solved in terms of the temporal flow of neural activity in the attention control model introduced above. In that all is neural activity, yet it is neural activity with very specific functionality at different times of stimulus processing. Thereby the ownership experience flows smoothly into that of content; they are bound together so as to produce, by sculpted inhibitory and excitatory connections between suitable modules, the immunity to error of 'I' so crucial to consciousness itself.

The Other Side of Consciousness

There is a vast richness of the understanding of the nature of consciousness from the two areas of Western phenomenology and Eastern meditation, which is noticeably absent from the Western cognitive science approach I have just discussed. It is difficult to select from the panoply of insight, but some brief comments are in order, in the light of the important discussions in recent writings on the subject. Thus, the British philosopher Strawson recently reached the conclusion, from a phenomenological study of his own consciousness, that 'there are eruptions of consciousness from a substrate of apparent non-consciousness'. From a different philosophical viewpoint it has been noted from meditation experience that 'Between moments of experience of self are gaps in which there is no sense of self or of separateness from what is being experienced'. These are of great importance to the model presented here. That is exactly what arises from my attention copy model.

To see how the 'gappy' nature of experience would be present, let us focus once again on the arrival of the copy of the attention movement control signal on its buffer site. This persists for only a hundred or so milliseconds before it is annihilated (or reduced). It was claimed earlier that the 'ownership experience', crucial to provide consciousness with the feeling of 'being there', was provided solely by that signal. Thus the experience of self at this most primitive level is expected to occur only in fits and starts – created by the attention copy signal arriving on its buffer, then annihilated when it has done its work and is destroyed by the buffer signal breaking through; that, I suggest, is the essence of the gappy experience itself. This is supported by the fMRI observation of parietal (and other) sites solely activated by the switch in binocular rivalry, as well as the motion after-effect data I reported earlier, where again there is a switch of perception, and so of attention.

The relevance of the briefly occurring attention copy signal (which I earlier had called the 'reverse echo' of attention movement, giving the feeling of presence and ownership to experience) to phenomenology is made even stronger in terms of recent analysis discussing the German philosopher Immanuel Kant's demonstration that the self cannot be experienced or even defined in terms of any empirical quality at all. This can be reconciled with my attention copy model as well as with descriptions from Eastern writings, some of which I already touched on in Part I. These writings claim that meditation training can ultimately lead to a state of consciousness termed 'pure'. This is empty of any content, but is not empty. It is sometimes called the pure consciousness experience (PCE). As quoted from the writings of a Japanese Zen mystic:

> But it is not vacant emptiness. Rather it is the purest condition of our existence.

In ancient Indian writings the pure consciousness state is described as follows:

> It is unseen, incapable of being spoken, ungraspable, without any

distinctive marks, un-thinkable, un-nameable ... He who knows it, thus, enters the self with his self.

What can be so indefinable yet be called a state of 'nirvana' and be attempted to be attained only by considerable concentration and practise? To answer this let me summarise the process of the creation of inner experience according to the discussion of the attention copy model of the previous chapter:

- The input scene is analysed into its features and objects.
- An appropriate attention guidance signal is created by the goal module, thence biasing the attention movement signal generator to send out an attention amplification/inhibition signal to the correct input and distracters.
- A copy of this control signal is buffered, so preserving the signal, and creating the experience of ownership of what is to come.
- In the meantime the attention control signal is sent to the earlier feature maps in posterior cortex to selectively amplify the chosen input features.
- The amplified input signal arrives at the sensory buffer and annihilates (or reduces) the copy signal sitting on its own buffer.
- The amplified signal is now accepted on its own sensory buffer site, and experience of the attended input now arises in close succession to the sense of ownership of the experience.
- A new input is then chosen for selective amplification, and this goes through the above steps, replacing the previous buffered input after a competition.

The state of nirvana mentioned earlier can now be understood as suitably extended activation on the attention copy buffer, obtained with no amplified external input of any sensory sort. This would very likely be achieved by lengthy meditation training to create a suitable frontal goal state, which would cause it to generate the self-perpetuating state on the attention copy buffer. At the same time the activation brought about on the attention copy buffer has to be developed to be strong enough to fight off all competitors arriving from associative cortices in all modalities onto their sensory buffers. The appropriate goal state to achieve such a level of inhibition of all sensory distracters must be a very complex state, needing years of meditation training. Given that, the resulting subtle goal thereby leads to the pure conscious experience. The attention copy signal of the PCE thereby continues its life on its buffer, leading to the pure consciousness experience continuing, with no concomitant sensory buffer activity allowed into awareness. Pure consciousness is thus the ownership of one's own ownership experience. The inner eye thus looks only at itself!

The exact nature of the temporally extended activation on the attention copy buffer during pure consciousness is expected to be of a variety of forms. It may be a uniform one, occurring across the whole set of attention copy buffer modules in different modalities (involving the continued inhibition of the sensory ones to prevent any sensory experience creeping in). On the other hand, there may be alternate buffer activations able to produce this experience of nirvana. In any of these activations there will be no sensory quality at all, only continued experience of 'pure' ownership of one's own attention apparatus (although with some hint of spatial extent, as reported by some meditators). That is close to the desired goal of a self-referential system. However, the referent has no content since there is no external input coupled to the attention copy buffer site, not even arising from the internal bodily environment.

The conclusion of this discussion is that the discreteness of conscious experience is a natural component of a version of the model. Moreover, the pure conscious state can be understood as arising from activation solely on the attention copy buffer brought about by internal intention with no amplified inputs of any sort.

The above explanation of pure consciousness leads to expectation that a further 'pure' consciousness experience could arise by learning to activate an extended goal state composed of the PCE goal state, plus separately those for normal life.

There is some hint of the existence of a further state, differentiated by a switch-over between the two states. This is denoted as state IX by the American philosopher/meditator Austin, which he termed 'the stage of ongoing enlightened traits' in his table of advanced extraordinary states of consciousness. In this state IX there is a higher level of sensory perception, as compared to no registration of the external world in pure consciousness (denoted state VIII). This difference implies that state IX may, according to the attention copy model of the consciousness and the PCE, be a continuation of state VIII (the PCE state), being achieved without complete destruction of the external input on the sensory buffer but with continued parallel self-activation of the attention copy buffer. This is the parallel processing of both PCE and normal consciousness, as expected from the extended goal. Note that the PCE state, together with those developing from it, will still be expected to be unitary, since constructed by reduction of all sensory and motor feedback from peripheral cortical sites.

In conclusion, the attention copy model of consciousness is consistent with the existence of the Eastern meditation state of pure consciousness.

The model is not in accord with the Western cognitive science approach to the mind, in which there is nothing but content. For the attention copy model there is the crucial brief period of ownership of the amplified and about-to-be-experienced content of the input.

Relations to Other Scientific Models of Consciousness

Here I will only consider scientifically based models, leaving us only with those models using either classical physics or those based on possible quantum effects. The first type uses the neuron as the fundamental unit of information processing in the brain. These models use neuron firing as the main signature of conscious experience (as also at the basis of all the unconscious processing). On the other hand, the quantum approach has more difficulty in tackling the activity of the neuron per se, for the neuron is a noisy little beast, firing in a spontaneous and random manner all the time. This would prevent certain quantum features from being easy to attain, such as the existence of collective quantum states involving vast reaches of the brain. These are only observed in matter at very low temperatures, without any noise to jitter them out of existence.

Quantum approaches

As just noted, quantum models of consciousness must investigate sub-neuron processes to try to detect the manner in which various quantum effects – wave function coherence, collapse of the wave function or suggested quantum gravity effects, among others – can play a crucial role. In order for these effects to be able to extend across regions of the brain in a coherent manner, smaller systems than neurons must be considered. It has been proposed that these units are composed of the internal skeleton of the neuron, the so-called 'microtubules'. These are protein structures inside each axon, soma and dendrite of the neuron, being involved in transporting material throughout the cell. With a diameter of only about 20 nanometres, these structures have been proposed as able to support a coherent quantum state. This coherent state can then, it is proposed, be extended from one neuron to the next, without loss of quantum coherence, by means of gap junctions (known to occur in about 10–15% of all synapses between neurons in the brain, thereby allowing direct electrical contact between neighbouring neurons). The resulting quantum coherent state is then suggested as breaking up – or decohering – by quantum gravity effects at a very short scale. The British physicist Roger Penrose and the American anaesthetist Stuart Hameroff proposed that consciousness involves a quantum gravity-driven 'decoherence of quantum superpositions'. Stuart Hameroff wrote that Penrose described this process as ' ... a shearing off into separate, multiple space-time universes as described in the Everett 'multiworlds' view of quantum theory ... '. Various even more exotic extensions of these ideas involving microtubules have been suggested, such as through features of super-strings, or through quantum electrodynamics.

There have been numerous attempts to bring these various approaches to consciousness, using the concepts of quantum coherence and decoherence, closer to observed brain activity. In particular, it should be possible to deduce characteristic features seen through brain imaging during conscious as compared to unconscious processing, as observed in differences in particular correlated brain activity across various modules, both with specific spatial and temporal features; this is still under investigation. The nature of any conscious inner self and how it may be created by such collective quantum coherence is seemingly remote from the quantum approach.

40 Hertz and Gamma Synchronisation

For a period of about a decade until a few years ago, the '40 Hertz story' was all the rage for a brain-based explanation of consciousness. '40 Hertz' denotes a coherent state of nerve cell activity, with common nerve cell activity oscillating at 40 Hertz across a variety of regions. It was first suggested as the basic mechanism to achieve the binding of the different features of an object split across different regions of cortex. This 'binding' problem – of creating the unified concept from these different feature activations – is one of the important features of consciousness empha-sised earlier, and included in the 'contents of consciousness principle' in the previous chapter. Much experimental work has found that 40 Hertz is indeed a component of binding, as well as being present in brain activity involved in attention. Thus there is support for the thesis that 40 Hertz is a necessary brain activation mechanism for consciousness. There is, however, no support for the claim that 40 Hertz is a sufficient signal for consciousness. Indeed, the original results, suggesting the 40 Hertz signal as that of binding of features across those of an object distributed across cortical regions, were observed in anaesthetised cats. These cats clearly were not conscious. Nor is the original claim of identifying consciousness with 40 Hertz now backed by both of the original authors.

Even more problematic is the manner in which 40 Hertz could support the other features of consciousness besides binding. Thus synchronisation of brain activity will help explain how intentionality can arise, through feature binding for object experience, but such experience has more aspects than solely the binding of content. It has an owner, involved with the inner experience of 'what it is like to be', as noted in various places in the book so far. There is still a big gap from the synchronisation considered above to any form of inner self or owner. More generally, the nature of control by the self over brain activity is completely absent from globally synchronised neural activity: all components of that activity would be equipotent, unless other functional components are introduced.

In conclusion, synchronisation has to be accepted as an important component of brain processing, and especially in the creation of consciousness through binding. It must thus play a role in any final theory. But there must still be other components involved.

Dynamical Systems and Complexity

There has been a somewhat similar spirit of jumping on the 'band-wagon' for the dynamical system and complexity approaches to consciousness as there was to the 40 Hertz endeavour. A dynamical system is one for which the components of the system interact with each other in a complex manner, but in such a way that some general features of this motion can be described in general terms. One important aspect is how ultimately this motion moves along certain standard paths, such as staying at a single point, or moves around circles in different dimensions. These final 'paths' of the system are termed 'attractors'. Attractors of some dynamical systems, like simple models of the weather, have been found very difficult to define, resulting in their being termed 'strange'.

Many groups have followed such a dynamical systems approach, although allowing it to overlap at times with the 40 Hertz thesis. There has also been strong activity investigating the possible role of chaos and of complexity in brain processing, from both an experimental and a theoretical perspective.

At the most basic level, it is clear that a general dynamical systems analysis of brain activity is essential to achieve complete understanding of consciousness, alongside detailed experimental data. The equations of interacting neurons, and at an even lower level of the dynamics of the sites where an axon from one cell stops to give its information to another, the synapse, present a very difficult mathematical task. The general principles that can be brought to bear from dynamical systems theory would be expected to be of help in such analyses, using the concepts of attractors and many related ones that have been developed through mathematical analysis. However, it has not been clear, in such terms, how the neural dynamics underlying conscious activity (the neural correlates of consciousness) differs in the brain from that involved with unconscious states. There are experimental results showing that some brain regions have more activity when consciousness arises than when it does not. This helps to determine the sites of the neural correlates of consciousness. However, this advance, important as it is in its own right, gives no immediate help to explain why such dynamic activity leads to conscious experience, and more particularly what specific features of a dynamical system would be sufficient to create consciousness. Only through a theory in which functionality is assigned to various specific brain sites (as seen by brain imaging) and inclusion of suitable specific dynamical components can there be development of such understanding. That has not yet occurred. However, dynamical systems theory still plays an important role, both in general and in more specific details, as an important tool in attacking any overall model still to be produced.

There have been more detailed proposals about how consciousness arises, such as by the use of strange attractors. In this approach, rapid transitions can occur between attractors (representing information) by means of movement through a dynamical landscape using the strange attractors I mentioned earlier. Such transitions can be fast, and so agree with experimental data indicating such fast changes. Data on these speeds of change has been discovered by the American neurophysiologist/ philosopher Walter Freeman, providing an important basis for what he calls 'mesoscopic brain dynamics', such as that involving single brain areas such as primary visual cortex. This approach using such dynamical systems concepts, allied with detailed simulations, is important in understanding how the brain processes information at a relatively large but not yet global scale. Its value in singling out how brain activity can be more global and support consciousness is not yet so clear.

Complexity of global brain activity has been at the centre of the thrust of the approach of the American Nobel Prize winner Gerald Edelman and his colleagues in California. Brain activity has been analysed by this group to determine if there are regions of higher connectivity during conscious as compared to unconscious processing. Results have been obtained that show such regions exist. This has not necessarily helped in creating a specific model of consciousness. Yet again, this approach can be expected to form an important component of analysis of any final theory of consciousness, although it will not be enough on its own.

Centre of Narrative Gravity

In the provocatively titled book *Consciousness Explained*, Daniel Dennett put forward the thesis that consciousness is created as a 'centre of narrative gravity', from an ensemble of narratives created in the various working memory sites in the brain as information processing continues. To Dennett there is no place in the brain in which it 'all comes together'; there is no Cartesian theatre, as Descartes suggested, where consciousness is finally created (Descartes chose the pineal gland, as we now know wrongly).

There is much to support Dennett's picture of the dynamics of brain activity at a general level. How it is that the resulting centre of narrative gravity achieves satisfaction of the various features mentioned earlier in the book for consciousness is not at all clear. However, this is not a loss that Dennett laments: there is no place in the brain where it 'all comes together', he argues, so in particular there is no perspective. Yet that perspective does exist, as we know from our own inner experience. All need not be lost, however, since there may be certain detailed features that may help fill the gap to inner experience, such as the overall inter-module connectivity to achieve attention control. Yet again, Dennett's approach can be seen to be a partial theory, still to be filled in regarding how various higher-level functions are supported, especially attention.

The Global Workspace

The global workspace (GW) is another theory emphasising particular aspects of consciousness, put forward by the American psychologist Bernie Baars. It is based on the computational science concept of a 'global workspace', where material needed to be worked on by a number of processors is held. It corresponds to a global buffer in my terminology. In the process Baars claims that such activity possesses consciousness, in agreement with the contents principle I developed earlier.

The global workspace approach has been very fruitful in bringing together a number of ideas that stem from psychology with those from computer science; it has more recently been attempted to be placed on a brain basis The prefrontal cortex does not seem to behave in solely a global workspace manner but also as a dedicated set of executive processors able to guide the carrying out of suitably rewarded goals to enable maximal rewards to be obtained. How such executive function can be understood in terms of prefrontal brain circuitry is still to be explained in detail, although much progress is being made; the global workspace viewpoint undoubtedly adds a valuable overall additional functionality. We add that the nature of inner experience is a further aspect beyond the global workspace approach. Yet again, the global workspace gives a useful new view on certain aspects of conscious experience.

The Relational Mind

Yet a further incomplete theory emphasises the use of memory in the creation of content in consciousness, as I developed in my 1999 book *The Race for Consciousness*. I suggested there that such relational aspects of experience give it much of the meaning of internal content that it possesses. In a sense this must be so, since without past experiences of present objects they can carry no import for the person experiencing a given environment. However, this approach only emphasises one aspect of the basis of experience, that of memory, to the detriment of many others, especially that of the inner self.

Conclusions on Other Models of Consciousness

The theories of consciousness that have been described so far are all to be regarded as important steps towards understanding consciousness, but are still incomplete or premature. In their different ways they emphasise particular components of the total manner in which the brain processes information. Since the brain is awesomely complex, such a multitude of approaches to the way it works is to be expected and welcomed. Put together they can begin to fill in the details of how it does function. Yet as supports for complete models of consciousness, the various approaches (and numerous others for which I have no space to mention) are deficient. They are incomplete in three different ways:

1. Only partial: in general they are only partial descriptions of the nature of brain processing. None handles satisfactorily, for example, the manner in which there is action of the various neuromodulators (acetylcholine, dopamine, noradrenalin, serotonin). Other aspects of brain sophistication correspond to the complexity of the microcircuitry in the six-layered cortex, for which the circuitry is presently being laboriously uncovered, as well as numerous other components. It can be argued that the principles of how the brain supports consciousness may not need to be based on a perfectly correct model of the brain, down to the latest detail. However, to be able to extract further principles of global brain processing, it may be necessary to include in models more complexity than used so far in modelling.

2. Inner self: the most important criticism, already noted above for some past approaches to consciousness, is that the various models do not appear, even in principle, to allow for the presence of a component of consciousness without content. But we have already noted the strong

need for such a component, called the 'pre-reflective self' or inner self earlier. Thus, even if all of the complexity of the brain were understood, the manner in which a content-free inner perspective of experience could arise from brain activity would still be the hard problem. This is especially true of the models reviewed above. Even my own relational mind model, which was shown to possess many of the essential features of consciousness, did not contain any explanation of the perspective of the inner self. There was no owner of conscious experience. So it was not conscious in the sense we know it. You or I have a perspective on our external world and the sensations we receive from it; that perspective is completely different for you as it is for me, even if we were to be in very close juxtaposition. The same criticism applies to all of the other models above, as well as those not able to be considered due to lack of space. So in conclusion there is presently no model that can explain the inner self.

3. Pay attention to attention: most of the models do not emphasise the manner in which attention functions as the gateway to consciousness. Without this attention framework it is doubtful that any model of consciousness will be able to be properly related to brain processes. For example, how do they explain the important feature of immunity to error through misidentification of 'I'? Since the brain is the only ground truth we possess, such a gap between any model and reality, especially this component of it, is very serious.

The attention copy model of consciousness I introduced earlier begins to address the basic criticisms above. I have not spent time on the problem of developing a far more detailed model of the brain, based on the various strands I have suggested (item 1) above – it is more suited for publication through papers in the appropriate computer science, robotics and neuroscience research journals. That is a route I am presently following, as are increasing numbers of my computational neuroscience colleagues. I have properly addressed point 2, especially in terms of the ownership principle, and how the experience of ownership arises from the attention copy of the movement of attention control signal. I have also addressed point 3, and indeed I have made a strong feature of that in terms of the whole of this part of the book.

The attention copy model has many versions, in terms of the detailed architecture of the form of Figure 8. These variations on the main attention copy model and the related ownership principle need to be winnowed down to produce a more detailed model able to withstand the many rigorous neuroscientific tests to which it can be subjected over the next years. But there is already enough evidence, from the broad range of areas I have presented to you so far, to support my thesis that an attention copy of the attention movement control signal is the basis of the experience of ownership of the content component of conscious experience. It is that thesis which I will explore more fully in the next part of the book, and I will consider its implications for all mind users in the final part.

PART III

IMPLICATIONS

O the mind, mind has mountains; cliffs of fall
Frightful, sheer, no-man-fathomed.

Gerard Manley Hopkins

CHAPTER FIFTEEN

DISTORTED CONSCIOUSNESS

Being Distorted

I just can't remember it – it's on the tip of my brain, but just won't come through – shall I try another word? Yes – ah – let me see – come on, keep trying – keep on – oh no, my mind's empty – I can't recall a thing – damn, it just doesn't work, does it – damn, damn, damn – okay, so where's the what's its name? What's it called? My God, I'm losing it, aren't I? Words are fleeing from me – my brain is a – what's it called? – oh yes, a sieve – got that one right, didn't I? But who's that coming in through the door? She looks familiar, but what's her name? – 'Hello, dear, how are you? You look so well' – better to say nice things, whoever she is, hadn't I? 'Hello, daddy – I just came to see you' Oh – my daughter – I really don't know her properly do I? How do I know it's her? Perhaps it's someone else's daughter? 'Are you sure, my dear?' Oh no – the wrong thing to say – just better keep my mouth shut, hadn't I?

So it goes at an early stage of dementia – the 'what it is like to be', from inside a crumbling brain. Memory going, words unable to be accessed. People once very close are forgotten. More and more is lost to the mind and becomes unfamiliar. Those are stages that have been experienced by millions of people worldwide as their brains gradually decay away. They are the stages that will be followed by millions more until a cure for Alzheimer's disease (AD) and other dementias is discovered. Even their causes are still to be properly understood, let alone discovering any cures. But dementia is only one among many problems with a damaged or decaying brain, one distorted by forces outside the control of the experiencing person. It may be bad genes that cause something to go wrong as their brain develops, as is suspected in autism, for example. Their brain is out of shape in terms of the brains of most people, but in subtle ways. Or it may be that the person has had a stroke, so that parts of their brain are damaged so severely that the region can no longer perform the functions expected of it. Such can lead to the phenomenon of neglect, where damage to the right side of the brain, especially the parietal lobe, causes loss of awareness of the opposite side of space or of the body.

In some cases, nothing can be done to ameliorate the lot of the suffering person. In others some recovery may occur. In a car accident initial head trauma may be severe, but effects may reduce as damaged tissue recovers. For a certain period after an accident, some recovery of function, such as of language, can be achieved as the nerve connections regenerate. So language tuition is often used to help guide such connections as are left or re-growing to perform as successful a replacement as possible.

But one thing we can try to do, in all these cases, is to understand the experiences of such people with damaged and reduced brains. In fact, some diseases of the mind are at least presently regarded as all in the mind. It is only through what a sufferer tells a physician about the disturbing nature of their experience in these cases that the illness can be diagnosed. A schizophrenic can suffer from hearing voices telling them to kill someone, for example. Only by hearing from such sufferers about their horrifying experiences – to them as if there was someone invading their minds and taking it over – that the existence of their illness can be discovered. So it is only through their experience that we can learn about the deranged inner world that these people inhabit.

What is it like to be them? This is an important question to answer, especially for those whose world is invaded by voices or other experiences. We can ask: as they move around the world do they still experience themselves as 'I'? Is that 'I' reduced in substance? Or is it only certain contents, previously recalled with ease, that are no longer available to them? Does the world around them look faded, grey around the edges, or even become dangerous and menacing? And if so why? What has brought this change of experience about? What has produced an altered personality, as occurs in AD when a previously nice and gentle person becomes unpleasant and even violent? What causes a schizophrenic to lose their previous common-sense view of their world, where objects have to be separately interrogated as to their meaning and cannot be handled in the easy automatic way they could before their disease?

It is hard to answer this raft of questions. There are many different cases to consider because of the many and different types of damage caused to the brain. It may be a slow change that is occurring, as in AD or in schizophrenia. It can occur over years, although early signs of something being wrong are now becoming available, as in the case of the writer Iris Murdoch. Analysis has shown that her language began to incipiently decay away some years before her AD became evident. This has been noted by comparing the range of vocabulary she used in her successful earlier works as compared to her last work, *Joseph's Last Day*, which was not received well by the critics, but which appeared well before her symptoms became obvious. On the other hand, the change in behaviour may be sudden, as after brain damage, say in a car accident or after a stroke. There may be gradual amelioration of symptoms in some cases. So there can be dramatic changes as well as creeping ones. Some recovery can occur or there is tragic and irreversible loss. In either case the problem is to help understand what a person is experiencing – not only for the people themselves, but to help their carers and nurses to be able to get into their minds. This would help improve care, and allow the carers' empathy to relieve the lot of the sufferer. Even more basically, does the patient still have a mind, and what sort of experience does it provide?

We can answer these difficult questions in one of two ways. One is to go along with the developing symptoms and patient's responses, and use them to make a guess as to what the sufferer is experiencing. The other extreme is to create a model explaining consciousness in the normal population (itself very disparate), and then apply that to the specific cases met in the patient population. This cannot be done so easily for specific people, but only for the group of people suffering brain distortions of a certain class, such as AD or autism or schizophrenia or neglect. These are all different diseases, as careful diagnosis shows, so we should at first try to differentiate the varieties of experience across the range of diseases.

In Part II I presented to you a model of conscious experience, which I termed the attention copy model. I showed this to have a considerable level of support in brain science in terms of being able to explain many of the paradigms considered to be important in analysing conscious experience, as well as incorporating important components of the observed architecture and function of attention in the brain. So I will follow the second method in this part of the book, and try to explore both distorted consciousness in this chapter, damaged consciousness (caused by brain damage) in the following one, and self-caused distortions of consciousness in the next. However, I will also guide this exploration by constant reference to the nature of the symptoms, so incorporating what regions of the brain are observed to be damaged in the given disease, and also the nature of the inner experiences of the sufferers. Folding those damages into the attention copy model, and checking with the reports of the sufferers should allow us to begin to tease out the distortions of consciousness that can arise. Thus, we will be combining the method of taking descriptions of experience from the sufferers with the modelling approach. We will thereby also be testing the attention copy model or similar models as to their ability to help explain the broad range of changes of consciousness experiences as expressed across the patient population.

It is very natural, in a mind-user's manual, to consider such break-downs as the ones I have briefly covered above. On the other hand, a good car-user's manual tackles car breakdowns by listing those components of the car that could be the cause of the fault. Here I am trying to discover which faulty components of the brain, looked at through the eyes of the attention copy type of models of consciousness, can have caused the problem experiences. There are various clues, but no final answers. So I am still building the mind-user's manual before your eyes.

In any case, I am going beyond what is usually done in a car-user's manual since the brain is, as I trust you would agree, considerably different from a car. Here I am trying to explore what experiential changes are actually occurring in the mind of the person with the breakdown. In most cases the patient is still functioning, although at a reduced level. In the case of a car, it either runs or it slows down and stops. However, in these human cases the brains are still running, although not in the expected manner. In some cases the changes are so catastrophic that the patient can no longer function in the community: like the car, it has broken down. But the mind still has not ceased, but only gone on the wrong tracks. Nor is it possible, in many cases, to modify the fault by taking out a suitable part of the brain which is no longer working properly and replacing it with a new one (although that may be possible in the future when stem cells for given patients may become available). So we are exploring the equivalent of a car still running but, for instance, using up too much petrol, or one not properly following the commands of the driver (steering faults or some such).

Before we commence this exploration, let me remind you that the attention copy model divides consciousness into two parts: the content of experience, and the experience of the owner of the experiences. This latter is subtle in terms of its content: it was claimed only to consist of the ownership experience. So while the owner has implicit knowledge of the contentful experience about to arise, that very first spark of ownership knowledge is not explicit. Let me remind you how this division into two sorts of consciousness arose. The content of consciousness arises by brain activity arriving at a sensory buffer site with suitable strength to be able to be sent round for report and decision making to other such brain sites. These other sites can use the information sent from the first sensory buffer site for a variety of purposes, such as making a decision or responding with a particular action. In order to access the sensory buffer site, input activity, coded up to the level of meaning (semantics) must be amplified by attention. Otherwise it will not break through to reportability and awareness. To achieve sufficient amplification, an attention movement signal is generated to achieve that amplification by suitably moving the focus of attention in posterior cortical sites to where the relevant brain activity is situated.

To speed up this process, a copy of the attention movement signal is employed to give a prior 'wake-up call' to the sensory buffer site where this amplified activity is due to arrive. A buffer site is then posited as existing, on which the attention copy is briefly held, in order to be used to generate this wake-up call. The resulting experience created by the attention copy buffer activity is of expectancy of the content of the full conscious experience, about to be created by the activity (on the sensory buffer) of the attended stimulus activity. In other words, the owner knows in principle what is about to come into his or her consciousness, although until it has so arrived the experience does not have any content. There is no redness of the rose or the tulip, nor taste of the delicious food. Only when the attention copy has done its necessary preliminary amplification work on the incoming brain activity representing these exciting experiences will they then be experienced as required.

The basis of the attention copy model approach is that, as I said earlier and emphasise again, there is a bipartite division of conscious experience into ownership and content. Such a separation would, on first blush, be expected to lead to two possible types of changed experience in patients with brain decay or damage. Damage to some brain sites would be expected to cause loss of content; in other cases there would be loss of ownership. Dissociation should be expected between these two sorts of experience. However, on second blush, and after simulations that I and my colleague Nickolaos Fragopanagos at King's College London have performed of the specific attention copy model (of Figure 9 of Part II) in the attentional blink, it was discovered that such a division of phenomenal experience need not occur. Loss of the attention copy buffer can cause a resulting loss of ability to attain access to the sensory buffer of a given stimulus, surrounded by distracters. In other words, there is a strong coupling of the effects of the various components of the attention copy model architecture that does not necessarily allow simple 'first blush' dissociation of consciousness into its two main components. This is because these two components of experience occur sequentially in time: the ownership experience leads into, and helps speed up, the experience of content. So if the first is destroyed or damaged the second is expected to become vulnerable to loss as well. They can thereby both be lost together.

This lesson indicates that we must look at the various distortions of experience with care, and also through more general attention copy-type models separately in each case. Hints as to how experience may be distorted are then deduced from the various important features of the attention copy models, guided, for example, by the detailed modelling results of the model based on the architecture of Figures 8 and 9 of Part II in specific cases (as in simulations of the model or its variants in the case of the attentional blink), as well as from the knowledge of specific brain damage suffered by the patients/subjects.

Alzheimer's Disease

It is natural to start our more detailed discussion of distorted minds with AD, since I started the chapter with comments on it. AD is a disease of vast proportions, with no present cure, nor a complete understanding of its cause. Some clues are available, such as it having a genetic component and running in families (due to mutations in various chromosomes). Similar genetic defects can be causative in other brain diseases. A recent study from the University of Arkansas Medical School has shown, for example, that the biochemical glutathione is found in decreased amounts in patients with autistic symptoms. This chemical is known to be a powerful anti-oxidant, and its low level may increase susceptibility to free radicals in the body, leading to damage to the brain, gastro-intestinal tract and immune system, as well as helping to activate the mutated genes on several chromosomes.

AD is a disease that ultimately causes complete disintegration of information processing in the brain, leading to death. This may take from 2 to 20 years from initial suspicion of its presence. It occurs in about 60% of cases of dementia, and is especially prevalent in old people (with 25% of those over 85 succumbing to it). However, it is hard to diagnose except by post mortem. It has a steady and measured progress through a well-charted sequence of early short-term and long-term memory loss, with concomitant loss of less commonly used words (as evinced by Iris Murdoch in her most verbally meagre last novel *Joseph's Last Day*), then beginning to lose the ability to make mental calculations and operate appliances, becoming disoriented in time and place, showing lack of sensitivity about what to say in front of children, and progressing to use of empty words like 'thing' or 'stuff', further on not being able to comprehend complex ideas and language, then losing language ability, until the patient is bedridden and their brain loses the ability to regulate bodily functions, ensuing in death.

Most of these items in the spiralling downward progression of functions of the brain involve content. Initially the AD patient has a functioning 'owner' so they still possess the ability to know what it is like to be them. Even at the stage of severe personality modifications and loss of many words, there would be expected to be a preserved sense of their pre-reflective self. Only at the stage of becoming bedridden will one expect that sense of ownership to begin to falter and desert the patient. The attention control-type models help us to understand what is going on in the experience of AD: as the brain crumbles, different parts can go at different rates, so that the ability to move and buffer attention will gradually become reduced. When and how the patient loses the sense of 'being there' is difficult to say in general. It clearly happens by the end, but exactly when and how is difficult to predict with such a variable type of cortical decay. It most likely will differ in what is lost between individuals. But in all such cases there will be a gradual diminution of the sense of inner self arising from ownership, as that which can be owned in experience itself is reduced irreversibly by the decay of the brain.

In more detail for AD, there will be a stage at which the attention control system is unable to move attention in a voluntary manner. This will be due to the lack of operation of the frontal working memory system, with no voluntary goals being able to be held. The patient will then still be able to experience 'being there' in the world, but with no or little control over to what or where they attend: their attention will be driven by external events only. It will be expected that only later will the ability to move the focus of attention be lost by external stimuli demanding attention movement, so that there will be no attention movement signal. It will be then that the owner will have shut down completely; from then on all processing will be automatic.

Alternatively the attention movement signal may still be present in the sufferer's brain while any buffer for the attention copy signal has already shut down. If that were so, the patient would have a ballistic form of attention, but one without any 'owner' of the content being attended to. There would be no 'inner experience' as such, but only automatic processing, as in the situation above. That could be efficient, but would be that of a zombie. However, the resulting zombie would not have the speed-up of attention conferred by the use of a copy of the attention movement signal, as noted in the previous part. As mentioned earlier, it may even be that if they lose the ability to have a suitably buffered attention copy, they would not be able to help their brain activity for attended stimuli reach its buffer for report to other sites. In that case the person would not be even a slow and inefficient zombie, but one able to use only the automatic responses built up by earlier attended responses.

This set of changes could be followed in time by investigation of the modification of the pattern of brain waves as the AD progressed in a given patient. Gradual decline would be expected of the N2 signal, suggested earlier as the signal of the attention copy signal. The N2 itself is now known to have various components, and each of these could crumble away at different rates. The other important signal of awareness is the P3 (a signal occurring in the parietal lobes at about 330–450 milliseconds after a stimulus input); again, the rate of decay of the various components of this will be important to discover.

A different form of dementia is multi-infarct dementia, which arises by multiple small strokes. The results of this are similar to the decay of AD patients. However, the loss of cortical function may be more dramatic. The father of one of my colleagues ultimately died from it. At a late stage of his disease he appeared only to be able to respond automatically to objects placed in front of him. If a piece of food were placed before his lips he would open his mouth, move his head forward, and eat it. The same would happen if a pencil were placed in front of him. He did not know anyone who went to greet him, even his family members. The consultant told my colleague that there was almost no activity in the cortex of his father. Sometime between the beginning of his disease and this late stage cortical-dead situation, it is certain that my colleague's father lost his sense of ownership. That would have occurred gradually as parts of the crucial neural networks for the ownership experience deteriorated, possibly in parietal lobe and also possibly in prefrontal cortex. In his later automatic stage it is very unlikely he had any sense of 'being there', or even of any content as possessed by a zombie. So a similar problem arises for non-AD-type dementia: the content as well as the owner gradually decay away, with the owner ultimately being unable to help move the focus of attention anywhere. The detailed possibilities of changes of experience will be along the lines outlined above. In all these cases of dementia the owner will have been annihilated before the end comes, with only automatic responses being available to them.

Schizophrenia

Schizophrenia has very different characteristics from Alzheimer's disease, although sadly not in terms of the numbers of people who suffer it. About 1% of any population develops schizophrenia during their lifetime. More than 2 million Americans suffer from the illness in a given year, as do 600,000 British people. Schizophrenia appears earlier in men, usually in the late teens or early twenties, than in women, who are generally affected in the twenties to early thirties, although the overall incidence of the disease is about the same.

People with schizophrenia often suffer terrifying symptoms such as hearing internal voices not heard by others, or believing that other people are reading their minds, controlling their thoughts, or plotting to harm them. They also experience subtle changes in their experience of their selves, such as feeling too 'inner directed', with the outside world not meaning so much to them as before, and even losing its original natural meaning. This causes them to have great problems with everyday things, such as putting on their shoes. So schizophrenia involves things 'going on in my head' that can only be expressed by the sufferer. It is not like Alzheimer's disease, in which the behaviour of the sufferer disintegrates increasingly. In schizophrenia the sufferer can behave completely normally, possibly fooling health helpers that they are normal. Then they can strike and in some cases kill either a complete stranger or their nearest and dearest, as recounted earlier in the book.

The symptoms experienced by a schizophrenic may, in some more extreme cases, leave them fearful and withdrawn. Their speech and behaviour can be so disorganised that they may be incomprehensible or frightening to others. Available treatments can relieve many symptoms, but most people with schizophrenia continue to suffer some symptoms throughout their lives; it has been estimated that no more than one in five individuals recovers completely.

Accounts of the experiences of sufferers of the disease can be very clear. Thus the French writer Antonin Artaud wrote of his own experience when suffering very badly:

A terrible cold/An atrocious abstinence/The limbo of a nightmare of bone and muscles/With the sensation of stomach functions snapping like a flag in the phosphorescence of the storm/Larval images that are pushed as if by a finger and have no material thing.

This is a graphic description of images of bodily processes that would normally be suppressed in the mind. It is as if the normal inhibition of such signals from entering into consciousness has been lost by Artaud, a feature related to the nature of attention control. Such control seemed to have been damaged in his case.

A more general form of altered experience reported by schizophrenics has been noted by a number of close observers of the disease. Sigmund Freud noted that:

The libido of the schizophrenic withdraws from the outer world onto its own ego.

Another close observer of schizophrenics, Minkowski, in 1927 noted of them in general that:

His personal inner drive does not seek to identify with reality, but becomes like an empty slate.

A further psychotherapist, Morselli, in 1930 reported that his patient Elena said:

In truth, I am closer to the soul, to Dante's Paradise, in that world, but I feel removed from life, devoid of emotion and detached from everything.

Based on their own observations of schizophrenics in various stages of their disease, as well as from reports like those above, a group of modern psychotherapists have begun to explore the crucial experiential nature of the disease. Thus, the psychotherapists Bruno and Sarter noted in 1999 that there is too strong an attention of the patient to their inner world, and summarised this as:

Such hyperattentional dysfunction might represent the primary cognitive abnormality seen in schizophrenia.

Joseph Parnas, the Copenhagen expert on the disease, wrote in 2000 that in his view the general problem of the experience of the schizophrenic is:

The patient does not feel being fully existing or alive, fully awake or alert, or fully present and affected.

He and his colleagues reported in a scientific paper in 2003 on the results of a study of 21 long-term schizophrenic patients that:

Diagnosis of schizophrenia was associated with elevated scores on scales measuring perplexity (loss of meaning), disorders of perception, disorders of self-awareness, and marginally so, disorders of cognition.

Thus there seems to be damage, for a schizophrenic, to access to automatic responses/representations of objects (as in Artaud's case and many others), as well as damage to goals, monitors and attention control, with some form of hyper-reflexivity or over-attention to oneself. There is also an alteration of the status of normally unconscious semantic-level brain activities – these can intrude onto sensory buffers, again as in Artaud's case. Or there can be a loss of common-sense meaning of everyday objects, as noted in the study by Parnas and his colleagues.

Recent more detailed studies have been made that help clarify the cognitive changes brought about by schizophrenia. In particular, a number of cognitive deficits have been observed in the disease which allow us to relate what might be happening to the various parts of the attention copy-type model of the movement of attention. I discussed, in the previous part of the book, how consciousness could be created from the more detailed attention copy model of Figure 8. The knowledge of which components of the attention control system are being damaged in the disease can now help us understand the manner in which the experience of the schizophrenic will be altered. At the same time this alteration of experience, as reported by many schizophrenic patients, can itself throw light on the model of Figure 8 and the more general attention copy-type models of consciousness being considered here.

The list of cognitive deficits includes various breakdowns in the ability to move attention around rapidly. One feature is that there is a larger than expected signal, measurable by EEG, and called the P300. This signal is thought to arise when recent memory is updated, as when a new experience occurs. For schizophrenics it was observed that this signal is larger than for normal people. This may be related to the 'hyper-attentionality' of schizophrenics mentioned earlier: they are attending too much to the inner world of their brain activity, dwelling on aspects of it, even those noted by Antonin Artaud as normally unavailable to conscious inspection.

Recent research has also uncovered a lessening of the ability of schizophrenics to monitor consistency between behaviour and goals. This breakdown is notable in the ascription to others of the voices schizophrenics may hear inside their heads; these have been shown to be produced by sub-vocalisation by the patients themselves. They have lost, however, the ability to monitor this production effectively, so think someone is broadcasting the message into their minds. A similar feature of errors of ascription can occur with movements they make, so a schizophrenic can say, for example:

My grandfather hypnotised me and now he moves my foot up and down.

The force moved my lips. I began to speak. The words were made for me.

These illusions of lack of control are explicable in terms of a control approach to motor actions as governed by the brain, and by an attention control-type interpretation of inner experience. The error in attribution of 'who is doing the action' has been suggested as arising from damage to the monitor used to specify an internal willed action being made, against a target action having been set up. One or other of the processes of setting up such a target action, or its being compared with what has actually occurred, could lead to loss of the experience of the action as being willed by oneself. However, an attention control-type system is needed to give the lack of sense of a willed action itself as an 'inner feel'. Without that only a zombie will be doing the actions, without knowing it; the zombie would have no inner experience to report as deranged.

The source of the illusions created by such damage to brain activity is subtle. But even more subtle must be the change to experiences of the self complained of by some schizophrenics. These were noted already in the quotations I made earlier from the writings of Bruno and Sarter and of Josef Parnas. Some descriptions are very disturbing. One young man wrote of his constant attempts to hear his music player properly, but could not get it correct: he continually heard it as if he was 'hearing himself listening to the music'. He could not get the music system so arranged that he could hear the music directly. All was echo, as is the account of his own experience by another schizophrenic:

My thoughts come back again like a playback.

Other schizophrenics display brilliance in arguments about the 'inner nature of reality', but yet are not able to crystallise their thoughts in any way related to the real world. It is as if too much attention is paid to what is going on inside their heads, not enough to what is coming in from the outside world.

Such a characterisation is possibly too broad to cover both positive (when inner voices are heard) and negative (in which little contact is made with the external world) schizophrenia. However, it can be conjectured that the negative cases are too involved in making sense of the over-attention, and ultimate break-up, of their inner world, and that this is a second stage after earlier positive symptoms disturb them by their bizarre character. In this sense, then, there is very likely a gradual breakdown of the attention copy-like structures creating their inner experience. Initially this is able to handle the misattributions to others of self-willed actions. Later, as more breakdowns occur in the attention copy circuitry in the brain (with increased activity in the specific attention copy circuit, so causing increased concentration on the inner experiences, and decreased access to automatic responses to familiar external stimuli), the patient's mind becomes increasingly driven to consider itself. This would end in negative symptoms.

There is also some relation of this aspect of schizophrenia to the experience of pure consciousness mentioned in Part II – although the latter is actively looked for (by setting up a goal reducing the input to the brain of the external world through meditation or prayer) while the schizophrenic's descent into the spiral of their own inner self – thinking more and more about itself and shutting out the outside world – is completely involuntary. It is thereby more frightening for the schizophrenic to comprehend and face up to than the meditator. Schizophrenics have no control over their descent into an inner hell, switched on very likely by their genetic make-up combined with special external factors, and so making them lose themselves to the world.

Autism

A similar feature to schizophrenics' neglect of certain aspects of the outer world is noticeable in autism. However, the inner experiences present in the two diseases are very different. Autism is a disease that about half a million people suffer from in the UK, with two million in the USA, with a range of symptoms from extreme to much less severe in the case of those said to suffer from what is called Asperger's syndrome (supposedly suffered especially by university professors, due to their solitary state and savant-like behaviour, learning more and more about less and less, some would say). A famous Asperger's case is that of Temple Grandin, presently a professor at Colorado State University in Fort Collins, Colorado. She is a remarkable woman, who has had a successful international career designing livestock equipment, having obtained a PhD in animal science at the University of Illinois in Urbana. She writes of her experience:

> Two of the subjects covered in this chapter are the frustration of not being able to speak and sensory problems. My senses were oversensitive to loud noise and touch. Loud noise hurt my ears and I withdrew from touch to avoid over-whelming sensation.

She has also suffered extreme levels of anxiety, partly due to the fact that when she was young she could speak hardly at all. As she wrote:

> Not being able to speak was utter frustration. If adults spoke directly to me I could understand everything they said, but I could not get my words out. It was like a big stutter. If I was placed in a slight stress situation, words would sometimes overcome the barrier and come out. My speech therapist knew how to intrude into my world. She would hold me by my chin and made me look in her eyes and say 'ball.' At age 3, 'ball' came out 'bah,' said with great stress. If the therapist pushed too hard I threw a tantrum, and if she did not intrude far enough no progress was made. My mother and teachers wondered why I screamed. Screaming was the only way I could communicate. Often I

would logically think to myself, 'I am going to scream now because I want to tell somebody I don't want to do something.'

Her lack of early speech, and continued motor problems (she cannot toe a line, a test used for drunk driving) could be due to the reduced size of her cerebellum, the hind-brain at the back and underneath the cerebral hemispheres (as shown in Figure 2). More generally, autistic subjects are known to have a cerebellum considerably reduced in comparison to normal people – possibly the cause of linguistic difficulties for many autistics (as also observed in children who have had parts of their cerebellum removed due to a tumour). Like many such people, Temple Grandin cannot modulate the level of the sounds she is hearing – in general they find them too loud, as well as having difficulty in screening out background noise. Autistics also have profound abnormalities in the neurological mechanisms that control the capacity to shift attention between different stimuli. Autistic people also like to have deep touch sensations, although they find it difficult to be hugged by other people.

There are many families with affective disorder in their family history. The relationship between autism and affective disorder has also been noted. Family histories of high-functioning autistics often contain gifted-ness, anxiety or panic disorder, depression, food allergies and learning disorders. Some of the most successful high-functioning autistics have altered childhood fixations into careers, such as the person who turned his childhood fixation on numbers into a bank teller's job. The farmer who brought him up found goals for his number fixation; he told him he could count the corn rows if he ploughed the field.

Discussions with other high-functioning autistics have revealed visual methods of thinking on tasks that are often considered non-visual. A brilliant autistic computer programmer told Temple Grandin that he visualised the program tree in his mind and then just filled in the code on each branch. A gifted autistic composer told her that he made 'sound pictures'.

The understanding of the altered experiences of autistic people has been explained by the British psychology team Uta and Chris Frith as that an autistic person had lost a sense for other people's internal states – in other words for their minds. Effectively they were not able to comprehend easily that other people had internal mental states and desires – a lack of a so-called 'theory of mind'. This helps explain some of the problems experienced by autistic people in relating to others, but does not seem to be closely related to the perceptual distortions and movement problems experienced by Temple Grandin and other autistic people. Thus, a woman wrote very recently to *The Times* newspaper to state that her son aged 6, diagnosed with autism, has great problems learning words and sentences. This is a typical feature of those with cerebellar damage at an early age. At the same time these autistic people can possess wisdom and expertise in a very specific area, such as the ability to draw complex pictures of buildings, or to calculate complicated arithmetical tasks. One young man aged 25 (who did not, however, have many other autistic symptoms) was able to rattle off the value of the constant pi to one thousand places, without thinking about it with any special care.

In terms of the attention copy model of consciousness, it is clear that autistic people can suffer from a sensory overload, so they can be frightened by the noises or bright lights in their surroundings. This could be related to the loss of portions of their cerebellum, as involved in the overall circuitry for monitoring errors in movement. It is now understood that the cerebellum is also involved in cognitive/sensory processing. So it may be that the cerebellum is part of the monitor system introduced in the attention copy model of Figure 8. If so, then there are expected to be some decrements, possibly mainly in handling what would otherwise be automatic processes such as keeping sound and light stimulus inputs to a required level, and to allow touch to be handled properly as well. The resulting too high levels of sensory inputs will thus cause difficulties in the overall attention control circuit, with the monitor extended to include the cerebellum, now damaged. Moreover, other people would prove difficult to deal with due to their unexpected alterations in their speech and behaviour patterns. This again may relate to the suggested role of the cerebellum as involved in predicting future patterns of movement and sensory inputs from what has just gone before: if those predictions are not able to be made efficiently then other people, in particular, would appear dangerous, unpredictable machines.

The Varieties of Damage

In Alzheimer's disease there are quite different features of alterations of consciousness, as compared to neglect, for example, as seen by the attention copy model. In AD there is a gradual loss of content, with specific content gradually ebbing away and with it going the associated ownership. The edges are increasingly chipped away of the inner self, until there is no inner self left at all. Automatic processes then take over to keep the body alive, until they themselves disintegrate.

There is a very different set of distortions of experience in schizophrenia as seen through the eyes of the attention copy model. Here the inner self undergoes various distortions, one important component of these being too much strength given to the relevant neural activities in those components involved with the attention copy signal. This helps explain the remoteness felt by some patients as well as the loss of a common-sense view of the world around them: they get into a state similar to that of pure consciousness, where the external world is prevented from entering. The descent totally into the inner self is expected in a later stage of schizophrenia.

In all, a person's experience when suffering either Alzheimer's disease, schizophrenia or autism can all be helped by looking at the diseases by way of the attention copy model. We have not finished with distortions of consciousness yet, although the next group we consider are brought on swiftly by traumatic events – by stroke or brain damage.

CHAPTER SIXTEEN

DAMAGED CONSCIOUSNESS

The modification of conscious experience, as brought about by explicit and immediate damage to parts of the brain, can be enormous. The change can be very sudden, as in a car crash or by a stroke. Within a day or so the subject has an enormous change to their inner experience, be it of total unawareness of the left or right side of their world, loss of social rules, or more subtly when they are caught by events and objects on one side of their view impinging from the other side, as in extinction. These changes are far more dramatic than the creeping modifications of personality and mental powers caused by Alzheimer's disease, schizophrenia or autism. Sometimes with these rapid changes in experience there is a concomitant denial by the subject that there has been any loss of function. The resulting problems are possibly more difficult to handle than those of the crumbling brain, although ultimately when mind has disintegrated too far in the crumbling brain it is as if the subject had experienced brain damage in a more dramatic fashion.

Neglect

A stroke is caused by the loss of the blood supply to part of the brain, due to clogging up of the capillaries from various causes (such as a clot) or their rupture. After such loss of blood flowing to support nerve cells, there is a catastrophic loss of oxygen to the cells, so causing a number of them in the related areas to die. This leads to loss of the functions being performed by the particular brain sites at issue. A very common area of loss of brain tissue due to stroke is the right parietal lobe, sometimes with accompanying loss of prefrontal cortex. Such a loss can be devastating to the ability of the person either to perform actions with the left side (called apraxia) or to be aware of sensory inputs on their left side (sensory neglect).

A typical case report, from a patient's husband, is as follows:

On 10 October of this year, my wife (47 years old) suffered a deep vein haemorrhagic stroke located above her right ear which affected both the frontal lobe and parietal lobe. She was transferred to the Hershey Medical Center's Rehab hospital about 16 November. Surprising everyone, she has responded to rehab well. They initially thought she'd not be much more than an intelligent veggie but she's just blossomed. She walks, talks, eats by herself and in general is well on the way to recovery. I'm told her mental recovery is progressing well and there's no reason to expect anything less than an almost full recovery in this area. She's blind in her right eye since birth and the stroke affected her left eye. She was partially paralysed on the left side but this is responding very well. She suffers from left side neglect. The eye department evaluated her remaining vision and told her she has lost a full 50% of the vision she had left and that she'll never be able to drive again. I've been told that this will never get any better and I've also been told that it may improve!

These types of deficit arise in a brain with good functioning of the early sensory brain regions, but with loss of awareness of a particular part of the left visual field (as in the above example). A physician can test such patients by holding a pencil up in that part of their field of view: they report nothing. Or they may have no awareness of their left leg or left side (as in the above report). Patients have even been known to complain about the foreign leg of some other person who has got into bed with them; it is only their own, but not recognised as such! They may persist in trying to remove this foreigner from their bed, and an almighty struggle can ensue.

So what has happened in neglect is quite different experientially from that in Alzheimer's disease or schizophrenia. In neglect a particular region of either sensory or motor 'space' has been blanked out of the patient's experience. But they are still themselves. They still have the 'I' as strongly as before. It does not crumble away from within, as in Alzheimer's disease. In terms of the attention copy model it means that there is loss of brain tissue supporting buffer sites coding for the specific content of an experience, such as coding for a specific region of space or of the left sides of objects, or the left side of their body. Such content has completely vanished along with the neural tissue, partly justifying us considering that region of brain tissue as coding for the content of that experience. There may also have been loss of the ownership experience for the corresponding experience, and I noted earlier it may be that the brain works so that once ownership is lost then so goes the content: it just cannot rise up into consciousness since it is not supported enough in its battle to emerge into the light of conscious experience. This is because the attention copy signal, carrying the signature and experience of the owner, is not available any more – it has been destroyed at the same time that the tissue supporting it was destroyed by the stroke and resultant loss of oxygen.

Neglect is thus possibly a case of loss of ownership for specific contents in experience. Schizophrenia, on the other hand, is the opposite in some cases: too much experience of the inner self, cutting off the outer world, initially distorting it by misattributions of excessive inner brain activity as arising from outside under someone else's control, but finally turning the inner self in on itself so that much of outer experience is inhibited from entering consciousness.

Extinction

There is an interesting reduced form of loss of content of experience in extinction. Suppose two stimuli, one on the left and the other on the right, are presented simultaneously to a patient. For example, suppose two pencils are held to the left and right in front of the patient. A patient with extinction will most likely report the right-most pencil, but not have any awareness of the left-most one: it has been extinguished. However, the patient can report a single pencil held on either side of them without difficulty. The corresponding brain waves when the two pencils are presented have also been shown to be reduced on the right-hand side of the brain in this case: expected by the cross-over of information from the eyes to the brain. There appears just not to be enough neural activity on the right for patients to register the left-most pencil, and as a result they are only aware of the right-most one.

This phenomenon is also explicable in terms of the attention copy model, with a competition occurring in the brain between the left and right hemisphere attention control systems battling for supremacy. With the right-most hemisphere damaged by the stroke, the left one in a patient will win, the competition destroying enough activity in the right hemisphere to make the viewer blind to the left side of their field of view.

Frontal Lobe Damage

The frontal lobes are the powerhouses of higher thought, as well as supporting our social rules and memories. The sad, famous case of Phineas Gage, which I reported earlier, is a clear case of the importance of frontal brain structures that enable decent social relations to be handled by the person. What is more, I noted that Phineas Gage did not lose consciousness after the terrible damage caused to his frontal cortex by the tamping iron blowing through his brain. Prefrontal cortex does not therefore seem essential to consciousness, but if lost, takes with it its content, which is crucial for the ability of being in control of one's social life. Such damage can also occur through stroke.

One very specific feature of such loss of control is the 'alien hand syndrome', which can be caused by a stroke or other sources of brain damage. It is an eerie phenomenon: one or other hand of the subject takes on a life of its own. For example, the alien hand, as if completely independent, will suddenly reach out and pick up a pen on the table in front of the patient. Even more bizarre was the case of a patient who had stroke damage to her left medial frontal cortex resulting in her suffering alien hand symptoms. As reported in a neurology journal in 1981, from analysis by three American doctors from Temple University in Philadelphia:

> *The patient would reach out spontaneously with the right hand and then would not be able to release her grip voluntarily. She was unable consciously to inhibit this behaviour although she was quite aware of it and was obviously frustrated by her inability to prevent it. She tended to restrain the movement of the right arm by holding it by her side with the more 'obedient' left arm. At times the right arm was noted to interfere with tasks being performed by the left arm. This 'intermanual conflict' was observed at one point when it was noted that her right hand came up to keep her glasses on after she had begun to remove them with her left hand. She was aware of these conflicts but was, again, frustrated by being unable to prevent them consciously.*

The conflict between the hands in such patients can be far more extreme. One patient with alien hand syndrome reported that he had to sleep with his alien hand under his pillow otherwise it would try to strangle him as he slept.

We can see that the attention copy model of consciousness can explain the loss of conscious content for social rules as arising from prefrontal neural tissue coding for social rules and planning powers that are essential for efficient relations with others. The alien hand syndrome may be a reduced form of a situation in which the motor plans the patient is trying to carry out cannot access the brain tissue controlling hand movements on both sides. So the 'alien hand' will indeed be 'out of control'. It will perform automatically tasks it has been trained on, such as picking up pens, grabbing hold of door handles, and so on. That it can take on an apparently 'evil' character, as seen from the patient's point of view, even to the extent of trying to strangle him or her, is also explicable in terms of plans being accessible by unconscious motives; as we know since the time of Sigmund Freud there are indeed many such plans in the human psyche.

Anosognosia

This is one of the strangest deficits brought about by brain damage, but a very well attested one. In it the patient has no consciousness of their deficit. This is known to happen in a relatively large proportion of patients suffering strokes leading to neglect, of a variety of sorts, such as hemiplegia (paralysis on one side of the body due to damage to brain of the opposite hemisphere), Anton's syndrome (unawareness of blindness) and anosognosia with hemianopia (where there is partial loss of sight on one side, but no awareness of the deficit). For example, in hemiplegia, the patient, when asked to lift up both arms, will only lift up the healthy one, but maintains that he has raised the disabled one as well. As an expert in hemiplegia reported:

The patient behaves as though he knew nothing about his hemiplegia. Requests for movements with the paralysed left arm or leg are performed by him merely with the healthy one, or not at all, but at the same time he is convinced that he has carried out the task. The patient may pay no attention to the paralysed side, but even refuse to look at it or turn away to the right. If such a patient is shown the affected arm or leg as being attached to his body, he will often remain indifferent or will declare that it is not his or that someone else's is in his bed, and the like. It is as though the patient experienced the paralysed limb as absent. (Gerstmann, 1942)

The exchanges between a doctor and such a patient under examination can be quite bizarre, as in the following, published some years ago in a scientific paper:

Doctor (D): Where are we?
Patient (P): In the hospital.
D: Which hospital?
P: Santa Orsola.
D: Why are you in the hospital?
P: I fell down and bumped my right leg.
D: What about your left arm and leg? Are they all right?
P: Neither well nor bad.
D: In which sense?
P: They are aching a bit.
D: Can you move your left arm?
P: Yes, I can.
D: (Puts her right index finger into P's right visual field) Can you touch my finger with your left hand? (P does not move)

> D: What happens?
> P: It happens that I am very good.
> D: Have you touched my finger?
> P: Yes.
> D: Can you touch your left hand with your right hand?
> P: (Doing it without hesitation) Yes.

The patient showed a severe form of anosognosia, but could recognise her left hand and touch it without any searching for it, so had no deficit of awareness for sensing touch. Similar accounts have been published in numerous scientific journals about other forms of anosognosia, and how there can be specific modalities (in touch, action or vision) in which there is no knowledge of a deficit while in the other modalities there is knowledge (although not of the deficit in that given modality).

Two competing approaches have been proposed by psychologists to explain anosognosia: the motivational approach (that it is caused as a defensive adaptation to the stress caused by the illness), and the cognitive approach (that it is due to the loss of a specific cognitive process after damage to a special area in the brain). Each of these approaches has numerous specific theories exploring how the cause is worked out in more detail. However, the motivational approach in general predicts that there will be gradual increase in anosognosia as the disease consolidates; this is not what is observed across a number of cases. Furthermore, denial of all sorts of deficits is to be expected, which again is not found to be across a number of cases. Also, many of the cognitive theories depend on a unified brain site for monitoring higher-order intellectual activity. But then lesions of this site would lead to anosognosia of all deficits (if a patient has a number of them brought about by stroke). Such a blanket form of anosognosia is not what is observed, but there is dissociation, so that a patient could have anosognosia of loss of sight but not of their inability to move their left leg. More appropriate theories have been proposed which have a number of monitor systems, one in each modality; these have the best explanatory power for the phenomenon.

The attention control model developed through Figure 8 and in Part II is a development of such models of anosognosia, being based on attention as the controlling 'power'. The attention copy model of consciousness thereby possesses monitors for each modality, as well as working memory buffers for content and for the copy of the attention movement signal of the focus of attention. If there is loss of both of these buffers – for content and for ownership – then there will be loss of the experience associated with that content. Thus, loss of the content and ownership buffers for vision will lead to blindness; that for motor control of the leg will lead to apraxia in the left leg. In both cases there will be awareness that such a loss of capabilities has occurred. However, loss of only the buffer for content will lead to loss solely of the content experience but the owner should still feel there: in other words anosognosia. Extensive evidence from autopsy of sufferers indicates that the areas in the brain lost in anosognosia include regions of parietal and temporal lobes already noted as being the sites of such buffers for content and ownership. This supports the thesis that attention copy-type models are able to explain how this subtle effect of loss of awareness of a deficit could occur.

Amnesia

Amnesia is one of the first symptoms to be noticeable in Alzheimer's disease. However, there have been several cases of severe amnesia brought about more rapidly either by surgical intervention or due to viral infection. The former is resorted to as an attempt to prevent an otherwise constant flow of epileptic seizures making the patient's life impossible, but which are untreatable by any other method. Removal of the hippocampus leads to a state of total amnesia for the past for all events much earlier than the operation. Thus, H.M., in the well-known case quoted earlier, would look at himself in the mirror and not accept that it was his face, aged some 20 years on after his operation, which stared back. However, this and similar cases do not have any change in their consciousness, except that they cannot remember the passing of time in terms of a series of images allowing them to make sense of their present in terms of their past. Thus, their sense of 'being there' is not damaged. They lose only the content of those years that have passed since their operation: after the operation those periods were not part of their past at all. Their 'I', on the other hand, is still active, only reduced by being unable to call on past reflective memories including those of events up to only a few minutes ago. A number of cases show that they can, however, manage to handle the previous minute or so in their lives, so that they do not lose a sense of continuity of themselves.

A more extreme case of memory loss occurred 20 years ago to the British conductor Clive Wearing. He had suffered a freak dose of herpes simplex, which is the well-known virus causing cold sores. This attack robbed Clive not only of much of his past memory (although he could still remember how to read music) but also of what had just happened. His was a case in which even the continuity of self was at stake. It was as if every few minutes he re-awoke to find himself. He documented in his diaries, for example:

> 7.40 am: I wake for the first time
> 7.47 am: This illness has been like life and death till now. All senses
>   work.
> 8.07 am: I am awake.
> 8.31 am: Now I am awake
> 9.06 am: Now I am awake
> 11.37 am: Now I am perfectly completely awake (1st time)

He has since made some recovery, especially in recognising the nature of his memory loss, and being able to compensate for it. To us the case offers an interesting insight into how consciousness hangs together over time. That has always been a problem to philosophers. Here we have a clue about how it happens when it goes wrong – part of a user's manual at least to point out what is going wrong and how, although in this case no cure is offered (without new cell growth available).

What Clive Wearing has lost appears to be more than the regions of the hippocampus that were carefully snipped away by surgeons in the patients I mentioned earlier. The virus that ate away parts of Clive Wearing's brain was not so careful, very likely also destroying temporal lobe tissue near the hippocampus needed to support laying down in long-term memory the working memory activity also thought to be basic to memory. These neural buffers are crucial for holding activity over short times like seconds, the times you need to hold items in your head for almost immediate use (such as remembering a phone number and then making the call). This may not be remembered permanently, but is important to give the continuity of experience.

In the attention copy model, if the working memory buffer were to be damaged, then the 'continuity of experience' would be damaged. Short-term continuity occurs by the ability of the buffer site to hold activity for long enough to bridge the gap from one moment to the next. In our case that gap is several seconds; remember that many aspects of experience are bundled up into a 2–3 second packet of content. A line of a poem or a stanza in a song lasts about that length. Psychologists have shown that people's movements are gathered up into packets of about 2–3 seconds of fluidity, and then a new batch of connected movements occurs, and so on.

Clive Wearing appears to have lost the brain tissue allowing him to bridge between those seconds of time, so he keeps losing 'himself'. By that I mean that he has no memory of the previous batch of 2–3 seconds, so that when he arrives at a present moment, beginning a 2–3 second sequence of experience, he has no past such sequences to latch on to as to what had been happening. No wonder he kept repeating over and over 'I am awake', since he does not have enough memory overlap with his very recent past brain activity to keep his sense of being a continuous person going. He has short-term continuity but no longer-term form. His consciousness of his continued presence is thus continually renewing itself anew.

Dissociative Identity Disorder

A quite different sort of personality problem has caused much controversy over the past decade, but has now become a little more acceptable by renaming the claimed disorder. It used to be 'multiple personality disorder', but that was unacceptable to some due to the claim that only one personality was normally possible per person. This claim sounds a little silly in view of there not being a clear definition of a person's personality. Be that as it may, the new name of dissociative identity disorder (DID) properly defines what is happening. In these cases the behaviour of a person at different times is so different from that at other times – indeed, as if different personalities or identities possessed the person's mind at different times – that it is as if the identity of the person has dissociated. This is different from schizophrenia, where a sufferer claims that others are invading his mind. But it is still his mind, not someone else's. For sufferers of DID the dissociated persons who inhabit their mind at differing times each behave as if possessing a sense of 'I': they are not invaders of the given person's individual mind, but taking over command of the 'I-ness' as they come into play.

A case in point is Pamela Edwards, whose 'alters', as they are called, are named Andrew, Sandra, Margaret and Susan. They each have very different characters. A report on Ms Edwards noted that one of Ms Edwards' personalities was very controlling, but did not properly connect to the outside world, so sometimes put Ms Edwards into a difficult and even dangerous position. As in many earlier cases of DID, the alters seem to have been created as a strategy to handle great trauma, usually brought about by childhood abuse. The alters allow the memory of the trauma itself, and the associated burden of guilt, to be shifted away from the main personality and so a relatively equable life can be lived, But in a threatening situation the stability of the fragile personality has to be faced by resorting to an appropriate alter who can handle the relevant threats.

All is not necessarily goodness and light between the alters. In Pamela Edwards' case they appear to be causing a danger to her health and sanity due to some of the alters becoming overbearing and trying to attack each other. As Judy Williams, her one-time foster-mother and now full-time carer reported, as she began to understand Pamela Edwards' predicament:

> I became aware there was this argument happening within Pamela. I turned round to see her in the midst of shouting. Pamela with one hand was going 'slap' across her face and saying 'Don't you dare f***ing hit me' and the other hand was going back. 'You f***ing hit me'. There was this fight going on in one body. The table went over, Pamela was on the floor with her legs crossed. She was in a terrible state saying 'I'm sorry, was there an argument?' It became clear that it was Andrew who had had a fight, and then it became clear that they were people and that the people had names.

The nature of the DID protection process is to be understood in terms of the more general character of the personality of anyone. This is composed of memory banks under the attention control system (for access and guidance in response) composed of memories of past episodes, with their associated remembered rewards and punishments. These provide a set of social rules and rule schemata for organising response in various social situations. The episodic memories are an important bank of examples to help in dealing with novel social situations. The totality of these memory and rule stores constitutes what is usually termed 'personality'.

When an episodic memory becomes too traumatic, with an associated set of punishments that are too great to be too close to consciousness for comfort, then they must be covered over and made inaccessible to conscious access. DID achieves this by carving up the personality memory banks, so that it is very difficult for the personality of one alter to tap into the personality memory banks of others. Some alters may become dominant, so that they can indeed know about the personality memory banks of some other alters, but the basic episodic memory basis of the trauma must be hived off from them all. That initial process of shutting off memory banks could be the basis of the further DID process itself. It could alternatively be a process of dilution of the trauma, it being shared in parts between the alters.

A neurological basis for DID in the construction must be in the hippocampus itself, now recognised as the crucial organ for the laying down of episodic memory. It is shaped like a sea horse, so there could be separation of memories laid down at different sites along the sea horse's backbone. This would be accentuated by separations of cortical sites for other components of these different memory streams, such as for report by speech (differing levels and types of speech occur among the alters) as well as differing facial characteristics for muscle tensions, etc.

The deeper question is: are there different 'minds' inhabiting a person with DID. My answer is that several 'I's may be needed in DID. Each 'I' is represented in the attention copy model of consciousness as the activity of the copy of the attention movement control signal. There are several such 'I' sites (buffer sites for the attention copy signal) in each of us, as I noted in Part II. In that case there would be some dissociation of 'I', as I noted in Part II had already been investigated by Tony Marcel. There could be even further dissociations happening in the case of Pamela Edwards, in whom different alters seem to be able to exist simultaneously. Each of the separate buffer sites are only providing a content-free ownership experience for each of these alters, as I have emphasised in the previous part in my discussion of the attention copy model. Such ownership experience will persist across each of these different alters. In this case there will be movement of the 'I' from one alter to another, or even simultaneous existence of several different inner selves inside the subject' mind.

In all such cases the phenomenon is explicable. It may be difficult to cure, since it has arisen as an efficient defence mechanism against the trauma. Removal of the alters could again expose the trauma, which would be too painful. The subject has reconnected their brain to function in an abnormal fashion, although one valid for them in dealing with their early trauma.

Depersonalisation and Derealisation

These are disorders that quite often crop up in clinical practice. They are defined in the American Psychiatric Association's Diagnostic and Statistical Manual (DSM-IV) as 'an alteration in the perception or experience of the self so that one feels detached from, and as if one is an outside observer of, one's mental processes or body (e.g. feeling like one is in a dream)', and 'an alteration in the perception or experience of the external world so that it seems strange or unreal (e.g. people may seem unfamiliar or mechanical)'. The condition has been reported in temporal lobe epilepsy as well as in various brain diseases such as cerebrovascular disease, postencephalitic states, migraine and mild head traumas. Thus, according to a report from the nineteenth century on the problem:

Some [epileptic] patients declare themselves quite unable to describe the type of sensory anomalies they experience. One said 'perceptions emerge into consciousness in a way that cannot be defined but only described by saying that they seem as if they were different. The singing of birds sounds different to me, as do the utterances of my relatives, the air feels different, and the body feels as if made from another material'.

Numerous other researchers have noticed the relation between depersonalisation and temporal lobe epilepsy. Most patients with depersonalisation also report a lack of emotional feeling, possibly related to the unreality feelings. A patient was reported as saying:

> I feel as though I am not alive, as though my body is an empty, lifeless shell. [I am hearing music] but there is no response in me. Music usually moves me, but now it might as well be someone mincing potatoes ... I seem to be walking about in a world I recognise but don't feel. I saw Big Ben alight last night, normally a moving sight to me, but it might have been an alarm clock for all I felt ... My husband and I have always been happy together but now he sits here and might be a complete stranger. I know he is my husband only by his appearance – he might be anybody for all I feel towards him.

Such people also may have loss or dulling of pain experience: the experience of pain in this state is reported 'as if it were being done to another person'. There is also a frequent feature of absence of thoughts, images or memories.

This state has been proposed as arising as a hard-wired vestigial state important for dealing with increased alertness with profound inhibition of emotional responses. This state may arise when emotions 'get in the way', such as in the case of one patient with medial prefrontal damage who was socially dysfunctional in everyday life but could handle in a cool manner the manoeuvres needed to survive when skidding in his car on an icy road. Thus such inhibition (or permanent loss) of emotion guidance in decision making can stand us in good stead in certain conditions.

It has been proposed that it is excessive inhibition from the medial prefrontal cortex that causes the depersonalisation disorder. Once an anxiety threshold has been reached then this region damps down emotional responses. This model fits well into an extended version of the attention copy model of the previous part, in which bias from emotional modules in the limbic brain can affect decisions and cognitive processing in an attention-controlled brain, through biasing activity on the monitor or on the attention movement signal generator. But if there is too much anxiety generated by excessive activity in the monitor module then this could inhibit emotional bias signals totally. That would lead to a number of the depersonalisation symptoms.

The overarching feeling of 'not really being there' is expected to arise partly from this loss of emotional activity, which has been inhibited by the medial prefrontal cortex. However the 'depersonalisation' experience may have additional components that can be explored through the attention copy model. A person in this state may complain of 'feeling dead – I am not really there – I feel like a ghost'. There are even stronger features to consider, as reports from patients indicate:

It feels like my soul is trying to leave its shell, and I am fighting with all my strength to hold it inside this body ... I must be going insane to feel myself wafting away ... I know it's only a matter of time.

Everything looked 'off', like it turned into a stage set or fake replica of how it should really look.

The world looks like I'm dreaming or like I have unwittingly taken LSD.

There are feelings of patients that they are the only person in the world, or increasing doubts of the existence of external reality, or of existing without a body, being only thoughts.

These experiences are clearly difficult for patients to bear. But if the monitor in the attention-controlled brain was over-functioning, not only would it inhibit emotions but also causes difficulties in the access of sensory stimuli to the appropriate buffer working memory. There is some evidence that this is actually happening, for a group of Greek scientists observed recently that there was about a 50% reduction of the sensory buffer working memory activity (the so-called P300) in a group of 15 depersonalisation patients compared to a matched group of 15 normal people. This could arise from the excessive level of inhibition not only damping down emotional experience but also making the content of experience 'thinner' (as evidenced by the 50% lower P300, the brain signal denoting emergence of a stimulus into awareness in a person's brain). This would give a dreamlike feeling to the world, as if it were unreal. The further experience of expansion of the self – 'the soul trying to leave its shell', as reported above – could also arise from this mismatch between the strength of the content of experience and the strength of the ownership experience. It will be important to measure the size of the N200 wave, suggested in the previous part as the signal for the existence of the owner. That could be expected to be larger than normal, at least in cases like the one reported.

Obsessive-Compulsive Disorder (OCD)

This occurs somewhat frequently in the population, causing people to perform ritual acts, such as washing their hands many times until they are bleeding, or repeatedly checking to assure that they have properly closed the refrigerator door. Lady Macbeth is a famous fictional case of OCD, with her nightly hand washing to remove the blood from them and assuage her deep-seated guilt about her husband's heinous murder of their honoured guest and king, Duncan, in Shakespeare's *Macbeth*.

It is now known, through careful brain imaging experiments, that OCD is caused by the inappropriate build-up of connections in the frontal lobes (including sub-cortical sites) that lead to the issuance of commands (in the subject's head) to perform the ritual act again and again. A method of curing OCD has been developed in which the sufferer has explained to them the fact that incorrect connections have been set up in their brain, so causing them to keep repeating their act. They are told that this behaviour is purely arising from these incorrect connections, and is not anything to be ashamed of or feel that it cannot be controlled. They are advised to attempt to distract their attention by doing something else entirely when the 'voice in their head' starts to urge them toward the ritual act. Repeatedly battling against this urge, by understanding it as something that can be handled as part of the incorrect connections in their brain, and by choosing rewarding alternate activities to perform when under the urge, allows the sufferer to begin to reprogram their brain and regain control so they are no longer under the control of the urge.

This story of 'retraining one's own brain' is reminiscent of the practices of meditation to achieve pure consciousness. The brain is well known to be adaptive to all sorts of situations – at all ages we can learn new things (although at different speeds for different ages, granted). So there is nothing especially extraordinary about such retraining to rid a sufferer of OCD. Yet it is a symptom of the power of the human mind to be able to achieve such results – the power of 'mind over matter'. Yet such power is attained by putting new goals and understanding in the sufferer's mind, so they can retrain their brain to function more effectively. Looked at in this manner, it is the power of 'matter over matter' through the power of matter to create patterns of activity leading to alterations of the patterns of activity through retraining connections. Such OCD experiences are understandable in terms of the attention copy model of going from matter to mind.

Explanations by Attention Copy Damage

I have covered only a limited number of rapid changes of conscious experience that are visited on the vulnerable human brain, usually through no fault of the brain's owner. In the process we see that the attention copy model of conscious experience can help explain the changes of experience in the various cases. For neglect there is just complete loss of awareness of the particular parts of the outside world handled by the part of the brain destroyed by the stroke. All other parts of consciousness seem complete, both for content and the feeling of ownership, of 'being there'.

Neglect, more clearly than other deficits, has a further component of consciousness modification – that of loss of awareness of a deficit, so-called anosognosia. The defects in the loss of awareness of the deficit in the relevant modality, in vision or motor sensation, need careful analysis. There are three possibilities in terms of the attention copy model: there is both loss of ownership and content, or loss of only one or other of these. However, these possibilities can be winnowed down by evidence from anosognosia, and by the difficulty of having content without anyone owning it. This latter reason arises from the detailed manner in which the experience of ownership fosters the development of the experience of content, and without the prior activity associated with ownership there will be no content. The former evidence is based on the nature of anosognosia itself, and the related brain regions observed to be damaged in the patient: I suggested ownership without content as the cause of anosognosia.

Dissociated identity disorder involves a different set of distortions of personality and phenomenal experience, but one able to be comprehended in a view of personality founded on a core 'I' experience with associated content founded on memory banks defining the personality of the experiencer. These memories can be dissociated from each other as might be caused by trauma, so that different personalities can exist under different environmental conditions. It is these alters (separate personalities) that are created to handle the trauma memory that are at issue. They provide a new view into the nature of personality and its possible disorders, and one consistent with that provided by the attention copy model of self.

Depersonalisation disorder has a different basis, arising from excessive inhibitory activity from the monitor, in the medial prefrontal cortex. This can lead to the dream-like or unreal aspect of the world, due to a lower signal level on the sensory buffer. At the same time the sense of self may become overbearing – explaining why some patients feel they are all alone in the world. Again, there appears to be consistency with an attention copy approach to the mind.

A similar remark applies to obsessive-compulsive disorder. It can be treated by the paths from matter to mind to matter by generating suitable mental states using input activations along the lines of the attention copy model. If the sufferer is told about the brain basis of OCD and how it can be removed by brain retraining, then the process of giving in to the ritual urges begins to be lessened and ultimately is prevented altogether by the retraining of the appropriate brain connections: these are observed modified in the frontal lobes once the sufferer is cured.

CHAPTER SEVENTEEN

DISTORTING CONSCIOUSNESS

Bring It On!

Some revel in the possibility of changing their consciousness. They think it is to be manipulated at will to give them new and more exciting views of the universe. They may even become trapped inside their own minds by the new mental spaces they have found and tried to explore, and require specialist help to return to reality (if ever). Or they may just get hooked on one or other mind-bending drug, and need to keep on taking the potion. Either way, they have to keep on distorting their otherwise 'mundane' experience so that they enter other mental spaces than normal ones. On the other hand, and from quite different motives, others want to manipulate the consciousness of all those around them: these we usually call politicians.

There are also other ways of travelling to new worlds and having new experiences: through the arts, literature, music and visual art; these have all expanded enormously over the last century. The advent of electronic games and music systems has now allowed people to surround themselves with enormously challenging and mind-expanding auditory and visual experiences: they are certainly transported into new artistic spaces. New art, new books and new music pour onto the market and may even be sampled for free on the Internet. I will not leave these new outlets for mental exploration out of our discussion.

A further avenue being explored by an important proportion of humanity is religion. Through meditation and prayer claims are made about how there can be access to untold knowledge and power, in particular that of God. Again, this is an important avenue being pursued to gain new experience, even up to the ultimate experience, it is claimed, of contact with the creator of all experience. In the light of my earlier remarks in Part I on religion, we can only view these experiences as part of those constructed by the brain. It is not their actual occurrence as being 'in the brain', but their interpretation which is at issue here: the ultimate origin of the experiences. Do they have purely a brain origin, or is there a further causative agent at work? We will turn to that in due course.

We can now view these attempted alterations of experience in the light of the general model of consciousness I presented in the previous part. I termed it the attention copy model. It was based crucially on there being two components to consciousness: an 'owner' and that which the owner owns – the contents of their consciousness. I will now apply this general model to these various new routes into experience.

Drugs

Through hard drugs of addiction, such as heroin or cocaine, experience can be made rewardingly different for a short period. Through other drugs like LSD, ecstasy or ketamine, normal experience can be shredded through the mincing machine. Strange experiences then arise as if from new 'inner spaces', as has been claimed. Less extreme drugs like cannabis or tobacco, or substances like alcohol, can modify experience in more subtle ways, partly by addiction (tobacco) or by removing some inner constraints (cannabis or alcohol). There are further subtle changes of experience, especially for continued users: some cannabis users (those with a schizoid personality being at greatest risk) become increasingly psychotic; habitual and excessive alcohol users suffer hallucinations of seeing things ('pink elephants') in their drying out period.

These changes are beginning to be understood in terms of details of brain chemistry. For cannabis-based psychosis and ultimately schizophrenia, the cannabinoid system in the brain is regarded as the basis, especially the way that this system becomes sensitive, through continued use of cannabis, to produce greater amounts of dopamine when normal objects are experienced. This means that many things take on an unnatural significance, as well as ultimately becoming fused into the meaning of one's external world. That way paranoia set in, as is apparently occurring in ever greater numbers in various countries with increased use of cannabis. With ten times the number of young people smoking it compared to 20 years ago, the increased incidence of paranoia is to be expected, given the genetic preponderance of 25% of the population to possess a variant of a gene that normally breaks down dopamine produced in the brain. It is reported that ecstasy, at 50 pence per tablet, is now being taken by 12-year-olds in the UK, with the youngest reported case being of an 8-year-old sampling the drug (with bad consequences).

How do we explain these alterations of experience under drugs from the point of view of the attention copy models of this mind-user's manual? In general, the action of addictive drugs is very complex, involving various neuromodulators that are still not properly understood in brain science. There are at least three components in this change of experience:

1. Addiction sets in, so that the person is no longer able to function effectively unless they continue having enough of the drug. The world can only be experienced by the drug addict when in the 'high' state produced by the drug; otherwise the world is increasingly grey and unrewarding.
2. Alterations of sensory experience occur, and even hallucinations.
3. Changes of personality take place, so that psychotic trends or withdrawal from the environment may occur.

The first of these is very important to understand, especially since it can cause much damage to society as a whole from addicts turning to crime to fuel their addiction, and with some addicts finally dying. There is presently considerable research into the basis of addiction.

However, the bottom line is that it is not remarkable that the world looks rosy when a drug addict is on a high, since that is what drug action achieves. Thus the modification of the fusion of reward and sensory input by the rewards from drug addiction is not as surprising as the initial fusion of these two aspects of experience in the first place for all of us. Reward and penalty are all around us; they make our lives worth while. They are the basis of emotions. Thus the real problem facing us reduces to the question: how do emotions emerge into consciousness? But then I suggest that is really no different from asking how any content emerges into consciousness. And that has already been proposed as occurring, in the attention copy model, through the early wake-up call of a copy of the attention movement control signal. This call gives ownership experience to the content (the 'what it is like to be' component), with the actual content (emotional/rewarded or just straight perceptual content) arriving after this ownership preparation has occurred, so as to let the content then be used in further report and executive actions like planning, thinking, etc.

Meditation

In my earlier discussion of meditation in Part I, I considered the high point of the meditatory experience as that of pure consciousness. In this, all contact with the external world is strongly inhibited from entering awareness. What then occurs at that point of maximum control over one's inner world is that the subject's attention is focused purely on itself. It is the 'inner eye' viewing only itself. Here the inner eye does not denote any organ similar to that of vision.

The inner eye is the ultimate control system in the brain, that of attention. It is able to attend to itself due to its attention control character. For example, in the attention copy type of model the focus of attention is moved around by means of a separate control system, which generates a signal to move the focus of attention in lower levels of the cortex. A copy of this movement of attention signal is used to speed up the process of amplifying suitably relevant neural activity in these lower sites. It can also be used for fast correction to errors about to be made in that movement.

Such attention assignment could be made not only to lower brain activity, representing the stimuli of the outer world, but even to the system at the heart of generation of this signal to move the focus of attention. A suitable goal to achieve such a new focus of attention – to attend only to itself – would have to be developed. It would not be a trivial thing to do. No guidance is coming from the outside world as to how to achieve this state of inner viewing. But yet there is one overarching maxim to hold in one's mind throughout meditation: do not think of the outside world. This can be achieved through one-pointed meditation, where a high level of control has been arrived at so that only a single stimulus is attended to at a time. Then even this stimulus is sent out of attention. While this approach can help guide towards the ultimate goal of pure consciousness, as many writers on meditation have attested, it does not give an easy goal. It is not as if the goal is: 'pick up that cup over there'. It is instead 'be unaware of the totality of the external world', which is much harder to achieve.

Yet after years of meditation the state of stillness or pure consciousness can be arrived at by those with suitable diligence. Again we have accounts of this state, some of which were reported in Part I. We are now in a position to attack the delicate question of how the connections of the meditator's brain might be reshaped, through this meditation process, to achieve this remarkable state of consciousness. I note here that what is at stake is the possibility of building a bridge between the deepest experiences at the heart of the world's major religions and the explanation of those experiences solely in terms of the brain. This would be a big step, if possible, since it would bring an initial fusion of science and religion.

As appropriate for this mind-user's manual, I will consider this question explicitly from the point of view of the attention copy model of the previous part of the book. This model was analysed in some detail in the previous part, and shown to be capable of explaining various crucial aspects of consciousness, including the state of pure consciousness. Let me expand on this a little here.

Consider meditators engaged in their meditation. They are trying to inhibit all external input from creeping in and disturbing the state they ultimate wish to create, that in which there is no external input and only a recurrence of the copy of the attention movement control signal. To achieve this several connections must be established and strengthened as part of the model of Figures 8 and 9 of Part II. In particular, the activation of the special pure consciousness goal state must be made strong enough to bear the weight of the attention control signal generator fighting off all incoming distracting stimuli so as to have attention turn back to itself by this specific goal state. The connections to inhibit distracter input must be strengthened at the same time in this meditation process.

The initial attempts would involve new activity in frontal cortex acting as the seed for the subtle goal state driving pure consciousness. This would then guide the creation of a movement control signal whose copy would be required to inhibit as much as possible of incoming sensory input trying to access its appropriate buffer site. Such inhibition would not necessarily be already present in the attention copy contact to these buffer sites, but would have to be built up by gradual and difficult learning over the meditation periods. As I noted, using the technique of one-pointed meditation would allow a focus on the attention copy buffer to be set up from which to send out inhibitory signals to all other activities trying to access any sensory buffer site. This is a tall order, so will take some time, as is noted from the reports of meditators. However, there is no reason why it cannot ultimately be achieved. At the same time the relevant goal activity would itself have been concomitantly developed. The control having thereby been built up would be expected to help the final step. This is of the removal, by further learnt inhibition from the attention copy buffer to the relevant sensory buffer, of the single object being attended to. The state of pure consciousness would thereby ensue.

The attention copy model can thus begin to explain how this amazing state of pure consciousness can be created. The model can also help explain why it takes such a long time to achieve this remarkable state, since the connections are not naturally present in the young person, nor will they develop as they grow to adolescence. That the process of meditation has been created across the world, through very different styles and practices, all leading to such a state, is support for its universal character in the brain, and also for the adaptability of the brain.

Religion

God is supreme to billions on this earth. What God means to this vast number of people will be very different from one person to another.

However, in each of the clusters of belief – Christianity, Islam, Judaism, Hinduism, Sikhism, Buddhism, and so on – the idea of God is more or less similar. And all of them require some form of insubstantiality or immaterialism in their God. God does not exist in our universe. If God did so exist, then he could not be all-powerful and all-embracing, but would be subject to the laws and constraints present here in our physical world. Such a possibility of immaterial 'entities' is difficult to understand for anyone believing in only material objects. As they tend to say, 'If there is no matter there, how can you even think about it?'.

Those who have stayed with me so far with the mind-user's manual will, I hope, already have found strong support in my exposition for the claim that all the experience of a person arises only from that person's own brain. All the multitude of colours of consciousness – some of which I have discussed here – can be explained, I claim, by the attention copy model I presented in Part II. This model already has considerable support in brain science, and further support is constantly arriving. A supernatural cause does not, on these grounds, appear necessary to explain consciousness and mind.

The Arts

To be able to discuss the arts with any clarity, we need to answer the basic question: what is art? A recent claim has been made by a certain literary critic that anything can be art, but that literature is possibly more superior to the other arts as being more universal and self-critical. This latter claim is very likely false, since art can look at itself very quizzically (think of a Magritte painting or the famous Duchamp urinal), and painting and music (especially of a popular form) are everywhere.

But a question relevant to the mind-user's manual is: what is art for? Why do people visit art galleries, or have copies of paintings on their walls? What value does such exposure add to a person's life? In general, it is clear that it extends the windows of the mind. When I look at the two paintings on the wall of the room where I am writing this chapter, in one I see the Barnes Pond with its beautiful trees and bushes and lazy water, and in the other the elegant sweep of the antique Hammersmith Bridge over the translucent Thames. I am transported to each of these environments and remember the smells and sounds from past times I have spent at each. Even if I had not been to the sites in question, as for a beautiful sea scene by a friend in another room, or a delicate 1860 watercolour of a forest with cattle walking along a path, I can still be transported to places I have never been.

However, some modern art is even further away from the real world. If I consider a Jackson Pollock, covered in its abstract lines like the tracks of elementary particles seen in a bubble chamber, or other abstract paintings solely with a single square, what can I pick up from that? These more abstract paintings, I suggest, have value for us as representations of our early visual experience. Here I am using the word 'early' in both its developmental and its 'levels of processing in the brain' meanings. For the first, an infant will pick up simple shapes at an early stage and only later begin to recognise greater complexity. For the second, all of us have such increasingly complex levels of processing, so that the simpler shapes are not usually part of our conscious visual repertoire. Only by emphasising these abstract and simple shapes, by putting them on a canvas and exhibiting them under suitable lighting conditions, can we begin to regain the importance of such early shapes and structures. We are undoing some of the filters that we developed in early experience to allow us to be more sophisticated in our take on the world around us.

How does this view of the experience of art relate to our inner self – to the experience of ownership contained at the core of our own experience, and represented in the attention copy model of the mind? Here we come to a theme that will be all-powerful in the next part of the manual: art adds to the content of experience, so allowing us a richer mental life, with greater internal rewards. As such it helps us be more satisfied and fulfilled. It does not necessarily change our inner self of the 'owner of experience' that I described in some detail in the previous part. But it does grant that owner an enhanced and more rewarding domain of ownership. It extends the domain of experience that the owner can regard as theirs. That will be true for the development of all sorts of behaviour, both in ourselves as humans with very complex brains, in animals with less complexity, and in autonomous robots we will try to build in the future. The range of such expansions of experience should be looked at with a little care, since it can lead to the production of psychopaths (be they humans or robots) or those with paranoid tendencies. However, the more detailed form of such guidance in development will be considered more fully in the next part.

Pain

Pain is usually regarded as being visited on us in a manner that is out of our control. As such it should have been considered in the previous chapter, devoted to those alterations of consciousness brought about by external agency. In that sense pain is a mechanism for drawing attention to a part of the body that is damaged, telling the person, 'Do not use this, and get it cured'. On those lines, I remember pulling a hamstring in my left leg very badly some years ago. I went to a physiotherapist and got some immediate relief from the pain, but was told to exercise the leg, in spite of any pain that might arise. I did, and the leg did not seem to recover – I continued in agony and was in despair – thinking I would end up in a wheelchair for life. But then, in desperation I drove down to my cousin's wife, also a physiotherapist, this time for sports injuries (which my hamstring damage definitely was – it was caused by my suddenly sprinting off from a standing position). I told my cousin's wife what the previous physiotherapist had said. 'Rubbish,' she riposted in her forthright Australian manner. 'Pain is telling you not to use the leg – so rest it until the pain has gone'. I took her advice to heart, and after some days of good rest, I recovered.

But why is pain painful, I hear you ask? I think that it is so because it is a continual attention control signal from the pain centres in the somato-sensory and insula cortex. This signal is persistent until the pain goes away. Until then it functions to direct attention to find the source of the pain and repair the body so that it is no more painful. As such this is a very good example of survival value for a brain signal. People born without pain nerve fibres are very much at risk, being prone to terrible burns to their hands, for example, from hot oven plates or an iron that has heated up. Such people usually do not live beyond 30–40 years of age, due to the many accidents to which they are prone.

Pain, then, is a continual drag on the control system of attention, in the language of the attention copy model of consciousness. It is constantly nagging away at the edge of consciousness, or even in the middle if the pain is severe. It will then drive away all other thoughts. So the attention copy model can explain how pain is painful and extremely deleterious to quality of life. It is not something we should genetically engineer away, however, due to its important survival value. But it is possible to help severe intractable pain by means of attention control and meditatory techniques. This is understandable in attention copy terms, since the pain input to the attention movement control module will then be inhibited, by learning, so as to attend to other aspects of life. Thereby the pain will be reduced. Such an approach may be all right for a Buddhist monk who has meditated for many years and who is now in pain. But it is not so easy for the many people who have not meditated and learnt to control their attention, so that in those cases chemical intervention will also (or alternatively) have to be employed.

All these aspects of pain are visited without the wishes of the sufferer. Yet there are those who wish to visit pain on themselves, as if it were enjoyable. They will cut themselves with scissors or razors. Recently the sportswoman Dame Kelly Holmes acknowledged that depression had led her to harm herself by cutting her arm repeatedly with a pair of scissors. Apparently such self-harm is reaching epidemic proportions, according to a spokeswoman of the mental health charity SANE. It is a way of releasing 'intolerable mental pressures'.

Dame Kelly Holmes reported that she was in constant pain from a damaged right calf, and locked herself in her bathroom, turning on the taps so no one could hear her crying. She went to her bathroom cabinet and opened it.

> That's when I saw a pair of scissors on the shelf. I picked them up, opened them and started to cut my left arm with one of the blades. I made one cut for every day that I had been injured. With each one I felt I was punishing myself, but at the same time I felt a sense of release that drove me to do it again.

Such a sense of release may have arisen from the removal of attention from her painful calf, and also the process allowed her to feel more in control of her body. The pain she was causing in her arm was what she was inflicting on herself. She was now in charge.

Yet again, the attention copy model would indicate that such a process of self-harm can lead to regaining the sense of control – the self-inflicted pain being that caused by the person, giving them back the self-control over their pain they had lost from that heaped on them from their environment (either internal in the case of Kelly Holmes' aching calf to external in terms of abused or wronged children or adults).

Hypnotism

Under a hypnotic trance a person seems to be playing along with the hypnotist, following their suggestions willingly but in such a way that they appear to have given up executive control. Only deep rules of conduct (not committing murder, for example) are not followed up, so it is claimed. Hypnotism appears therefore to arise from the ability of the hypnotist to persuade the subject to turn off their frontal lobe executive system. In other words the internal goals set up by a subject, controlling attention and response, will now be those decided on by the hypnotist. Moreover, these goals, if of actions to be carried out at a later time, do not appear to be consciously accessible to the hypnotised subject. How could that occur?

In an attention copy-organised brain, goals are set up in prefrontal cortex to guide attention to various stimulus representations in the subject's brain. Those who are hypnotisable may be able to have external goals inserted in their minds (in their prefrontal cortices, more precisely) in such a manner that they play a crucial role in decision making when the right context comes up, but are not accessible to attention amplification into awareness. Such unconscious goals would thus function more at an automatic level than at an aware one. There are automatic response circuits in the brain, arising, for example, through overtraining of responses. It would therefore be reasonable to suppose that, in hypnotisable and suggestible people, such automatic goals can be set up more easily than in non-suggestible people. The latter may have stronger attention control systems, and especially attention monitors, able to alert the overall attention control network to attend when any attempt is made to reduce monitoring of inputs in relation to goals, and so preventing hypnotic responses to later contexts.

Sleep

Like pain, this is usually regarded as a part of behaviour which is brought on from outside, at least outside the brain. It is usually claimed that tiredness leading to sleep arises from fatigue brought about by constant activity during the day. Since we still do not know the reason for sleep it is hard to argue the case scientifically. It could be for one of a number of reasons: to protect us from dangers in the dark by hiding away and resting, to replenish specific tissues and chemicals used up in the hurly-burly of the day, to reprogram our brains so that the day's news is part of the background by incorporation into the semantics of the world, and so on. Some of these reasons are now to the fore. But there is further structure in sleep: it is divided into what are called rapid eye movement (REM) sleep and slow-wave sleep (SWS). Thus there must be (possibly different) reasons for each of these forms of sleep.

From the point of the mind-user's manual, both of these forms of sleep possess some form of mentation. If sleepers are woken immediately after a period of REM or SWS they usually report dreams, in the one case, and some forms of reasoning in the other. What do they signify for the life of the mind? Is it present when asleep and in what form?

Before we can properly handle this, we should note that there are different levels of dreams. The normal level is when a dreamer is out of control and is moved around from situation to situation in a manner that he feels he cannot stop – especially in a nightmare. There are dreams, had by a few, called 'lucid dreams' in which the dreamer is able to control the content of their dream to a large extent. According to those who have experienced lucid dreams, they can develop their prowess of controlling the dream over the years.

Mentation in dreams, as discovered by brain imaging and by probing dreams from dreamers with brain deficits, are mainly based on activity in the posterior cortex. This area of the brain will supply the content of the dream, as is now accepted. A lower activity in prefrontal cortex will lead to lower levels of goals, and possibly to no explicit goals at all. Thus the spectrum from normal to lucid to very lucid dreams could correspond to increasingly active prefrontal cortex, bringing with it increasingly active goals and hence direction of the situations in the dream. Nightmares would arise from activity in limbic brain components; this is not always present, however.

The phenomenal experience in dreams fits with the attention copy model: it arises from the dragging of attention around, with ownership experience associated with such attention movement as in the attention copy model. The feeling of being out of control would then arise due to the inability to set up frontal goals; these would arise spontaneously or from automatic schemata that would also lead to the feeling of being out of control. But the dreamer is still there as owner of the experiences, but is out of any feeling of control by being buffeted around by the deeper unconscious and emotionally important memories acquired over the past day or so.

To Expand the Mind or Not?

There are many methods by which a person can distort their consciousness: through drugs, meditation, religion, pain, looking at paintings, listening to music or reading, through sleep, and so on. In some there are artificial mechanisms to modify the experience (as in drugs); in other cases the person has to work hard to obtain a meaningful level of change of experience (as in meditation). In between lie the arts, which can move a person a little or a lot. Such self-determined alterations of experience are all explicable through an attention copy model of how consciousness arises in the brain. These experiences expand the richness of life. This is sometimes irreversible, as when drug addiction sets in or paranoiac tendencies are brought to fruition in a genotype already prone to such a possibility, a genotypic condition now thought to be possessed by about 25% of the population. So mind expansion can be good for you or bad for you according to its type and your genotype. But this is nothing new; it now expands from poisons and bad food to mental states. So the general message on this from the mind-user's manual is: take care!

CHAPTER EIGHTEEN

DOES FREE WILL EXIST?

Traditional Free Will

Iadvised you at the end of the previous chapter to take care about the sorts of mind expansion you do. But do you have any say in the matter? Do you really have free will in making your decision, as the title of this chapter questions? In any action you take? Let me first discuss the notion of free will.

To have free will is to be able to act freely. When an agent acts freely – with no constraints on it whatsoever – it can thereby rightly be said to exercise its free will. What the agent does is entirely up to itself. Various alternatives are open to the agent, and it then determines which of these it pursues. The agent is the ultimate source or origin of its actions.

This description of free will is the standard one. The controversy starts when it is asked if there ever could be such a free will. This is partly because the definition I have given is still ambiguous. Is the agent allowed to decide on actions that are outside the bounds of the laws of physics? But then what are the laws of physics, and if they exist why are they so sacrosanct?

It is relatively easy to answer the second of those questions: the laws of physics have to be accepted since they have been shown to give a correct description of how matter behaves under present conditions. Of course if you want to fall into a black hole or the centre of the sun then the laws may be different from the standard ones holding here on earth. But we are talking about realities and not airy-fairy possibilities in other universes.

The first question – what *are* the laws of physics? – is more difficult, since these laws have changed over the past 100 or so years. Whereas before then, Newton's view of the material world was sacrosanct – his Three Laws of Motion were universally accepted after an enormous amount of testing – now we know that we live in an uncertain quantum world in which all may ultimately be unified into ten-dimensional superstrings or even super-membranes. The implications of that picture for matter are still being vigorously fought over and are presently very indistinct.

Yet we should not despair about what appears to be the shifting sands of the laws of physics. For we humans, only the natural force of electromagnetism is relevant to the workings of our brains, and the laws involved there were already put in place nearly 150 years ago by the brilliant Scottish scientist James Clerk Maxwell working at King's College London. Maxwell's equations, as they are now universally called, describe with the required precision what is involved. How electromagnetic radiation interacts with matter is still being teased out, as recent studies of the unknown but possible childhood leukaemias under power lines and the similarly unknown but possible effects of mobile phones on frying children's brains show. However, there are no cases of people picking up radio or other waves directly through their brains (although a few allegedly do through the metal fillings in their teeth – a very different feature).

For the brain the laws of physics are well defined: Maxwell's laws and those of Newton. This presents ultimate constraints one has to accept on the possible responses a person can make, without them using enormous forces, such as a beam of particles accelerated in one of the world's big particle accelerators. The constraints preclude people from realistically proposing they can zap someone else's brain by a radio beam from their own brain – witchcraft at work? – no way, since the energetics would be just too vast, and a person just cannot have enough energy by a factor of millions. There are an infinite number of similar responses that are outside the bounds of science – such as levitating oneself out of harm's way as an avalanche comes down, or levitating down from the top of a tall building in Superman style. It's just not on.

This is where the going gets rough between the laws of physics and those who want real freedom of the will. There are those who propose that free will is real, and since it could clash with the laws of physics it is those laws that must go out of the window. These so-called incompatibilists (the incompatibility being between science and free will) are still arguing from the unbridled free will point of view. The German moral philosopher Immanuel Kant in 1788 put the position as strongly as any by saying that to claim that free will must be compatible with the laws of physics is 'a wretched subterfuge – a petty word jugglery'.

The battle is not quite between incompatibilists and the laws of physics but incompatibilists and determinism. The latter is taken to imply that all the positions and velocities of the atoms of the universe were fixed once the initial conditions were fixed in the Big Bang. Since then the atoms are just running out their due courses predestined for them. So whatever our initial conditions were at birth, all is predestined until our death. That is more correctly what the incompatibilists are fighting against. They claim that determinism is wrong.

This claim does not necessarily go against the laws of physics if they themselves do not support determinism. It has been claimed by some writers, bending quantum mechanics to their purpose, that due to its uncertainty, the quantum mechanical world is not governed by determinism. However that is false: quantum mechanics is a highly causal theory, where by this I mean that any cause precedes its effect. But then determinism follows. And the latest versions of quantum mechanics, even down to superstrings, have causality built into them up to the highest energies or down to the smallest lengths (so-called 'microscopic causality'). So the present laws of physics are very strongly in favour of the world being deterministic.

However, there may be an alternate way to introduce an effective breakdown of determinism into the world: through the mechanism of chaos. No one can predict the weather more than about three days ahead, in general. Such a dynamical system can have its overall flow pattern altered by very small changes in local regions that then spread out across the whole weather system. That is chaos: the butterfly effect – a butterfly flapping its wings in Beijing can cause a rainstorm in London. So while there may be strict determinism it is not very useful if there is not predictability in the long term.

However this does not really help the incompatibilist cause, since for real free will there needs, from their point of view, to be uncaused acts or those actions that appear to have no causal precedent. This will therefore only be possible by a breakdown of causality, leading to these uncaused acts being the moral responsibility of the freely deciding agent. So some incompatibilists hold that, since we have good reason to believe that we are morally responsible, and that moral responsibility requires free will, then free will requires indeterminism. They then have to live with the uncomfortable disagreement between science and their moral imperative.

However, there is another group of 'free willers' who accept determinism but still claim there is some form of free will. They use a meaning of the word 'free' according to which free will is compatible with determinism, even though determinism is the view that the history of the universe is fixed in such a way that nothing can happen other than it does because everything that happens is required by what has gone before.

These so-called 'compatibilists' believe that to have free will is to be free from constraints: freedom is a matter of not being physically or psychologically compelled to do any particular thing. Your character, personality, preferences and general motivational style may be entirely determined by events for which you are in no way responsible (by your genetic inheritance, upbringing, subsequent experience, and so on). But you do not have to be in control of any of these things in order to have the freedom of choice the compatibilists claim. These constraints do not actually compel you, because freedom of choice is just a matter of being able to choose and act in the way one prefers, given that you are who you are. So this approach is compatible with determinism, even though it follows from determinism that every aspect of your character, and everything you will ever do, was inevitable before you were born (barring chaos setting in).

These philosophical discussions are all very well, but why are we so concerned with them? They never seem to get anywhere in any case. There are two basic reasons they are important, especially in a user's manual for the mind:

1. We each of us have the impression of effortful acts of will when we are trying to tackle a hard problem.
2. We also wish to have a way of introducing moral responsibility into decision making, so that we can develop rules of development by means of appealing to these moral imperatives. In the past this was achieved by religious rules, such as the Ten Commandments. However, religion is no longer universally accepted as the bedrock of morality, not can it act universally in that manner, such as for those who lose their faith later in life. Do they correspondingly lose their morals?

The first of these reasons is a fact of life. A supreme example of this is a man who suffered loss of all the feedback over his body, up to his neck, due to a viral infection. He has to make a supreme act of will just to walk around, attending most vigorously to the stance of his body at every step. If he sneezes he falls down. He is exhausted after returning from any trip. So he can vouch for this feeling of 'making an act of will'. It is very real to him.

The second reason is more difficult to analyse. It is undoubted that society is becoming more dangerous due to the presence of those who have been brought up with little in the way of a moral code or discipline. This is evident in threatening behaviour on the streets and the danger of breakdown of discipline in schools. For example a recent headline in a UK national paper read 'Schools should be allowed to punish disruptive pupils', and another read 'Penalty for parents if pupils on suspension break curfew'. The same paper carried a report of a girl of 12 being slashed across the face several times by another of the same age in her class, which was being supervised by two teachers. The report noted that, 'Without warning her attacker stood up from her desk, said to her victim 'I f***ing hate you' and attacked her.' The victim had to have 30 stitches and will need plastic surgery; she will be scarred for life. More discipline is undoubtedly needed.

But the more difficult question we face is: can we find a true moral imperative, that all should abide by? Many have searched for it. One of the appeals of some religions is to try to return us to those moral imperatives of their faith. The believers are threatened by there being no longer the need to 'Honour thy father and thy mother' or obeying others. People seem free from obeying any moral precepts at all. All seem to have been sucked into the maelstrom of the material age in which we live. In the process, it is claimed, we have all lost moral responsibility – even up to severely and painfully disfiguring those we dislike, like the 12-year-old mentioned above.

But there are many counter-examples to this moral responsibility always being for good, even if being claimed to be from religion. There is now an increasing realisation that some evangelical churches in the UK are fostering the notion that children can become possessed by the devil, or become witches, and can only be saved by their death. This culture is also suspected of leading to ritual deaths of young boys, some of whose remains have been found over the past few years. All of these cases imply that the claim that God is telling people to behave in this way is no justification that it is morally satisfactory.

To add injury to insult, a recent shocking case of murder caused by claiming knowledge of the absolute morality of God was that in a park in the southern city of Basra in Iraq. Students had gone to the park to have a picnic and enjoy themselves. As one reported, men attacked them:

There were dozens of them, armed with guns and they poured into the park. They started shouting at us that we were immoral, that we were meeting boys and girls together and playing music and that this was against Islam. They began shooting into the air and people screamed. Then with one order they began beating us with their sticks and rifle butts.

Two students were killed and many injured. The whole episode was controlled by a follower of a radical cleric. Yet again God was taken to require such murders and infliction of pain, as the preservation of the so-called 'moral laws of God' is above that.

As shocking a case has been reported recently where a priest assumed absolute morality, and, aided by four nuns, deliberately killed another nun by crucifying her for three days without any food or water, praying for her all the time. But the priest was apparently only following hallowed traditions in the Romanian Orthodox church of exorcising those possessed of the Devil. The standard Orthodox texts on exorcism are full of stories of 'an epic struggle between evil and the purifying spirits', as one report on the case wrote.

The victim had strong signs of schizophrenia before her death, and was given to rapid mood swings, so that she appeared to the nuns in her convent to be possessed by the Devil. The priest was reported as showing no remorse when he was arrested:

God has performed a miracle for her. At last Irina has been delivered from evil.

Indeed, from the evil of the murderous priest. He showed no sign of seeing anything wrong in his murderous act. Thunder claps from an approaching storm were apparently the only sound as her coffin was brought in to the church of the monastery for later burial. He is reported to have said:

This storm is proof that the will of God has been done. People must know that the devil exists. I find his work in the gestures and speech of possessed people, because man is often weak and lets himself easily be manipulated by the forces of evil.

Speak of the devil! Shades of the witches of Salem. Arthur Miller: turn in your grave.

You could claim that the cases I mentioned above involved physical suffering of the children or a nun: that cannot be a good thing. Therefore these cases are not 'good' examples to argue against the claim that there are 'good' moral precepts based on one religion or another. However, inflicting physical pain and murder are extremes at one end of a whole spectrum of imposed constraints, both physical and mental. These constraints can be purely mental, where young people, or even older ones in the case of the murderous priest mentioned above, are indoctrinated by religious mores and scriptures to behave in certain set ways: not to eat certain things, not to do certain things (think Ten Commandments), etc. The society thereby created may be one in which all live in harmony with each other. Yet that could also be achieved by a community of zombies, so there must be more to human life than that.

There are several other features of free will that we should take note of before moving on. Is it the case that actions can be taken which are purely automatic? In that case, where does free will come in? There are certainly such actions, even some, such as a killing carried out while the killer was, so he claimed, sleepwalking, that come under the heading of automatic. They could be excluded from our discussion of free will if we restrict ourselves solely to conscious free will. This leaves out of the discussion, and thence out of the question of moral responsibility, such automatic actions. However, we now know that much of our mental activity carried out by the brain is unconscious. So why should we still not consider a person responsible for a heinous action even though they were not conscious of it? The unconscious forces at work in their brain still need to be regarded as a cause of the heinous act, and hence modified in some way to prevent any repeat. It is somewhat like the claims made by Nazis in the 1939–45 war about their horrible acts of mayhem on the Jews: 'I was just doing my duty – carrying out orders,' these brutal murderers say. But they were prepared to do so, even if they might claim they were effectively in an automatic response mode, obeying every order, as every good soldier is trained to be.

In neither of these cases can there be said to be a diminution of responsibility. It is a different sort of responsibility from that of acts carried out under conscious will, but still carried out and guided by their brains. And each person is the possessor of their own brain, and its ultimate guardian and architect from the commencement of adulthood. There is no doubt this is a controversial area, as it is in modern legal systems such as in the USA. There the mental state of the actor is necessary to be clarified before he or she can be said to be criminally responsible for an act. My conclusion in all such debatable cases (was the actor aware of his or her actions?) is that in any case society must be protected from further possibly deadly assaults even if he or she were not. The McNaughton Rules on responsibility in the UK determine if the person is responsible in the consciously willed sense. If so then they may be sent to prison. If not they are usually incarcerated in a mental hospital for a suitable period.

Making Decisions to Respond

In order to search for how we might face up to an increasingly lawless and egotistic society, we have to turn to how decisions are made in the brain. What is going on in a person's mind when they decide to commit a murder, snatch a mobile phone, rape an old woman, slash someone else's face or just push someone aside in order to get on a crowded train? More generally, we are all making decisions all the time – should I go in to work or work at home? – go in early or late? – go out for a meal this evening? – and so on. How are such decisions reached?

As we grow we attach values to things in the world. The infant starts with the nipple on his/her mother's breast, graduates to the nipple on his/her feeding bottle, then to the plastic juice mug, plastic plate and spoon and then finally to sitting at the table with adults. The infant also graduates from children's toys to big child's toys up to adult ones and other pursuits. Approbation gained from obeying parents' requests and praise for special steps – like the first walking steps or first words – is elevated into working for approbation over a larger range of endeavours. Finally, adult approbation is searched for, from the actor revelling in the audience's applause to the gong bestowed by the Queen for good works.

In all these developments, value maps are created in the brain that code how much reward is to be expected from a given stimulus or course of action, and therefore how much the object is valued. It is the shape of these value maps – what stimuli turn a person on, or turn them off – that determine a very important component of their character. Most recently, however, a pessimistic statistic has been arrived at by scientists studying the inherited genetic make-up of identical and non-identical twins, as to their propensity to psychopathic behaviour. It is such behaviour – a cold and calculating way of manipulating people around them, with no sensitivity to other's needs – that is so damaging to society. Such people can form a nucleus of misrule. Sadly it would appear from the study that psychopathic traits are mainly genetically determined. In the battle between nature and nurture, the latter loses out badly in trying to remedy a psychopath's personality and tame it. Even so, it is important to do what can be done with such hard cases, and even try harder to attempt to provide such personalities with loving interactions, wherever possible. Recent suggestions in the UK that children at the age of 3 be assessed for potential future psychopathic behaviour, and application of possible remedial action, is a step towards trying to help such children be less dangerous to society when they grow up.

Whence the Illusion of Free Will?

There are many problems in society. For example, nature beats nurture at handing out psychopathology. Also, in any family the relation between parent(s) and children may crumble due to pressures of work and money, or just pressures from society in general. So much being owned by so few may lead to envy, or the welfare state may lead to apathy. Among so many religions on offer, none may be accepted. Morality may be difficult to instil in growing children's minds. Or the feeling of failure in modern society or its apparent degradations, as seen by 'chosen ones', may lead to extreme religions and to extreme acts, such as terrorism.

All would appear to have the freedom of will, be it conscious or unconscious. So how can they be prevented from performing heinous acts to gain personal satisfaction – turning to robbery or to murder to take from those more fortunate? In modern society this is prevented by prison. It locks up transgressors, both hopefully to re-educate them and to keep society free from them for a suitable period of time. Prison is a clear loss of conscious free will. Yet prison does not seem to work – there are many repeats of criminal activity by those who have already served a prison sentence. They are 'criminalised' by the prison system, and find it difficult to get out of the ways of villainy.

These criminals, when out in society, appear to have free will in plenty. They use that apparent freedom of their will to commit further crimes. So the apparent existence of free will in these cases implies that a deeper look at what is happening here is needed. Do these criminals even have free will? But that is the thin end of the wedge: do any of us really have free will? The message I have given so far is that free will is an illusion, and we must accept the way our genes and upbringing drive us forward to do as we do. So we can apparently not do anything to help those in need from their misguided actions. But that is far more fatalistic than is actually warranted by the position I have described.

Is Free Will a Total Illusion?

To repeat, the message I have given so far is that free will is a total illusion, and we must accept the way our genes and upbringing drive us forward to do as we do. But according to the attention copy model of our minds (and even more general brain-based ones of many sorts), one would expect that decisions are going to be made that are maximally effective for the person. They will always work to obtain maximum reward by their actions: a person will attempt to act so as to maximise their future rewards. Here the criminals do not seem to be doing that. They act so as to maximally get themselves banged up again. What is happening?

One answer to this conundrum is that none of us really has a truly free will. We have an illusion of acting freely. But that sense of freedom is itself hopelessly encircled by constraints. These arise from our past exposure to events. The villain keeps to his villainy – he knows nothing else, so it actually does give him rewards associated both with the ill-gotten gains and his general criminal sub-culture, in which he may gain recognition. So the criminal continues his misguided way, with the result that he is liable to go back inside relatively rapidly.

More generally, each person has their own circumscribed horizons. I could no more sing at a pop concert than could Nelly the Elephant. Nor could I fly a fighter plane at Mach 3. I am what I am by what I was. So are we all. This means we have to work out how to prepare ourselves, as we grow from infancy to childhood to adulthood, so that we end up as a maximally 'free' creative individual, but one not causing grief to others in society and respecting the 'freedom' of others.

Yet that is not really possible: as children we are under the control of our parents and our teachers, our culture, and ultimately our politicians (who can screw us up as badly as our parents did, as Philip Larkin graphically pointed out). Here we meet a fundamental problem: how to create that environment which gives maximal growth to a child to produce a creative being as an adult? Are there any mechanisms to achieve this?

How Are Decisions Made?

To begin to answer this question, we must look at the way that decisions are made in the attention copy model of the mind. The mind is indeed acting like a machine, but I would claim it is one that is subtle and beautiful enough to explain all of our experiences. I have given considerable evidence so far in the book that is the case. Now we can ask: how are the brain and mind really used in decisions?

This is a question that has caused a lot of controversy recently over recent results on the timing of decisions and their awareness. In particular, the work of the American neuroscientist Benjamin Libet, which I have mentioned earlier, has caused a lot of heart-searching, especially in the manner which Libet has interpreted his results.

Libet found that the timing of decision making in the brain is very subtle. Using EEG measurements on subjects, he asked them to make a willed response by moving a finger, at the same time noting when they became aware that they were about to make the action. The results were not all that surprising: activity that was associated with motor preparation was detected some 500 milliseconds before the action in the motor planning region of the cortex. However, the awareness of the movement only occurred some 150 milliseconds before it happened, about 350 milliseconds after the beginning of the unconscious activity. This is not surprising: we are supposedly unconscious of about 90% of our brain's activity, so the fact that we are unconscious of the beginning stirrings of the plan to move a finger is no great shakes.

The interpretation of this result by Libet was that consciousness, being such a latecomer into the decision-making and planning arena, is not causally efficacious. It can only provide a veto on the ongoing plan. However, that itself is controversial, since the original plan to move had already been set up as a goal in the subject's prefrontal cortices by the experimenter some while before, by asking them to move their finger whenever they wished. So there is already an influence on what is to be done, the subject having consciously accepted to agree to the experimental conditions.

What is most controversial about Libet's interpretation is that he claims that the conscious component itself has no unconscious precursor. This is where free will can enter so happily to the free willers. For now the conscious veto acts as free will itself, pure and simple. Free will is once again ensconced, and morality can regain its absolute reign – not that any moral code can be seen to be favoured over any other from this experiment. Yet we are all conscious responsible beings again, not unthinking machines, so it is claimed from these results. As put by the philosopher T. W. Clark, 'the underlying concern is that if the self reduces to the brain, and conscious control reduces to a sub-system of the brain, then the individual doesn't have real, contra-causal free will and can't be held responsible'. Libet claims his results avoid that dreadful view of ourselves.

I already remarked that such a possibility as uncaused processes does not fit at all with the fundamental understanding we now have of the material universe. Causality and determinism, in a quantum framework, persist down to the very shortest distances that experiments have been performed in high-energy particle accelerators. I see no way that a person could employ forces above (or even approximately near) what are achieved in those gigantic particle machines to achieve the dream of the free willers: uncaused processes.

Given that avenue is closed, we can look at Libet's results again, but now from an attention copy model of mind framework. As I have already pointed out, consciousness comes into play early in the 'willed finger-moving' experiment when the experimenter talks to the subject and tells them the rules of the game. These were remembered by the subjects, and used to set up a movement of the sort the experimenter desired, along with them noting when awareness arose of the movement itself. Thus a monitor process was occurring in the subject's brain: to detect such movement, as compared to no movement. The monitor would alert attention to be directed to the moving finger, but in the process detecting a copy of the movement command, so as to alert the buffer sites of consciousness, both that of the owner of the conscious experience and shortly thereafter of the content: 'I am moving my finger'. Such is the way the attention copy model of mind explains the experimental results, together with more precise predictions of how neural activity would flow in the brain between the various attention control modules.

The 'free will' that is left to the subject is that of using memory banks, with stored goals and social rules for dealing with other people – 'not to get angry with the experimenter', for example – to guide motor responses. This guidance may also be automatic (unconscious) if there has been a lot of training of the subject, or if the subject is attending to something else entirely at the same time. So the best we seem to come up with for free will is a guided form. Actions are only taken inside the constraints such guidance provides. If the guidance is not fine enough to define a single response then further guidance may be sought by searching memory banks for similar situations. If that fails then reward values may be thought about consciously and a checklist of pros and cons constructed. If that fails then 'the dice man cometh', and randomness of some form would have to be used to reach a decision.

Free Will in Society

It is obviously false that each person takes actions all on their own. They live in society and must try to accommodate other people. Indeed, part of education, be it by the parents (if they care), by the teachers (if they are allowed to) or by the peers, is to achieve an adult who can live in society without too much hassle. So free will is not only a personal faculty but also one involved in the responses of others in society. If laws are made in society the person is expected to keep them. Society as a whole can be regarded as an organism, and it can then be asked: does society have free will? It does in a democratic society, where voters can send various politicians to power or prevent them reaching office by voting accordingly. Even the politicians usually have constraints on them as to what powers they can take to themselves. Thus, a society itself can be said to have free will in terms of its voting powers. The recent debacle in the referenda over the European Union's new Constitution in France and The Netherlands shows this free will of society at large at work against the (in this case unelected) politicians.

This free will of society is also present in the responses of others to one's actions. So the social constraints mentioned earlier on the responses a person can make in a given situation arise as a part of the general features of society, and the needs of others also to be able to lead a life as free as is possible. Thus the free will of a single person has to be set in this much more uncertain larger framework. We do not expect uncaused causes to be at work, for example in terms of the European referendum debacles. These were responses of the majority to conditions in the European Union and its proposed Constitution that they did not like.

We see, then, that the quest for free will, when moved from a single person to the person in society, looks different. There are so many more unknowns in how a society will respond. But in any case there is still the question of the placing of responsibility for actions taken which harm others (or oneself). Is it on society itself? And if so how can this amorphous organism be made to bear this responsibility?

Living with the Illusion

Free will, of either conscious or unconscious form, is an illusion. Decisions are made in the brain in terms of past successes and failures of similar situations and responses taken. To enable society to be peopled by maximally effective members, a new approach must be taken to how infants and children are guided to adulthood. This can only be in terms of how we understand their inner experience and how they can be made to be maximally satisfied with their adult powers and personality.

But we have to turn to society to determine where responsibility finally lies for actions taken by individuals in that society. The nature of the individual's experience must be taken into account in looking at this problem. In particular, we must try to discover if the brain-based approach to experience which is at the root of this mind-user's manual can guide us as to what might be a class of appropriate societies, if any such exists.

Overall Conclusions to Part III

In this part I have looked at a range of activities and experiences of humans in modern society, and tried to understand their nature through the eyes of the attention copy model. This has proved successful as far as it goes, but this book is not meant to be only a popular scientific treatise on the mind but also a manual for brain users. This part of the book has indicated in what way the basic framework of the attention copy model of consciousness can handle all thrown at it across a vast range of experiences and in society. If only in a preliminary manner, I have started here to scratch the surface of the enormous range of implications for humanity and its society which are opened up to further discussion in terms of the attention copy model of the mind.

PART IV

IMPROVING THE MIND

The proper study of mankind is man

Alexander Pope

CHAPTER NINETEEN

IMPLICATIONS FOR SOCIETY

Responsibility in the Family: Upbringing

The family is the beginning microcosm for the infant. As has been said, 'The hand that rocks the cradle rules the world'. The importance of early upbringing has become ever clearer to child psychologists. Even the first year of life is critical in the development of socialisation and loving relationships. Reward and what are the beginnings of the 'rules of life' need to begin to be instilled then. This does not downplay the importance of the 'terrible twos', where the battle with the authority of the parents takes place and internalisation of the beginnings of appropriate behaviour really begins. Nor do later family connectivity and interaction not play very important roles. Another old saw is 'The family that plays together stays together', again summing up a great deal of family wisdom.

At the same time as giving the infant and child love and sustenance, the family must provide a good level of guided stimulation. Learning words and then to read, developing curiosity for how things work – these are all traits that should be fostered in the growing child. Loving guidance in all this is needed, again with the structure of authority not wielded too strongly by the parents, but necessarily there all the same.

Helping a child develop to the best of its ability does not necessarily mean that it should be hot-housed through arithmetic and reading so as to be ahead of other children. But our brains and minds were designed to give us an advantage in the competition of life by providing us with a conscious control system unique in the animal kingdom. It is that which indicates that we need to sharpen such control as much as possible. Reaction time, the time it takes to respond to a sound or visual signal, is a measure of how rapid we are in such control. The capacity of our buffer working memories (such as the number of elements we can remember over about 2 seconds) also gives us a measure of how much we can carry in our minds for further thinking, and is another important measure of general intelligence. So games helping these develop are useful. However, trying to bring a child on faster than its brain is developing will not be effective and could be counter-productive if the child is made anxious about its inability to achieve what its parents desire.

For example, studies on children across many cultures have shown that all children develop their mental capacities at about the same rate, independent of culture. This has been observed even for physical activity, which in some cultures is prevented up to a year or two by the child being carried around on its parent's back in a sling. Such children, when tested on various physical tests after a short time out of the constraints, do as well as free-running children from other cultures.

Responsibility in Society: School

It is in the school that a child can begin truly to flower with regard to its intellectual and sporting prowess. The basic purpose of the school is to impart knowledge to children, so that they can function effectively both in obtaining a job and earning money as well as being able to make their own decision as to what course of action to take at any time. Such 'teaching' of decision making is not usually transparent in schools, but is clearly ongoing from the function of the school as a mini-society. It prepares the child to develop its decision-making skills by having these being made in a well-defined environment, with specific rules of behaviour, and some of the pupils gaining positions of some power as prefects to learn how to wield it.

These are the ideal ways a school should function: as a learning environment and a mini-society. But schools come in a large variety of shapes and sizes, as well as involving children from a range of homes and social classes. So the nature of responsibilities of those setting up and running schools is varied, as is their success in carrying out the two ideals above. Some schools have pupils who wish to learn and come from homes that support and even actively foster such learning. But others are composed of those who find lessons boring and irrelevant to them, and who come from homes in which learning and behaving in a reasonable fashion are foreign.

A recent television program ('Classroom Chaos') exposed the depths that can be reached in some schools, as seen through the eyes of a teacher with a hidden camera. Her pupils were seen to take no notice of her, and in some instances became quite threatening to her if she tried to stop them from behaving so abysmally. One child was even heard to snarl at the teacher: 'You can't touch me – I know my rights'. Such schools might be expected to be in a minority, but this is not necessarily so, as seen by the increasing number of teachers leaving teaching, as well as the increase in those reporting physical attacks on them by pupils.

On the other hand, there are the top schools which produce the best-educated pupils in the country. In the UK these are often the private schools, where middle and upper class parents pay exorbitant fees to send their children for what in many cases is an incredibly good education. There has been a flight to such schools since the demise of most of the grammar schools. Only by beginning to look carefully at what education is appropriate for a given pupil can we begin to properly cater for all abilities. Different people need different levels and contents for their knowledge. Let me consider my own case.

I myself was educated in a grammar school, and owe to it the chance to go on to Cambridge University by winning a scholarship to Christ's College. Without that I would not have been able to enter, but it was my grammar school education that provided me with a stimulating environment to make me want to be a scientist when I grew up, like my father.

From my own experience and what I have observed in various environments and countries during my university career, I would suggest that education is a crucial factor in creating citizens who are able not only to contribute value to their society through their work but also to help mould that society into a decent and life-enhancing place to live and grow. Without a universally effective education, an underclass will come into existence, which will be self-perpetuating and very hard to eradicate. Only an enormous effort will enable the children born into that underclass to be educated out of it.

How does the nature of the understanding of the mind as created solely by the brain impact on these aspects? Not much, it could be claimed – it is already folded in to the way education has been created. I do not agree. There appears to be no hint in any of the educational schemes I have described so far (except possibly in the content of courses, such as the treatment of creationism) of there being any sort of non-brain-created soul involved. But there is still a lot of mileage to be gained from looking at the mind through the eyes of the attention copy model.

A brain-basis of intelligence and consciousness indicates that various ways of improving aspects of attention may help a student's study abilities. This is already being pursued by students in the USA, where it is estimated that up to 20% may take mind-enhancing drugs to improve their attentive or memory powers. There is the use of such drugs in the US military to help reduce the need for sleep, and in airline pilots, concentration could be enhanced to improve the safety level in long-haul flights.

An increasing range of drugs is now available. Among these are Ritalin and ampakines, important in aiding concentration and memory. Another important drug in the mind-improving pharmacy is Modafinil, which acts mainly on the frontal lobes to improve alertness and decision making. As a co-author states, in a new report on these drugs and their use in society (which came out in July 2005 from the Foresight gatherings): 'Many of these new drugs seem to have few harmful side effects and are not addictive while also offer particular benefits. The question is: is it right to try to stop them or should people be free to choose?'.

The USA is already ahead on this, with the 20% figure of students given above being for the use of Ritalin. This was originally a drug prescribed for ADHD in children, but students who have taken it found it helped them concentrate better and also to calm down before exams. In the UK prescriptions for Ritalin have increased from 2,000 per year in 1990 to 150,000 in 2002. Modafinil was originally used to treat narcolepsy (when a person keeps falling asleep even while moving around) but is now being used by business executives to help them stretch their waking hours.

As an expert in this area (a professor of clinical neuropsychology at Cambridge) said recently that the progress in drug research has allowed production of 'clever' drugs with few side effects and clear benefits; they would become popular across society and be, he opined, taken like taking any stimulant, such as coffee. Another expert in a recent review in the scientific journal *Nature*, wrote 'Humanity's ability to alter our own brain function might well shape history as powerfully as the development of metallurgy in the industrial revolution or genetics in the 20th century'.

I have already described how we can understand how meditation can alter experience through analysis of what changes in connections between modules could occur (with practice) in the attention copy model of awareness. There can be a similar discussion of the action of these drugs in terms of an increase in the efficiency of transferring neural activity between neurons in certain areas, or by how certain chemicals essential for cognitive activities are increased by taking the drugs. Thus Modafinil and the ampakines improve transmission between nerve cells. Modafinil is thought to increase this communication by augmenting the amount of the chemical glutamate which is used to excite one brain cell by a previous one in the information chain in the brain. Ampakines act by increasing the strength of the AMPA component of the excitatory synaptic receptors in brain cell. Ritalin seems to act differently, by increasing dopamine – the messenger of brain reward. As such this is the drug more likely to be abused for its rewarding, but addictive, properties.

A completely brain-based approach to the mind is very strongly indicated by the way these drugs are taking off as lifestyle accessories.

Not only do they provide sufferers of dementia, Parkinson's disease and schizophrenia with hope of amelioration of their condition, but they have already been shown to grant increased cognitive powers to many in society at large. These aspects indicate yet once again that mental life is completely controlled by brain activity. The attention copy model can be used to investigate in detail scientifically how these experiential changes are brought about by the drugs. That will no doubt occur in the next years.

Returning to the problem of achieving a suitable education for all (and help educate away the underclass), the new brain-improving tools I mentioned above and new understanding of motivation and its importance in education should enable a strong attack to be made. Even if the home is unable to provide a suitable atmosphere of 'loving control', the school may begin to allow the developing child grow more in self-respect in its intellectual abilities through a strong enough structured daily environment. That is a stern task for the teachers, but one increasingly able to be attained.

Laws and Responsibility in Society

I earlier covered areas where the law for personal responsibility and the findings from modern neuroscience impinge on each other. In particular the problem of being responsible for one's actions, if they are unconsciously controlled, is one that the law in a number of countries has met by various variants on the concept that a person cannot be held responsible for their unconsciously decided actions. However, this is not to say that there are no responsibilities for these actions having been taken in the first place.

Consider a person who committed a murder while in an automatic state (dreaming or pre-epileptic, say). The person may have, in general, an aggressive, even psychopathic personality. Thus there is a responsibility held by society to have tried to modify this personality before the act of murder was committed. It was very likely that such personality traits were not noticed by the relevant members of society (psychiatrists, psychotherapists, the killer's general practitioner, etc.). But that does not absolve society of responsibility from the killing.

A case came up at appeal to the Judicial Committee of the Privy Council of the UK of a man who had killed his girlfriend, but pleaded provocation because he was a known alcoholic, and had committed the killing under the influence of drink. He was ultimately convicted of manslaughter, not the far weightier crime of murder, which was being appealed against by the Court of the Island of Jersey. The basis of the court judgment was that:

> *The disease of alcoholism from which he suffered could be taken into account in considering whether the provocation was enough to make a reasonable man act as he had done.*

The plea was based on whether or not the defendant was provoked into losing his self-control, as well as whether the provocation (of his girlfriend taunting him by telling him she had had sex with another man) was enough to make a reasonable man act in that way. But it was accepted that one could not apply the standard 'reasonable man in society' description to those with mental abnormalities, and also to those for whom drugs or alcohol had caused loss of control under provocation. Effectively provocation was relative to the mental state of the responder to the provocation. Yet the Law Lords strongly called for a review of the law on all aspects of murder, since the case, and others like it, involved the need to specify more carefully how to regard the level of self-control and provocation in terms of the specific mental problems a defendant might have. This indicates that the law is presently uncertain how to properly handle cases where the level of self-control and of provocation by others has to be considered very carefully in judging if a person had 'cold-bloodedly' gone about murdering someone or was essentially out of their mind (with drink or drugs) and so could not be held fully responsible for any ensuing death.

It is clear that these dilemmas are not easy to resolve in a society in which there is increasing understanding of the way that actions can be generated without the associated control to consciously prevent them getting out of control. But society has to clarify the situation. Only through just law can society attempt properly to assign responsibility, and thence handle its responsibility to others in society, to justly deal with people who are out of control and would cause danger in specific situations. Society may not fully acknowledge that it does have such responsibility, although the call of the Law Lords indicates that there is unease over such problems.

In a similar manner, if a child is not noticed as developing a psychopathic personality, even though the observation of that psychopathology could have been made with our present knowledge, and later the child as an adult commits a series of horrific crimes, then society is responsible for the failure to make that observation. Pressure from others in the society should alert those able to do something about it, these being the lawgivers, psychologists, etc.

By responding to pressure, society moves on to play an ever more responsible role in the life of each of its citizens. That can be seen in the creation and use of behaviour orders, such as the 'anti-social behaviour order' in the UK or the use of a curfew for certain age groups in French cities, which are helping keep some of the worst offenders, with their threatening behaviour, off local streets. These legal methods are to be seen as the thin end of the wedge. One can even conceive of a time when the genetic spectrum of a foetus will be scanned for psychopathic components, with resulting termination or continuation according to the results.

We have now moved from responsibility for unconsciously controlled actions to clearly controlled (but out-of-control) actions. The attention copy model-based understanding of the mind indicates that the source of antisocial behaviour arises from the social rule base and empathy to others (in limbic and frontal circuits) built up by an individual in their earlier years. That is why there is also responsibility of the family if these break down. The only way to treat severe breakdown, in danger of consigning the individual to the criminal sub-culture, is to lock them up. However, just locking up and throwing away the key may only be needed for psychopaths. For others careful retraining is needed. Given the cost to society of many recurrent recidivists, the retraining route seems the only option.

An area of human experience where law and human needs have recently been clashing is over the right of someone to be responsible for their own death, or to be kept alive, if they become incapable after some point of making their wishes felt. This battle erupted more violently in the USA over the case of a severely brain-damaged woman Terri Schiavo, whose husband had requested she have the right to die peacefully by having her feeding tube turned off by doctors treating her on a life-support machine. The case divided the USA, pitting President Bush against the US Supreme Court and Republicans against Democrats (who were for turning off the feeding tube) over a ten-year period. The Supreme Court ordered the tube off, and Terri died peacefully.

Terri Schiavo had collapsed in 1990 at the age of 26. During the following five minutes her brain was starved of oxygen, and she suffered severe brain damage. She had left no will, so her husband argued that his wife would not have wanted to be kept alive in a rather degrading manner, by a feeding tube connected to her stomach. Her parents claimed their daughter could respond to them. However, an autopsy performed on Terri's brain after her death showed there had been too much nerve tissue degeneration for any possible conscious thought. So it would seem that the husband's action was justified.

Not all cases of this type are as simple. There have been several cases of patients recovering consciousness after long periods of coma, although in most of these cases there may be a further relapse, and even if there is not, the resulting cognitive abilities of the patient may be severely impaired, such as in speech and in thinking. So it does not necessarily mean that recovery of consciousness means recovery of all functions.

Another difficult case has involved the fight by parents to keep alive their infant who was severely disabled from birth. The parents went to court to require doctors to give suitable treatment to keep alive their daughter, who was born three months prematurely with brain damage, damaged kidneys and chronic lung disease; she is also blind. The infant has never left the hospital of her birth and is now two years of age. The judge said that the infant had only developed to the fitness of a three-month-old baby and had a severely reduced life expectancy. Should she be kept alive at all costs, or be allowed, if she has further complications, to die gracefully? The doctors prefer the latter course of action, the parents the former.

How does the attention copy model-based view of the mind face up to these cases and the legal aspects? If there is enough nervous tissue to support the attention copy model of dynamic processing, there will then be full awareness (possibly limited as to content due to peripheral degeneration). Loss of some of the component modules will cause a resulting loss of the relevant experiences. It is very difficult to give general rules about how great the extent of such loss needs to be before there is complete degeneration of experience. But this area needs to be explored using the latest brain imaging machines to help detect those crucial sites to create the experience of an inner self. It may be that there is seen to be no inner self, but there is content. I hinted some chapters ago that loss of the inner self may also make it difficult to have any access to the sensory buffer sites. In other words, if there is no inner self, then there is no content in consciousness. Thus both are there or neither is. Such a simpler story needs to be fully justified, but if validated might help make understanding experience in such very damaged minds more possible. It is unclear in the case of the severely disadvantaged two-year-old that she has all of the necessary components for the attention copy model to imply she has consciousness; her problem is compounded by her lack of sight and of possible brain damage hampering her growth of a perceptual/conceptual basis for understanding the world. Thus, which is content and which is owner is not presently clear. The case for her being severely mentally handicapped for the rest of her life will be much clearer as she develops.

Such advances as I am considering could help in handling the delicate problem of how to use the scarce resources of the National Health Service (NHS) in the UK, and those in other countries throughout the world, in such 'vegetative' cases. For example, consider the case of Duncan Wilson, who was left in a coma following an asthma attack resulting from a mugging in 1996. His father has refused to let him die, and visits his son most days. He is hoping for a breakthrough that could bring his son back to his original conscious state. However, there is presently concern in the NHS over the possible costs arising from a High Court ruling that supported a terminally ill man's wish to be kept alive artificially. The UK Government has strongly criticised this ruling, and would like it over-turned. At least if we could begin to attack problems like that of Duncan Wilson by means of an attention copy-based approach to Duncan's continuing experience, we might help reduce this financial load, as well as help relatives who may be hoping against hope (as in the Terri Schiavo case).

Another controversial area where law and society are sometimes at odds is on the legal rights for abortion. There is in any case a running battle between those who believe it is a woman's right to decide if she wants an abortion and those who are 'pro-life' at any stage from conception, even it is only a foetus of 9 or 16 cells. Such is life to them; it should have all its legal rights as a human being. The controversy has been particularly stirred up by publication of three-dimensional ultra-sound scans of foetuses at various ages in the womb. They appeared at even below 20 weeks to be moving round under their own volition and, more remarkably, to be smiling. Were they already able to have conscious experiences?

This is a question very relevant to the attention copy view of the mind. We have a reasonably clear picture of the rate at which the foetal brain develops in the womb. Could it have set up by 20 weeks some simple level of attention control so that the foetus could be claimed to be conscious in an attention copy manner? I think the answer is that it is very unlikely at that age. Looking at the foetal brain (as seen from autopsies at different foetal ages), there appears to be only the beginnings of the complexity of the brain by about 25–30 weeks. It will be necessary to go back to the details of this development to explore it in more detail, but I would suspect that the movements (including the smiling) observed by 3D ultrasound before 20 weeks are solely reflex ones that an infant has when it is born, or are related to brain activity at brain stem level. In any case if a foetus can now be kept alive at 20 weeks, then I would strongly support lowering the upper age of abortion to that length of time.

Religion and Responsibility

God can be said to be the ultimate point of responsibility. If he caused it all, including all the chaos and pain, then he is undoubtedly responsible for it. But who ever heard of calling God to account? Picture the scene in the High Court. The Judge calls to the usher, 'Where is the Defendant?'. He replies doubtfully, 'He claims to be here, my Lord, as well as there and – well – in fact he claims to be everywhere'. I can see the Judge becoming highly incensed. Would he send out an arrest warrant? And if he did turn up would he plead guilty or not guilty? Being perfectly pure he could not be guilty. On the other hand, I can only repeat he is supposed to have started it all, so is clearly guilty. O paradoxes of religion!

On a more mundane note, a Muslim cleric recently advocated on his website that all non-believers be killed. Is he responsible if one of his followers goes out and kills a non-believer? Clearly the follower committed the murder, but he could have been completely under the control of his religious leader. In which case is not he blindly 'doing his duty' to Allah, so is not responsible? We have already seen it does not seem easy to pin any responsibility on God, so the next best person is the cleric. He is clearly guilty of incitement to murder. But is he as guilty or more guilty than his misguided follower?

Such responsibility of religion is much broader than the stark case I presented above. The indoctrination of young people may also be regarded as a crime. It is restricting their freedom to explore the universe at large. The answers to the great questions of Life, the Universe and Lots of Other Things is laid out, possibly for the rest of their lives, for the young person being indoctrinated. Do they have no legal right to be saved from such indoctrination?

It can be claimed that all education is indoctrination. That is clearly false: in the arts one is taught to appreciate a range of styles and attitudes. In languages there is more rote learning, but that is the nature of language, and it has no value judgement. Science is value-neutral, and any good teacher will show how our understanding of nature has grown gradually until we now understand the very small, well beyond the visible, even under the most powerful microscope, up to the very large, almost back to the beginnings of the universe itself. Without such knowledge modern society would be a closed book, as also would most jobs.

Yet religions are all part of the rich panoply of human history. They cannot be ignored as part of a young person's education. Without some understanding of the various religions, there would be a very one-sided view of history – all soldiers galloping around on battlefields and political wheeling and dealing. But so much of history is interwoven with religious causes and beliefs. So I would advocate that a broad view of religion – comparative religion – be studied, especially from the point of view of the continuity of the growth of faiths one out of the other or one in opposition to the growing decadence of another.

CHAPTER TWENTY

TRAINING ATTENTION

Introduction

A ttention is the name of the game, for my mind, and it should be for everybody else's, I strongly suggest. The basis of my approach, scientifically justified in Part II, with some implications explored in Part III, has been that we can only scientifically understand the mind if we proceed through the door marked 'attention'. If attention were sharpened up then we would expect that there would be a related sharpening of consciousness. It is clear that consciousness is the ultimate control system of the brain, so we can begin to make much more efficient our highest level of control through training our attention. That is why I look here at attention from a more practical point of view.

But why don't I go straight for the jugular and deal with consciousness itself? That would appear to be the way, for example, when employing meditation. But across a broad range of meditation styles it is clear that attention has to be brought under control first in the meditation exercise before there is felt to be any benefit to a person's consciousness. So let us go back to attention.

There is a new buzz in the air about our own minds, especially related to the increasing understanding of the importance attention plays in controlling our thoughts and responses. Attention helps initiate behaviour, and determines how effective a person is in carrying that behaviour through. Safety professionals recognise lapses of attention control as an important factor in a wide range of injuries, such as strains, sprains, slips, trips, falls, hand injuries and driving accidents (like the near-miss of the distracted car driver nearly hitting another car that I mentioned earlier in the book). Moreover, there are an important number of people who are 'accident-prone' due to their continued inability to keep attention focused on the task at hand. Just telling them to 'think before you act' or 'pay attention' does not help, since it only emphasises their problems over attention control but does not enable people to learn to modify their attention lapses. It is no good saying to someone 'You are doing that wrong' without also telling them of ways to 'do it right'.

There are now many ways recognised for helping the development of attention control. These include electronic games (which may play an important role in improving attention control only now being recognised), mind games like crosswords or the recent fad of Sudoku, various types of attention 'mind-training' meditation techniques (at numerous levels and lasting from a few months to many years), relaxation techniques, neuro-physiological methods, especially the use of various sorts of biofeedback to alter the proportion of low frequency to high frequency waves in the brain, as well as by eating suitably smart 'brain food'. With this wealth of techniques on offer, some requiring the commitment of considerable amounts of time and others also considerable sums of money, it is important to attempt to assess what is expected to improve attention and what has no hope.

There are relatively high levels of controversy in this burgeoning field. Claims made in cases of attention deficit hyperactivity disorder (ADHD), for example, about biofeedback as a replacement for drugs like Ritalin, are difficult to assess. Full scientific studies are still being carried out, and at the same time there are those peddling biofeedback wares that make claims based on informal reports from parents about changes in behaviour – 'it helped little Johnny a lot' – that are difficult to assess in accuracy. For example, a child who has had behavioural problems and suddenly gets interest and encouragement from a new group of adults as well as some new fiddling equipment used on them may well change their behaviour to continue getting the lovely pats on the back, even though the treatment they are actually receiving is not itself the cause of these changes.

Industrial Applications

A company advertises its course on attention as 'Paying attention leads to better safety, productivity'. As Robert Pater wrote in the magazine *Industrial Safety and Hygiene News* (October, 2000):

> *People rarely get hurt because they want to, or because they don't care, or are clumsy. All too often, the inability to control attention and attitude can be an insidious contributing factor in many injuries.*

He suggests a set of 15 rules for trying to avoid these dangers of inattention in the workplace:

> **1.** *Take control of yourself first. It can be seductive to blame workers for the inability to control their attention, but it is critical that everyone – safety professionals and managers as well – exert self-*

control. You can't effectively help others learn a skill you have not yourself attained.

2. *Assess the specific contributing factors to loss of attention and attitude control within your organization.*

3. *Improve medical management to identify and provide appropriate help to those with physiological problems. Some workers have medical conditions they may not be aware of – such as depression, diabetes, hypertension, Attention Deficit Disorder and many others – that can reduce attention control.*

4. *Use principles of positive motivation to elicit learning, acceptance and change.*

5. *Enlist positive, realistic, involved goal-setting. Goals help focus attention.*

6. *Implement a system of training that helps people control their attention while doing repetitive work.*

7. *Design jobs so they provide a sufficient level of interaction and feedback, have specific goals and established procedures, and provide a sense of challenge.*

8. *Enlist attitude development techniques such as mental rehearsal.*

9. *Heighten eye control and coordination. This is a critical element in controlling attention. Internally, the eyes help organize movement.*

10. *Offer methods that apply to home as well as to work. People are creatures of habit; it's easy to instil positive default behaviours that will transfer between work and home activities.*

11. *Develop a system for ongoing reinforcement and behavioural improvements in attention control.*

12. *Develop effective organizational stress management.*

13. *Make work and safety programs energizing. Solicit concerns, heighten enjoyment and laughter, and involve as many senses as possible.*

14. *Focus your training on principles, judgment, personal interest and individual behaviour, and personal control rather than memorizing rules and procedures*

15. *Help people develop automatic safe responses when there is no time to think. Training can help a person overcome fear-based reactions, supplementing them with safe default behaviours when there is no time for conscious decision-making.*

These rules are all excellent. But rule 6 seems to be at the basis of most of the other rules: *teach people how to train their attention.* If a person cannot hold the focus of their attention for as long as a job requires that may be because they are unclear about their goals (rule 5), or are not suitably motivated (rules 4 and 7). So the rules fill out some of the aspects of how attention is controlled (goals setting, strong enough motivation, eye control and coordination improvement, make the tasks enjoyable, etc). But the crux is rule 6: 'training attention'. That brings us back to meditation-based techniques. For even if a goal is paramount and there is great motivation and so on, it will not do if the underlying neural apparatus is not bright and burnished ready for use.

How can we polish up attention? I have talked about attention as a control system, and presented an engineering control model (the attention copy model associated with Figure 8 of Part II) to fill out that approach. In such a way I and my research team have been able to explain a number of subtle phenomena in attention and consciousness, such as the attentional blink (especially some very recent results published in July 2005), as well as in 'perception' of masked stimuli, and of phenomena occurring in the change blindness range of psychological experiments. So what are the rules I can advocate to you so you can polish your attention to be as bright and sharp as possible? Since rules I would like to suggest also arise from meditation practices (as well as other aspects), let me turn to that now.

Meditation and Attention

An important component of the practice of meditation is indeed that it must be practised. There is no way around some sort of practice, be it guided by one's own eyes and ears or by biofeedback from one's brain or whatever. Any basic inattention or more broadly rusty forms of attention control can best be corrected by changes in the circuits of the brain. In particular, the parietal lobe module sends out the attention control signal to move attention to a new place or object, and one has to modify its connectivity to lower-level cortices in occipital and temporal cortices in order to be more effective. These connections run some considerable distances in the brain and can only be modified gradually, with time spent in practice. Similarly, there may be a need to develop new and more motivated goals, so involving both your prefrontal cortices (for coding and holding the goals) as well as your limbic system (for more strongly motivating those goals). If the overall modification process were not slow but modifications of these circuits could occur in something like a one-shot manner, then our attention powers would be constantly chopping and changing. There would thereby be considerable difficulty in having stable attention-controlled responses to the external world, resulting in poor survival value – you would soon be dead out in that dog-eat-dog world. Your attention would be shifting around too rapidly for your effectiveness. So some steady work over periods of time must be done to polish up consciousness. However, the results can be astounding. In particular, consider so-called 'one-pointed' meditation. That involves training oneself to single out only one among a whole range of objects in the outer world to which you are attending.

Let me give you an example from my own experience. I was in the New York Metropolitan Museum some years ago. I chose to go to the Oriental section, where there was a magnificent display of Buddhist art and of artefacts of the great past of Buddhism and related religions. One particular tapestry totally caught my attention. It was from some time in the twelfth century, entitled, according to my memory of it, 'Catching the Tiger'. It showed the hunter in various stages of trying to catch the magnificent creature. The hunter crept up gradually on the tiger, studying him as he went closer and closer, and always concentrating on not being detected. These various steps of the hunt were displayed in the several parts of the tapestry. Finally, the hunter launches himself onto the back of the tiger, with only the tiger at the centre of his attention as the hunter grips on tightly. No other sensations are allowed in to disturb this one-pointed attention. I have tried it ever since, imagining the sequences of the tapestry, and found it very satisfying, especially cleansing to extraneous components in my mind.

I mentioned earlier that there is a controversy about what really works in this new field of human endeavour. The meditation process carried out for many years by Buddhist monks was tested recently by scientists from the University of Queensland and the University of California at Berkeley. They investigated 74 monks in India, who had practised meditation over periods from 5 to 54 years. In particular, the monks were tested on what is called binocular rivalry. In this paradigm one picture, say of a cat, is shown to one eye, and another picture, say of a dog, to the other (by special goggles). Usually there is an automatic switch from one of the percepts, in one eye, to the other in the other eye, and then back again, oscillating backwards and forwards between the images every few seconds or minutes or so. It is very difficult to control this switching process and especially its speed. The scientists found that the monks were able to have remarkable control over this switching, with one monk even able to hold one single image in his mind for 12 minutes.

Olivia Carter, one of the investigators from the University of Queensland, wrote:

The monks showed they were able to block out external information. It would now be good to carry out further tests using imaging techniques to see exactly what the differences are in the brains of the monks.

Buddhist monks often report that if something negative happens they are able to digest it and move on. People who use meditation, including the Dalai Lama, have said that the ability to control and direct your thoughts can be very beneficial in terms of mental health.

There are numerous other scientific tests indicating how some forms of meditation can alter the usual activity in the brain when meditation is occurring. A study of meditators by scientists from the University of Copenhagen showed much lower activity in the input areas of the brain, where stimuli are being processed at a low level, while there was increased activity in the prefrontal cortex. This is exactly what would be expected from any control model of attention in which goals sited in the prefrontal cortex have been created, and are being used, in order to achieve one-pointed meditation. These goals inhibit inputs coming in through the primary senses to cause distraction. In this way the activity in the lower cortical regions, corresponding to the primary sensory input, is expected to be lower than when the subject is not meditating, as was discovered experimentally by the scientists.

There is a further step beyond one-pointed meditation: no-pointed meditation. After reaching the back of the tiger in these meditation exercises, one then removes the image of the tiger altogether. In other words, you try to reach that state of stillness that I mentioned earlier. There is no content at all to which you are attending. Such a state of emptiness can only be reached by constant practice of 'one-pointed' attention control, so that ultimately the control you can exert over distracting stimuli (sounds, views of your environment, sensations from your own body, etc.) becomes so strong that they can all be squashed in your mind, even the one-pointed tiger. I am afraid I have not got that far in my own meditation. I said earlier that the 'stillness/emptiness' state is an amazing one. However, I also pointed out that this state has been strongly criticised by some types of meditators. In the words of the Buddhist monk writing about those trying to find stillness: 'They are like lumps of stone, who sit there doing nothing'. I agree. One-pointed attention meditation is a fine practice. But to wipe all out from your brain except your attention control activity and to contemplate that alone may not be necessary or useful in the normal world. It has still to be determined by careful investigation what are the benefits of the state of stillness. It is clear what those benefits are for one-pointed attention, as generating a well-burnished attention control system. I advise one-pointed attention as a very practical and useful state to attain in brushing up on your mind.

One-pointed attention is not easy. Many thoughts bubble up in the mind to distract attention away for the tiger or whatever object you are trying to attend to. As Malcolm Hunter wrote in an article on 'Psychotherapy and meditation':

Ideally, when one meditates, one's attention remains with the primary object. In reality, though, many people's minds do not stay focused on the primary object. There may be, for example, thoughts of the past or future, distracting aches and pains, sounds and so on. When the mind becomes distracted from the primary object the distraction is acknowledged and the meditator returns his or her attention to the object. If the distraction becomes overwhelming or predominant, this 'distraction' may then become the object of meditation and of non-intellectual investigation. Like changing gears on a car one may shift from object to object and from mindfulness of body to mindfulness of mind states, feelings or mental objects. For example, if a jackhammer started up outside one's meditation room, the vibrations of the sound (a physical object) could become the object of meditation (mindfulness of physical objects or body). One could also choose to be attentive to the unpleasantness of the sounds (mindfulness of feelings) or the thoughts that arise in regard to the sounds (mindfulness of mind objects). Alternatively, one could direct attention to the quality of anger that may arise (mindfulness of mind states).

So stick to the object but realise it will take time to build those links in your brain that allow that one-pointed attention to become really effective. At the same time please take to heart the earlier 15 rules – valid in the home and round and about as much as in the office – setting up clear goals, motivating yourself, and ensuring you do those things from which you can get enjoyment.

Electronic Games

One recent area of controversy over the dangers of overuse is that of electronic games. These have become a very big industry, as large as the film industry if not larger. But is it good to have younger people glued to a computer, laptop or mobile phone screen 'mindlessly' zapping away in a 'shoot-'em-up' game or a villains-and-police game in which the player takes the role of a very villainous criminal (as in Grand Theft Auto, which sold 1 million copies in the nine days after its launch)? Grand Theft Auto involves lots of shootings and splattered blood all over the place, in which the player inhabits the fantasy lifestyle of a Los Angeles gangster, complete with their own tattoo. Is this teaching that crime does pay? Is that one of the components making modern society ever more violent?

This has been discussed in a number of different ways. One is to lump the games under the heading of 'violence on TV'. In general, that seems to be a bad thing, with violent behaviour being seen to be promoted by watching violent videos and television or films – shades of poor little James Bulger (an innocent 5-year old who was abducted and killed by two 12-year-olds who had been previously watching a stack of very violent videos owned by one of their fathers, with the crime being carried out along the lines of one particularly violent video). So watching violent scenes in a passive way is not a good thing. However, an electronic game is not passive, and can involve considerable close attention to the various characters being met in the game in order to reach some goal or other. When one also considers online gaming, in which many people play against each other, using different roles than normal, then the level of social involvement and role playing is clearly high, as well as involving the need for close attention to the events going on around one in the game (providing the game does not involve violence committed by the player).

A recent book *Everything Bad is Good for You* by the cultural critic Steven Johnson claims just the opposite to where the above is going. He quotes from a 14-year old boy who sums up the frustrations felt by many young people criticised by their elders for not reading books by pithily noting that lots of books are rubbish. Steven Johnson claims there are limitless opportunities opening up for young people for complex problem solving when they have acquired these games skills, even taking them on to solving problems based on systems analysis, probability theory, pattern recognition and mastery of spatial geometry. This claim is partly backed up by a recent study showing that between 1943 and 2001 IQ scores rose 17 points, the steepest rise being since the 1990s. The greatest gain in marks was in abstract reasoning and pattern recognition. So on-the-spot reasoning abilities may be improved by this electronic wizardry gained by the young and nimble fingered on their electronic gadgets. These media gizmos pose the challenge of getting inside the logic of how they work; the young mind leaps at this and so gains a general problem solving ability. Related abilities, especially of multi-tasking, have been noticed by other commentators on media developments, some complaining about their own lack of skills in such areas as being woefully behind that of the young tyros with the nimble fingers and even nimbler brains. As Seymour Papert, co-founder of the MIT Media Lab, said recently:

Game designers depend on millions of people being prepared to undertake the serious amount of learning needed to master a complex game. If their public failed to learn, they would go out of business. Kids who talk about 'hard fun' don't mean it's fun in spite of being hard. Learning happens best when one is deeply engaged in hard and challenging activities.

And it is worth taking note that computer games have been used in therapy for the elderly, to provide excitement and improve motor skills.

Yet there is the other side of the coin. These practices are no doubt honing important skills for solving hard problems with their challenges (in gentle societies such as The Sims or nasty one such as that of gangsters in Los Angeles). But there must also be other developments in young lives. As John Beyer of Mediawatch UK said recently:

All these advances are morally neutral in themselves. But if you become skilful at brutally killing people on screen, it dulls the brain and consciousness and may damage the psychology of the player. We become desensitised and are less likely to be shocked when we see it in real life.

Even Steven Johnson admits there is not much of an aesthetic experience in games. A teacher of English would be right in claiming that there was no magic or depth of feeling in such games; a sentiment agreed by Steve Johnson, in spite of his lauding games. He goes on to claim that the intelligence of the games lies not in their content but in the ability to learn how to make the right decision. But this is the nub of the problem. What does he mean here by 'right'? As pointed out by Johnson himself, there is little subtlety in the games, no 'moral quandaries'. However, there are decidedly so in the books derided by Joe, for example. At the very beginning of literature the *Iliad* and the *Odyssey* contained considerable insights into humanity's moral problems. The ancient Greek dramatists still stand today as magnificent exponents of these moral problems. Oedipus was beset with one of the deepest problems of all, that of accidentally killing his father and marrying his mother. His solution: put out his own eyes! Yet that is a very bare description of a subtle interplay of the fates and man's waywardness, and of the subtleties of the moral forces that are present in society. Similarly with Antigone, bound to honour her dead brother, but yet ordered by her king not to do so.

It is from the heart of the moral problems of society that we recognise the paucity of a diet of electronic games. There is little internal content – be it involving moral decision or those involving accumulated wisdom. Without some appreciation being instilled of the great cultural creations of the past, all dealing with the deep moral problems still present throughout society, there will be an ever increasing expansion of the moral black hole whose event horizon seems to be growing as more and more youngsters are lost to their own morally thin devices – all 'up a creek without a paddle'.

In a similar manner, and speaking as a mathematician, there is no doubt there is dumbing-down in schools, especially in teaching mathematics and science. More remedial teaching needs to be given at university as entrants show up with ever decreasing mathematical skills as the years go by. Even worse is the switch away from science, noticeable in the UK by the closing down of various chemistry and physics departments. Even my own component of the prestigious University of London, King's College London, is closing its chemistry department, due to its high cost (involving lab space) and difficulties of recruiting suitable students as compared to more humanity-oriented subjects. Media studies, psychology and English are oversubscribed in numbers of departments across the UK. But these subjects will only produce those able to support ever more humanity-oriented jobs. Real intellectual challenges lie in the sciences, both in the hard sciences (physics, chemistry, mathematics, environmental sciences) and the life sciences (biophysics, biochemistry, molecular biology).

You can rightly point out that I cannot have it both ways: the expansion of student numbers in the humanities is a good thing since it brings students into contact with the moral lessons of the ages, while the sciences, being neutral, certainly are not at all concerned with such lessons. But we must be careful since what is studied in humanities today need not carry much of past wisdom on moral dilemmas. We move forward into post-industrial society jettisoning the past at our peril.

We do not want to prevent youngsters growing up, for example, depending for part of their education on hand-held gizmos: they must also grow up cognizant in some degree to the stored wealth and wisdom of the past. It is in the great books, paintings, music and scientific ideas that this wisdom has flowered. If it is not part of a youngster's mental architecture then their minds will be content-free. And while they may be very rapid in pressing the right button, they also need to be able to acquire the sagacity of the past to make their button pressing not so automatic but tempered with the wisdom of the ages. They will then be able to better appreciate the results of their action when they do press that button. Think of the President of the United States with his finger on that atomic button. Who would want him (or her) to be finger-fast but content free, zapping the first thing that moves!

Biofeedback

I have already mentioned that biofeedback is being used to help children with ADHD, and noted that it had been claimed to improve their condition. It has also been used to help reduce the frequency of epileptic fits, as well as help reduce stress to ameliorate heart attacks. Various biofeedback devices have been developed supposedly to help the mind. The most basic is the self-controlled (or biofeedback) EEG machine. Over three decades ago I worked with scientists who had developed what they called the 'Mind Machine'. This looked like a crown, with several little feet poking down inside the main belt of the crown. When the crown was placed gently on a person's head, the little feet penetrated through the hair, and rested softly on the scalp. Because the feet were metallic they provided an electrical pathway to carry the electrical activity of the brain, as observed on the scalp and by way of a set of wires, to a small computer. This carried out the task of separating out the brain-wave activity at the various sites on the scalp into waves of different frequencies. So the Mind Machine, it was claimed by its creators, really could look inside the mind. And anyone could use it (provided they coughed up the not inconsiderable cost). Now these machines and other similar but updated cousins are readily available on the Internet for a relatively small sum.

If you work to accentuate certain brain-wave frequencies over others does it do the user any good? This is related to the question of how much information about what is going on inside your brain is really given by such a machine. Consider a child with ADHD. They can work, in a biofeedback fashion, to achieve a brain state in which there are more high-frequency brain waves (so-called gamma waves above about 30 Hertz) than low-frequency ones. That is good for keeping an alert state of mind (as has been shown experimentally by those people possessing a good clutch of gamma waves having better attention control under various tests). But it will not necessarily indicate that the control machinery of the movement of the focus of attention is being developed to help them attend better. In particular, remember that the goal is that of being mentally alert. But then one must move on that alertness to attend to specific items set up as goals. And motivation must concomitantly be developed – remember the rules I mentioned at the beginning of the chapter. So why should the powers of attention be enhanced unless work was done specifically on them in the precisely relevant situations? I am not saying that such biofeedback may not be an important step forward for ADHD children. But there is still more of a way to go for them, I suspect.

I earlier raised the more general question as to whether EEG can 'look' inside your mind. There have recently been a lot of claims in the newspapers about how various sorts of experiments can let scientists look into the minds of their subjects. It is true that various approaches now allow us to detect, for example, if someone has made up a 'memory' of the past, or if it is a memory of what actually happened – the real thing. Also, various sites of activity have been observed in the brain corresponding with many of the components of cognitive processing. But it is still premature to claim that a person's mind has now become transparent to onlookers by these powerful brain imaging machines. There is still a long way to go to be able to be assured (or worried) that has happened.

There are other ways to invigorate the brain other than trying from inside. It can be helped along by the application of external magnetic or electric fields. For example, Allan Snyder, at the Australian Centre for Mind at the University of Sydney, has created a magnetic 'brain zapper', able to turn off certain brain regions (specifically in the left temporal parietal junction or TPJ for short, that was suggested earlier as being an attention control region for object stimulus activity in the brain). He and his colleagues hope that in this way the savant skills of autistic people would be allowed to shine through in normal people, having removed possible control from this TPJ region. His tests on four subjects have shown interesting results, with subjects becoming better at drawing. The effects of the magnetic zapping to their TPJ persisted for 45 minutes, so may have been due to new ways of doing things, or just short-term after-effects. Other researchers have also validated some of these effects. Allan Snyder claims this lowering of control is the source of creativity, which is stifled by the conscious inhibition system from the TPJ – shades of the 'user illusion' that I mentioned earlier, the book of that title being part of a more general attack on the value of consciousness. However, it is still early days to support any claim to the basis of creativity. It may be that consciousness gets in the way, but all things in their place and at due times: without consciousness, the hard work of developing attention control of a suitable effective knowledge base cannot occur, so that the unconscious creative processes would not work effectively later and so that in their mysterious ways their wonders they create.

Another area of great importance in biofeedback is that of the learning of control to enable a disabled person to move a cursor around a screen purely by their brainwaves. This can also be learnt by non-disabled people, who are thus helped to improve, for example, their golf game. Wes Sime has found he can help golfers by hooking them up to what he calls graphically enough his 'Peak Achievement neuro-feedback machine'. He discovered a clear correlation between certain brainwaves and either a successful or an unsuccessful putt. He then found that the most efficient brain state is one in which all the major brain-wave patterns are absent. It is as if the golfer's cortex had shut down. This fits well with the experience a practised golfer (and athletes in other sports) has of 'the zone' or 'going with the flow', where the mind, it is proposed, is got out of the way and purely automatic processes take over. But that would only be effective if the correct stance and flow of the golfer's body had been learnt to become automatic (as in the case of creativity, after careful hard practice work having been done). Once that has occurred, then the Peak Achievement machine can indicate that the golfer has come out of their automatic state, and too much attention to feedback signals from the body has crept in. I should actually term this 'crept back in', since he would have had to be attending most carefully while practising, before 'going with the flow'.

However, it is debatable if going with the flow is actually being on automatic. In an automatic state it is usual to be able to direct attention to a completely different task being performed at the same time, since the automatic task does not present any attention load. Efficient performance in any high-level motor task cannot usually be achieved with any other attention-demanding task. So it is unlikely that the golfers under Wes Sime or ballet dancers performing at the highest level are on automatic: they are very likely using predominantly their motor attention control system, allowing the flow of action sequences to be performed exactly as they had been learnt using fuller attended sensory feedback, although there is still undoubtedly the running of automatic action sequences built by training to achieve more efficient encoding and control. The motor attention control system would thus be acting more in a supervisory and error correcting capacity, and for overall motor guidance, rather than being used for the performance of each atomic action. Here we see the balance in sports between attention and automaticity. There is also a balance between automatic and attended processing in creative work, where automatic or unconscious processes play a crucial creative role, along with attention and goal setting to assess the products of that creativity, and set up its possibility (by the initial hard work of creating databases in the brain relevant to the tasks being tackled) in the first place. Creativity is quite a different form of activity than that of the highly trained sports person: in performance by the latter, learnt action sequences are run off automatically with motor attention control overall guidance and error correction; in the former unexpected new connections and associations are being made at an unconscious level, emerging into consciousness, and thence being assessed by goals set up in frontal cortices as to overall tasks. The balance between unconscious and conscious processing is crucial here. Too much conscious control inhibits the unconscious creative processes, but too much unconscious processing leads to an over-abundance of ideas although with a more difficult problem of assessment of their relevance to the requisite goals. The timing of these two processes is also important: a certain amount of conscious 'hard thinking' is needed not only for database construction but also for careful optimal goal setting. There is the crucial process, most important especially for a hard problem, of breaking the problem down into its component sub-problems and enumeration of the resulting sub-goals. Each of these sub-goals is then to be tackled by the mix of conscious and unconscious processing that I mentioned above. In that way real progress can be made in tackling the most difficult problems, even that of consciousness itself.

I have used this dual-level processing in my own work, with the conscious work involving creation of a suitably complex database from the areas of brain science, neural networks, engineering, psychology, philosophy and religion. I consciously realised that an important sub-goal was to probe attention. This then required creating a suitable neural model. Using some unconscious creative processes, I came up with the application of engineering control models, and so was led to consciously create a more precise database of control models associated with the brain. This led to the creation of the attention copy model. Some unconscious cogitation produced an identification of the attention copy as the brain signal for the experience of the owner. It is the result of this creative process I have explained in this book, although not exactly in the sequence I described above.

Pain Management

Pain is never far away. When I stub my toe unexpectedly or come down with some unexpected ailment, pain is there. Pain is an experience across all humanity. We are made to suffer pain. I suggested earlier that pain is caused by the constant drawing of attention to the damaged part of the body. In this way, pain is a constant drain on attention – getting in the way of your daily tasks – that does not go away until the body part has been healed. It has thereby great survival value. But pain has been misused across humanity – in torture and in war. In the heat of battle pain may not be felt, as in the case of the soldier whose leg has been shot away but does not notice it until the battle is over.

Over the millennia, and especially in the twentieth century, pain management has improved enormously. In the nineteenth century some doctors thought that patients' screams during an operation conducted without anaesthetic were an important part of the cure. Some even suggested that the patients' screams could be used to help diagnosis.

That has altered now, with drugs available to handle levels of pain previously felt excruciatingly by the patient. There are some pains that can not be so screened out, but at least brain operations or large doses of morphine have helped alleviate pain even more. But if pain is the dragging of attention, why not just zap the region in the brain that is causing that attention dragging? That is very attractive at first sight, but it is not so easy, since there are numerous places where such dragging signals are created in the brain. There are also numerous sites which control the dragging of attention, and these cannot be shut down without ending up, for example, with someone who now has neglect. Of course many of the pain control drugs cause a drowsy state as the attention system is damped down – but this is a controlled level of neglect, not a permanent one.

Pain also has an important cultural component. The Aztecs, for example, would flay victims alive for their gods as a matter of course. In some North American Indian tribes, such as the Apache, pain was to be borne without complaint. In those and other similar societies, pain was to be regarded with some disdain, and levels of pain thresholds were undoubtedly higher than in 'softer' societies. Some years ago, I tested the world champion fire walker after he had walked on a horrendously hot fire of wooden logs. He had a very high pain threshold – he could burn his feet quite badly during fire walking and yet not be concerned about it.

Pain has also been a way of finding the truth. Torturers' instruments are hideous in appearance, and if one considers the torture methods of the Inquisition – the rack, the wheel, the fire – those were brutal days. But also the period of Stalin had its brutal tortures in the KGB, as well as similar torture procedures used by other societies in the last century and even up to today. It has even recently been suggested by some legal authorities that torture is a legitimate way of extracting necessary information from suspected terrorists; that is very debatable, but then one has to balance present pain inflicted by torture to the possible pains of many innocent sufferers of the effects of suicide bombs or other devices that are being prepared.

Anaesthetics have at least made the pain arising from normal hospital operations, and their painful aftermath, able to be handled without screaming. As Lucy Bending wrote, as part of a recent exhibition on pain in London:

If bodily pain is simply something to be alleviated at all costs, then

*those beliefs that had made it possible to bear it with Christian fortitude
have largely made their exit. And the sufferer is left with the pain itself
and a bottle of pills, rather than an internal system of understanding to
assuage it.*

Such an internal system still exists through meditation. In stillness, if it
can be achieved in pain, there will be reduction of the painful sensation,
if not its entire annihilation. Indeed, one of the reasons to learn to control
one's attention is to enable external 'drags' or distracters to be kept out of
awareness. That would be true also for pain as a distracter par excellence.
Indeed, the battlefield cases of severe wounds unnoticed until after the
battle is over are cases where the heat of battle has caused such a dragging
of attention to the ensuing action that any pain has no chance of edging
its way into awareness. Thus better attention control, as described earlier,
should lead to better pain control.

Dreaming

Dreams have played a very important role across the millennia of
recorded human history. Think of Joseph and the seven full and seven
lean years. Think of the chemist Kekulé who, dozing in front of his fire,
suddenly dreamt the structure of benzene as a ring of carbon atoms as the
snake in his dream bit its own tail. So what is going on in our dreams?
Can they be harnessed?

Numbers of people have now come forward who claim to have had
'lucid' dreams, in which they know they are dreaming, and, after a certain
amount of practice, can even begin to control the contents of their dreams.
This is a remarkable power if true. It may help to answer the riddle of
what dreams are for. There are presently numerous answers, with an
attractive one being that they are playbacks from the semi-permanent
storage system in the hippocampus to the rest of the cortex. It may be that
the episodes stored in hippocampus during a given day are being
replayed verbatim to more permanent sites of storage nearby in the brain.
It could also be that these memories are being used to build what is called
'semantic' knowledge. Such knowledge has no remembrance of you being
there when you learnt it. For example, I do not remember where I was
when I learnt that 'there are about 60 million people living in the UK' or
that 'Washington is the capital of the US': I must have been there in some
specific place each time, but that is not part of each of these semantic
memories. There are also other ideas about dreams, such as that they are a
way of releasing pent-up emotions, or even that they are just a process
involved with dumping unwanted mental rubbish.

Lucid dreams have a venerable heritage. In 1665 Samuel Pepys recorded a very pleasurable lucid dream:

> in which I had my lady Castelmayne in my arms and was admitted to use all the dalliances I desired with her, and then dreamed that this could not be awake.

But Tibetan Buddhists were practising lucid dreaming as 'dream yoga' over 1,000 years ago. It is suggested in Buddhist teaching that after death you go into something like a lucid dream.

Dr Stephen LaBerge is a Californian neuropsychologist who claims to have proved the reality of lucid dreams scientifically. He has even invented a device so that a dreamer can tell if their dream is lucid or not. Called the NovaDreamer, it fits around the head like an ordinary sleep mask but has built-in photoelectric sensors. These recognise when the eyes are moving rapidly, as occurs in dreaming, and cause two red light-emitting diodes to wink at the subject. If you are having a dream which you don't know is a dream and these little red lights appear in your dream, then you know you are having a lucid dream.

The amazing thing about lucid dreaming is that you can script your own dreams. If you want to fly, then you can. If you want to overcome certain fears, you can confront them in your lucid dreams. So these dreams are quite remarkable to experience. However, all is not completely under control for all lucid dreamers. Sometimes the lucid dream can be a nightmare; knowing you know it is a dream may not help you handle it well or wake up. A young woman had a lucid dream in which she reports a group of men around her attempting to rape her, from whom she did not seem to be able to escape. When she finally awoke she found she was crying with fear. This and other cases indicate that lucid dreaming is not risk free.

Where this leaves an attention copy type approach to the mind is that in lucid dreaming there must be some frontal brain components that are active enough to enable goals to be reached, so controlling the dream content, as well as some parietal and mid-frontal cortical sites enabling self-awareness of being in the dream. It will be necessary to measure the brain waves of lucid dreamers over the following years, in order to understand better what control components of the attention copy model are involved. This would lead to a further window on the amazing control circuitry of consciousness.

CHAPTER TWENTY-ONE

INFANTS AND CHILDREN

Introduction

Infancy and childhood are the gateways to adult life, hopefully one rich in experiences and creativity. But for some the gateway is too narrow, and the gate not easy to control. The gate may even seem to be controlled by someone else, especially if they are being abused. How can the growing child be helped forward to be ushered most effectively into the responsible and creative life of an adult? How can the gate be kept open wide and be made as attractive to cross as possible? And be felt to be under the complete control of the child itself? In particular, what is the way that an understanding of the mind can help achieve this control for the growing child? These are very difficult questions, in spite of there being a vast range of experience across many societies, of bringing up children to adulthood.

First, there may be genetic difficulties that prevent the child from developing properly, either physically or mentally. Over the next decades such problems may be ameliorated by genetic therapy, but that may only be in the more extreme forms of genetic disorders. But there is in any case an uncontrolled spread of genes inherited in society, so that aptitudes of any form, arising from a combination of specific genes, will differ from child to child and adult to adult. And we are still very far from the genetic manipulations of the kind described in Aldous Huxley's still futuristic book *Brave New World*, to create children of controlled levels of intellectual abilities.

Second, the child has to survive its family environment. In many cases the family provides a supportive guide to the growing child, but in others there may be abuse and violence, as well as poor attitudes to school, learning and work. There is also the impact of the child's genetic make-up on its abilities to grow most effectively in the family.

Third are the hurdles of adolescence. It is now being realised that the adolescent brain is still developing. In particular, it has an extended period of plasticity in the prefrontal cortex, enabling a variety of different sorts of social rules and internal controls to be created and moulded through experience in the family and more importantly in society at large.

So this is a period when experiments occur in lifestyle, and frictions with adults can be highest. This is part of the overall remarkable flexibility of the human brain, allowing it to be sculpted to fit into almost any form of society – those with brutal dictators or with intransigent religious rulers, or those with milder and more democratic social structure and greater individual freedoms.

Fourth comes the school and learning among one's peers. Bullying, lack of attention, distraction by others in the class, lack of motivation, and many other factors play their role in determining if school will be a success story for a child, launching it into an effective adulthood with a good knowledge base, or instead as a child turned off books and learning, and finishing school by it finishing them.

Nature versus Nurture

I have already talked about the recent study, at St Thomas' Hospital, London, of identical versus non-identical twins. With a set of 10,000 twin volunteers, this was one of the largest ever undertaken. Various disturbing results have arisen from the study. One was that smoking accelerates ageing of DNA (in particular causing shortening of the telomeres at the ends of chromosomes) by nearly five years, and obesity accelerates ageing by nine years. There are already strong guidelines to parents to prevent their children getting obese (by feeding them a good diet, and making sure they get plenty of exercise), and not starting to smoke (emphasising the dangers). Also, various illnesses previously put down to environmental factors (back pain, for example) have been discovered from the study to have a genetic component (identical twins often had worn-out discs in the same position in the spine). Other problems with important genetic components were discovered to be osteoarthritis, short-sightedness, perfect pitch (a definite boon to a musician), acne, cataracts and migraine.

Many aspects of our behaviour are also now recognised to be partially triggered by our genetic make-up. As I indicated above, due to the varied genetic make-up of different individuals, there will be a broad spread of genetically based aptitudes. At one extreme are the psychopaths, where a twin study shows that callous unemotional behaviour has a remarkably high inheritability. At the other is genius, which is difficult to define but is also expected to have some genetic components.

Such statistics about the level of genetic determination of intelligence and behaviour patterns as are now being discovered have worried scientists over many decades, ever since the time of the British scientist

Sir Frances Galton, the founder of eugenics in the nineteenth century. He was a cousin of Charles Darwin, and was a polymath, expert in geography, meteorology and founder of the discipline of biostatistics. He had coined the term eugenics as the method:

to check the birth-rate of the Unfit and improve the race by furthering the productivity of the fit by early marriage of the best stock.

Eugenics led to the Mental Deficiency Act in the UK in 1913, which gave a legal definition of feeble mindedness (so legally defining the Unfit). However, in spite of the popularity of the general eugenics programme, it was never carried out in the UK. In the USA a number of states passed sterilisation laws for the feeble-minded. Carrie Buck, an allegedly feeble-minded Virginian, appealed to the US Supreme Court to prevent her sterilisation order. Justice Wendell Holmes denied her appeal, stating that the principle underlying compulsory vaccination also supported the non-consensual cutting of a woman's fallopian tubes. He wrote:

Three generations of imbeciles are enough.

Nazi Germany also passed similar sterilisation laws in 1933. But the world has rightly taken against eugenics since then.

My conclusion is that in the relatively distant future there will undoubtedly be genetic manipulation by parents to create 'designer' children more to their own liking as more is known about the functions of the various components of the human genome. But in the near future this will not happen. Our children will have to be given the best environment to grow into effective human beings, given a rather unknown genetic component in their make-up.

Bringing Up a Loving Child

The most formative part of a human's life is their first few years. As the headline of a recent article in *The Times* asked:

If children are not taught how to behave at home, what hope is there at school?

In other words, the child needs to know who is in charge. It even has to develop the very concept of 'someone being in charge', which is quite sophisticated. However, from the word go the infant sees things being done around them – milk and food being brought to them, being washed and changed etc. So having a carer in charge is a natural part of their life. There is certainly someone in charge in those components.

Yet is that carer at their beck and call? If the infant is allowed to set its own agenda for its parents, as advocated by the child guru Dr Spock in the 1970s and 1980s, and lapped up by so many parents then (and many even now), then it will have no clear idea of anyone being in control but itself. As the article states from which the above headline was used:

The blame lies clearly in the transference of the upper hand from adult to child.

On the other hand, if the parents, especially the mother, set the infant's agenda then it will begin to learn that the whole universe does not automatically come at its beck and call. The process of setting up a reasonably firm regime under the mother's control should not be done in too strict and disciplinarian a manner, but with love and compassion, as a number of recent child-rearing books have emphasised. In a similar way to training a dog, strong chastisement when it transgresses is not the point: loving guidance as to what should be done is the only way forward.

Many of the children of today, as they grow up, have not had such a clear framework instilled since infancy. They have not learnt the meaning of the word 'no', uttered in a strong, commanding manner, nor the bestowed hug or word of encouragement when they have done something new and creative but in the given framework of allowed acts.

As another recent newspaper article noted, about one particular teenager's experience:

She has had her first sexual encounter and made her first suicide attempt, she takes drugs and stays away from home for days at a time. She is 13 years old. You might think this teenager is the product of an abusive family background and a turbulent upbringing, but she is in fact a much-loved child of well-educated and considerate parents who have always given her everything. And that is her problem. She is suffering from pampered child syndrome.

The author of a study on the subject of such children is a clinical psychologist, Dr Margaret Mamen, who argues that such children are the product of a permissive philosophy. The children have been brought up to believe that they have the same rights as adults but are not ready or able to shoulder the responsibilities of adulthood. It is suggested that parents think of themselves as the 'management team': the parents are the managers and the children are not, but are presently the trainees. As Dr Mamen has made it abundantly clear in her writing that children must have a clear framework of behaviour given by their parents, so that the youngsters can know where they stand in their family world. Those are my sentiments entirely.

If there is no clear framework or structure for a child's behaviour, then it can become its own demon – think *Lord of the Flies*. Children may end up running in gangs, like a pack of wild animals, attacking those different from themselves. This can result in terrorised neighbourhoods, with the elderly in urban neighbourhoods complaining of being too frightened to go out into such a jungle. As one elderly person said, 'I daren't go outside at night at all – they zoom close to you on their bikes and stand in their hoods on the corners of streets and seem ready to pounce'. Part of this is a defence-reaction from the elderly to the new styles of the young, especially the hoods, which can make children appear more menacing than they really are. It is also a consequence of there being nothing for the youngsters to do in such neighbourhoods. But the impressions are there for a reason, I suspect.

Such lack of a clear framework may also result in bullying, leading to attacks on younger and more defenceless children (shades of James Bulger). One 12-year-old girl, who was feared by other children as the local bully, was recently found to have abducted a 5-year-old boy from his garden and led him into a wood half a mile away. She attempted to tie him to a tree by string. He was later found outside a shop, with a ligature mark round his neck and scratches and bruises. A doctor said that if the pressure had continued for a few seconds longer the boy would likely have been killed. The little boy told his mother later that a 'big' girl hit him with sticks and nettles, then tied a rope around his neck and threw it over a tree branch. Amazingly, the girl was allowed to go free (as reported in *The Times* of 4 October 2005); it is assumed that one of the conditions of her freedom is that she does not try to kill any more young children!

The early connections in the brain are laid down in the family learning experience. Such connections will be the basis on which later more sophisticated responses and understanding will be built. But without the firm foundation of knowing who has the loving upper hand this foundation will not be coherent. In particular, the early rules and 'right ways of doing things' in the family will not be internalised. That internalisation of moral codes (or lack of them) is a very important process, enabling a child to later develop into an adult governed by such codes in important social interactions through its life.

A loving family unit is most crucial for infant upbringing and to begin this process of internalisation. How discipline is achieved once an infant begins to move under its own steam and starts nursery school may differ between families and certainly between cultures. In the UK a 'naughty stair' or 'naughty chair' is so designated, with the child being sent to sit there if it has not obeyed some important requirement of its parents (such as getting dressed or clearing away your toys) until it is prepared to say 'sorry' to the relevant parent. This style of parenting has been increasingly found to be effective in correcting bad behaviour.

Is there any naturally bad behaviour in a brain based on the attention control architecture for creating its consciousness? The clear answer is: there is none. What I described in Part II as the basis of consciousness is value-neutral. It has no knowledge of what is right or wrong. This is a very crucial and seemingly dangerous feature of a brain-based consciousness. We know that there are genetically pre-wired connections determining certain reflex responses. But these are primitive, and in any case soon get overwritten by cortical control circuits quite early on in the child's development. So there is no brain-based moral code. To some, this 'brain is morally neutral' viewpoint means that humanity is no better than the most primitive of savages. 'Help!', they shout. 'Bring back God, who will tell you what you can do and what you cannot do'. The difficulty is to believe those who claim he has told them what morally is right and what morally wrong. There are so many differing views as to what is allowed, what is not, by whichever version of God you are tuned in to.

But let's not go down that road of listening to those who claim they know the infinite. If we accept the results now coming in from brain science, and the message of this book, that consciousness can be envisaged as solely brain based, then we cannot avoid answering the question: how can we find a way of bringing up a child so as to produce a decent contributor to itself and to society? One where each individual has the freedom to be themselves and develop themselves, so long as they do not impinge on similar freedoms of other members of that society. In other words: how to develop a society of creative, independent individuals, all of whom 'love their neighbours as themselves'?

The answer is important, since it is at the root of the creation of any civilisation or culture with a good quality of life for its citizens. The attention copy-based brain can create the wide range of cultures known to have occurred on earth since mankind began, with such an enormous range of values. But as I said, and I repeat, the attention copy-based brain is morally neutral. All it can do is learn what is rewarded, what is penalised, by the world around it, and search to get only rewards, avoiding all possible penalties along the way. So how can we find moral imperatives to constrain it along the lines of teaching it the word 'no', but at the same time in a loving and supportive environment? We cannot find it initially in the brain of any infant. It can only be in how brains interact and are brought up, in particular in how one brain teaches another.

The answer is in terms of the adaptive capability of the neural networks of the brain. I did not specify the detailed connections of any attention copy-based brain in Part II. These connections have to be developed under suitable training conditions. This is not a trivial problem to solve, given the enormous number of possible connections that could exist between the nerve cells of the brain (about ten thousand billion billion potential connections). The brain uses two separate methods to solve this problem. First, it relies on genetic guidance to set up initial sets of pathways along which a considerably reduced set of 'hard-wired' connections run from one part of the brain to another. Having set up those hard-wired connections in the foetus, when it is born the infant uses learning methods to modify some of these connections even further, plus adding some extra ones, especially those in cortical regions. Such learning will go on in stages, first with the sensory regions developing in response to stimuli, then the higher parietal and temporal lobes as the child moves into its teens, and last of all the prefrontal cortices, which may continue developing their structures even until the late 30s.

The second learning method of developing connections applies not only to the attention control system, but also, and possibly starting earlier, to the value system. Such a value system provides an estimate of the reward to be expected from a given stimulus, based on each past experience and the resulting rewards of such experience. Such value maps are at the basis of emotions, and provide emotional colour to all we see about us. Without expectations of reward we have little reason to act in any specific way, since nothing is expected to be rewarding or predicts that rewards are just around the corner. The brain bases of the emotions are still being clarified, but they are now known to involve various specific cortical and sub-cortical sites. These sites can be seen active in humans when angry or happy faces, for example, are displayed to those undergoing brain imaging. It is these value maps, and the associated emotions, that are crucial in making decisions. If someone is taking a gamble, several of these sites light up, depending on the level of reward and risk level of penalties.

Initially the value maps are just about empty in a newborn infant's brain. As the infant brain develops its value maps, it correspondingly begins to encode how important various stimuli are to obtain rewards from its parents. Which stimuli or actions are rewarded is initially totally up to the parents. They have the choice of what responses to encourage, what to inhibit. If they do not encourage sensible responses, then their offspring will very likely make their own and other people's lives a living hell (especially as the offspring grow more and more independent). If the parents are sensible and give the loving guidance, along the lines of 'guided creative fun' I mentioned earlier, showing in the process where 'no' and where loving rewards lie, then life should be much easier, for all concerned across society as a whole. So as I see it there is a moral imperative – on the parents, not the infant or child – to avoid releasing a monster on society as their dear little Joan or Johnny grows into adulthood. The rest is up to society – its moral, legal and education system, to give further loving guidance.

Adolescence and Learning

Chaos seems to be moving ever more into society – as clear from increasing disruption in classrooms and in streets, buses and trains brought about by ever younger children behaving more and more badly. These features are no doubt arising partly due to children being released into society by families who have not given loving guidance, sometimes no guidance at all, to their offspring. But society also has some responsibility itself for this condition. Drug accessibility, bad role models, irrelevant teaching in schools for some children, little in the way of amenities to keep the young occupied and help develop their skills to give them self-confidence, are among the many causes of difficult out-of-control young people. What can be done? More crucially what should be done?

Again we meet the question: is there a right way to bring up children and teenagers in society so they do not tear it apart? We are now moving on, in an attention copy-view of the mind/brain, from early learning, initially of brain connections to set up the very minimal infant control rules in prefrontal and other cortex, as well as the relevant reward maps in the limbic system, guided by learnt values attached to actions and stimuli, to much more sophisticated adolescence-level social rules for responding in society. There are new people to meet, new events to handle, all possibly causing emotional pain if there is no initial success in dealing with the situations in which adolescents find themselves. How can the blows of outrageous fortune that can rain down on the growing adolescent be cushioned? Of course, we have such problems all our lives, but we do mature and learn how to handle delicate situations. Teenagers are only trying out various responses, some of which may be very bizarre, even shooting others in their school, as occurs in societies in which guns abound. They have as yet unformed social rule bases in their still growing prefrontal cortices. They may not know what rewards are available in certain situations for certain responses. A vast uncharted area is ahead of them, which they cannot avoid navigating but which they are ill prepared so to do.

There is again no right and unique way forward, but only a general approach: to require that society does not make a cross for its own back by the products of its schools and universities. Again, there must be compassionate guidance. But guidance there must be. That involves a certain level of discipline. At the same time, the differences between people's abilities and aptitudes are becoming apparent as the child grows.

Here an attention copy approach is much harder to develop. The attention copy model was created by looking at single brains: they were involved in some forms of interaction with society, but only in a minimal manner. One way to understand the implications for society of attention copy minds and brains in interaction is to measure brain activity when the owners of these minds and brains are interacting with each other. Consciousness is clearly involved here, but more specifically it is the way that the memory and social rule brain banks are developed and used that needs to be better understood. That will no doubt happen in the future, but there is still a long way to go.

Some countries are resorting to more rigid methods to help those who have not been able to benefit from their school experience. In France, for example, it has just been proposed to set up 50 'boot camps' for up to 20,000 youths per year between the ages of 18 and 21, especially for those who are school dropouts and face social exclusion. As the French Defence Minister in charge of this development is reported to have said, 'I think a certain number of young people need not only professional training but also to learn how to behave. We are going to do for civilisation what we already do for young soldiers'. Discipline is tight: they have to wear a uniform, ask for permission to go out, and have to be back by 6.00 p.m.; they make their own beds, do their own ironing and scrub their floors. As an army spokesman is reported to have said, 'These young people have a need for authority and they need benchmarks'. At these boot camps the youngsters end up with training in the service industries such as hotels and restaurants. It is a pity they did not have that discipline in their earlier experience in infancy, imparted by parents and later by teachers, then they may not have needed such draconian measures as volunteering to go to an army-style boot camp.

Similar but smaller-scale projects are going along the increased-discipline route in the UK, or giving it support. For example, a project on 16 young so-called 'unteachables' was briefly set up to try to bring them back in from the cold of illiteracy and unemployability. As part of an experiment on teaching methods, they were first of all exposed to soft teaching methods (led by a guitar-strumming teacher who swore continually to show he was one of them), but these failed dismally, with them running even more out of control in their classes. They were then put in the care of a strict disciplinarian (a head teacher who had previously brought in similar disciplinary methods to save a failing school), who imposed detentions and sent continued miscreants home. The remaining children began to improve, with an increase in their attention span from 40 minutes to an hour and a quarter. There was an all-round improvement of behaviour. A child psychologist involved in the project is quoted as saying 'Although teenagers demand autonomy and independence, they actually need quite a lot of structure and clear boundaries. When they are given too much power the system does begin to break down. They need to know how far they can go and then they do better' – a fitting summary of what I have been writing.

CHAPTER TWENTY-TWO

INSIDE THE MINDS OF ANIMALS

Introduction

I have not so far touched on animals in any detail. But an attention copy model of human consciousness can also be searched for in animals. Do they possess the complex structures that I claimed in Part II were crucial to the attention copy model, and hence to the possession of consciousness? More generally, do they have a copy of the attention movement control signal, leading us to expect that there is an ownership mechanism at the basis of the consciousness creation system in the animal's brain, and so that they possess some sense of 'being there'? An animal could still be regarded as conscious in some sense even if it does not have the full attention copy apparatus. But either way it would be important for a further expansion of our understanding of consciousness.

As an example, suppose that the brain of a particular species were studied carefully while the animal is moving around, and no copy of the attention movement control signal were discovered, however hard the search went on. But still attention was being shifted around. Would the animal be conscious? It would not, according to my claims, have any sense of 'being there'. So it would be a zombie – all content, but nothing experiencing the content. I have hinted earlier that our brains very likely could not function like that. For brain activity to be made reportable, it is necessary for the attention copy to work as an early boosting signal to the buffer site from where content is available to other sites – in other words is reportable. No attention copy, then no consciousness, even of content. So it would seem therefore not possible for there to be zombies in this scenario. But that only applies to humans, and very likely also to apes, whose brains have very similar overall structure and sets of modules to our own. What about animals lower down the evolutionary tree? Are dogs zombies? Or cows? Or do they also have some inner self, a sense of being there?

Any approach to animal consciousness has to be taken with care. We have lived so long with animals as domesticated companions and especially as pets that we tend to anthropomorphise them. We only too readily read into their behaviours the same thoughts that we would have if we made similar responses as they do. But we have no proof that they are having such thoughts and experiences. Marc Hauser, a professor of psychology at Harvard University, has pointed out very strongly in his recent book *Wild Minds: What Animals Really Think* that animal minds cannot be approached by looking at anecdote or reading into them our own feelings. Nor should we go to the opposite end of the spectrum and claim that animals have no inner experience at all, especially as some scientists (and philosophers from the past) consider by fiat that only through language can inner experience arise. On the other hand, Marc Hauser makes the response to the question 'are animals conscious?' that it is not a very useful question since it involves a poorly defined phenomenon. He goes on to analyse more specific components of behaviour, such as the capacity for tool-making, problem solving, route planning, what capacity they have to learn by imitation, and so on. He uses neuroscience as a basis for this attack. From the position we are in here, we can now begin to use neuroscience to tackle seriously the problem of animal consciousness. For we now have a framework, a model, with which to clothe not only our own but other possible consciousnesses across the animal kingdom.

Animal Intelligence

We can use intelligence as a beginning marker of consciousness. Numerous recent discoveries have shown that there is a remarkable amount of animal intelligence about.

For example, a recent scientific article by two scientists, working in the Brazilian Capivara National Park, described how they observed wild capuchin monkeys using tools to dig up roots, to crack open seeds and to dig insects from holes in trees. Moreover, they used anything that came to hand as a tool – a stone used as a spade to dig up roots or other food, and also to crack open seeds or to crush lizards or to break open the outer skin of cactus plants in order to get at the soft pith inside. They used twigs to dig into holes in trees, modifying them by breaking off leaves or stems. The use of these tools was suggested by the scientists to have arisen from the pressures in the harsh and arid environment to develop tool-making powers, and so enable the monkeys to have a better chance of survival.

There was much amusement recently when sheep were observed using an excellent strategy of getting across wire cattle grids on the roads around their moorland grazing sites in the Pennines in the UK. These grids had worked very efficiently as barriers to keep the sheep in their proper grazing grounds for a number of years. But then the village of Marsden, surrounded by the moorland (and the grids), began to have sheep appear in the gardens, eating all that was available to them. One lady's garden was devastated – they didn't go for the grass but for the plants and flowers. They also munched away on vegetables being grown by the villagers. How did the sheep get across the grids? They have spindly legs, and they could not step on the cylinders of wire making up the grids without falling through. The grids had been specifically designed in this manner to prevent sheep trotting blithely across them.

Finally the solution as to how the sheep seemingly miraculously crossed the grids was discovered. A passer-by saw a woolly customer trot up to the grid, lie down, and roll over and over until it had got across the grid. Then for a delicious lunch, it thought! The marauding sheep had also developed other methods, such as jumping 5 ft fences (by the more athletic among them) or squeezing through gaps less than eight inches across. They were nicknamed the 'Marsden Munchers', and give us evidence that sheep are quite intelligent animals – they are not so woolly minded as previously thought. Scientists at the Babraham Institute near Cambridge in the UK have also discovered that sheep have good memories, and can learn to recognise up to 50 faces in their flock. A scientist friend of mine, who keeps the rare breed of Wenslydale sheep, told me that he thought his sheep were quite intelligent, and each had their own personality (not necessarily all nice).

Returning to the problem of language in animals ('if they don't have language they have no inner experience' is the dictum of many, across many cultures), a recent scientific study, led by Julia Fisher of the Max Planck Institute in Leipzig, has shown that some dogs, especially a collie called Rico, can learn the meaning of quite a number of words. Rico is a nine-year-old border collie who has been shown to have acquired the vocabulary and the language skills of a three-year-old child. The dog can recognise about 200 words and correctly identify objects by their names. He can even learn new words by picking out a new object, designated by a word he has never heard before, from a collection of familiar toys. He could retrieve 37 out of 40 familiar items randomly chosen from his toy collection. Rico's linguistic abilities were, it was claimed by the psychologist Paul Broom from Yale University, a vindication of the numerous claims made by dog owners of the communicative powers of their pets. There are also considerable linguistic skills in other animals. A pigmy chimp, Panbanisha, for example, developed a vocabulary of 3,000 words and could ask 'Please can I have an iced coffee?'.

Some birds are also known to have considerable intelligence as well as being able to display linguistic skills. Parrots are well known for their mimicry, and Dr Irene Pepperberg from the Massachusetts Institute of Technology taught a grey parrot called Alex to recognise and count up to six objects and to describe their shapes. She recently caused something of a stir in the animal intelligence world by claiming that her 28-year old grey parrot possessed the concept of 'zero'. If so this would be remarkable and put the parrot above the conceptual level of the ancient Greeks (who did not possess such a concept). Her claim was based on the response of the parrot to a set of objects. If she asked if there were five objects there, but there were not, then the parrot replied with a response meaning 'not applicable'. It is not clear how this response can be directly interpreted as meaning that the parrot understands what 'zero' means. Even so a number of her colleagues have been impressed by Dr Pepperberg's claims.

Signs of reasoning powers are also evident in rooks, jackdaws and other members of the crow family. In particular, crows are possibly the intellectual champions of the bird world. Various species of birds – from the crow family to parrots to emus, ostriches and partridges – were assigned an avian IQ index by Professor Lefebvre of McGill University in Montreal. The index reflects different kinds of original behaviour, such as tool fashioning and using (noted in birds of the crow family), the ability to memorise where food stores were sited, or the macabre habit of vultures sitting at the edge of minefields in Zimbabwe's civil war in the 1970s, waiting for their next meal to be blown up for them. As one might expect, predatory birds, as in the crow family, were at the top of the IQ index list, while those being preyed on, such as quail, were down at the bottom. Survival for a predator requires all its wits to catch its prey; for the prey all they need to do is fly fast or be well camouflaged and sit tight.

One special feature of the crow and its close relatives' brains is of relevance here: it is that they contain a proportionally far larger region thought to be similar to our prefrontal cortices than less predatory birds. Thus the carrion crow has about six times more prefrontal brain tissue, relative to its brain stem volume, as compared to that of the quail or partridge, typical non-predatory birds. This extra brain volume can provide the crow and its corvid relatives with the extra mind power indicated by their considerably higher level of intelligence. So the mind of birds depends crucially on their brains, exactly as do the minds of primates, and especially of humans.

In all, then, there is considerable intelligence across the animal kingdom, with increasing scientific understanding of its nature. However, we cannot conclude from that there is also consciousness. Intelligence requires some level of attention. A crow has to attentively search for a suitable twig to use as a tool, and then attentively shape the tool to properly fit the hole in the tree that it suspects harbour some juicy insects. But we do not know what brain architecture in birds creates that attention. We must search for that to make proper progress. It has yet to be done.

Animal Emotions and Socialisation

Another area of interest in animal experience is that of emotions and their involvement and use in their own animal societies. We regard ourselves as having developed emotions, beyond the basic ones of anger, fear, sadness, happiness, etc., such as embarrassment, shyness, guilt – being the social emotions clearly involved in how we see others see us. As to be expected, chimps display social emotions in their society as an important way of getting their intentions across. These emotions are also used in a socially guarding manner. Worried chimps will hoot out 'Ooo, ooo' to warn others of impending peril – such as a boss chimp approaching.

One important question in any animal society is the manner in which violent behaviour arises: is it innate or is it learnt? Apparently baboons learn to be violent in their society if it is a violent one. This was noticed by a study over a period of years of a troop of baboons. The more aggressive of them went foraging to a nearby dump, where they came down with TB and consequently died. As a result of this the general level of aggressive behaviour in the troop dropped off markedly. Even ten years after the major aggressors in the troop had died, the level of aggression still remained low. Even more specifically, it was observed that the top males did not pick on those much lower in rank than themselves, while in an adjacent troop, which still had its tally of aggressive males, the top males bossed much lower-level males, as would a bully pick on those of a much lower level of aggression than themselves.

There is yet no evidence, other than by anecdote, of the high-level social emotions of humans going far down the animal chain. That also does not appear strongly relevant to the presence or absence of consciousness in animals, however. It does indicate something about the level of knowledge of the self possessed by humans compared to other animals. But that is all. An animal could still have a primitive sense of 'being there' without being able to ponder on its own emotions or abilities. So we must move on to see if we can track down this subtle quality of animal experience and consciousness by guidance from attention, especially through the attention copy type of model of the mind.

Animal Consciousness

Can an animal's brain architecture support consciousness? That is a criterion that the sceptic Marc Hauser, whom I mentioned a little earlier, would accept as a viable way of going forward. He wrote:

> *Unlike Scrooge, who was given the opportunity to visit his past and look into his future, we must use the current design of an animal's brain and behaviour to infer the kinds of problem that its mind was designed to solve.*

These problems are ones of seeking out and gaining control of food and water, of finding a mate, and a safe place to sleep and so on. All of these use a number of skills, as Marc Hauser has emphasised: memory (remember where food stores are, for example), planning (how to get most quickly to the spot), socialisation (strength in numbers), attention (avoiding becoming food yourself by watching out for predators), and so on. Some animals are good at all of these activities; others are limited to only one or another of them. But even then it is not only the behaviour patterns being carried out that are relevant. It is what is going on in the animal's brain that indicates to us what sort of cognitive tools it might have at its disposal.

An interesting case of how this can open up completely new attitudes to an animal species occurred some years ago with the fruit fly. It even led to some wild claims that 'some neuroscientists think that a fruit fly's brain contains the rudiments of consciousness'. The situation was that, using remarkable experimental skills, the American neuroscientist Ralph Greenspan and his colleagues had skewered a fruit fly and put it in a wind tunnel. They had also implanted an electrode in its brain (which is minute, consisting of only a quarter of a million brain cells, and only the size of a poppy seed – compared to our hundred billion in a reasonable-sized skull). The scientists then discovered what appeared to be an attention-controlled increase in brain activity in the fly when a vertical stripe of green light passed in front of it. Moreover, the electrodes from three different parts of the fruit fly's brain rose and fell in unison as the green stripe of light appeared.

The scientists involved seemed to think that they had found consciousness in a fruit fly. Or at least they had found attention. I have been emphasising throughout this book how important attention is for consciousness. So why am I not hopping up and down with the results shouting 'eureka' or something like that, and ending with 'Conscious flies!'? The reason is that attention itself is a complex phenomenon. We have some idea in ourselves as to how it works, but it is not so clear in small brains like those of the fruit fly. Perhaps for them attention is guided in a completely 'bottom-up' manner, so that new and exciting stimuli drag any attention the insect possesses willy-nilly to take note of and amplify the activity in their brain representing the new stimulus. There may be no higher-order control at all. Possibly there is additional biasing by some representation of the reward value of the stimulus. But that is all – no 'movement of attention' signal at all.

Such a form of attention would work well for an animal with a primitive brain. It would not have to spend an important portion of its scarce brain cells creating an attention movement control signal, nor some more brain cells to bias that movement by storing goals. No – just leave most stuff out in the environment, and only worry about amplifying stimuli by their bottom-up salience – how intense they are, or what colour, or some such low-level feature. Somewhere in the brain there would have to be a competition between salient stimuli to find out the most salient. But that would only require one module, not numbers of subtly connected control modules along the attention copy lines.

If there did exist an 'attention salience' module in an animal's brain, then it could function as the attention control module in a more general attention control architecture, and thence provide copies of the attention movement signal to other sites. There would therefore be a possibility for consciousness to emerge, although there would still need to be other parts of the attention control architecture – in particular the working memory buffer sites for the sensory input and the attention copy – in order for consciousness to emerge, by suitable binding to input stimuli, for example.

As yet we do not have enough knowledge to say if the way the fruit fly attention system works is as a simple bottom-up system like the one I have described. We just do not know. Nor is it easy to find out, due to the smallness of the fruit-fly brain. On the other hand we have far more chance with the human and ape brain. The latter is somewhat like our own, but smaller and not so convoluted. Yet apes, including ourselves as humans, have both a bottom-up form of attention as well as the ability to plan and set up goals to control attention top-down, so indicating they possess a similar sort of attention control circuit. The ape brain even has similar lobes and modules to those in our own brains. Similarly, we now recognise the increased intellectual powers of crows and their relatives could support a similar attention control circuitry. Apes are also easier to study than fruit flies (with larger brains and considerably larger repertoires of behaviour), and are more likely to have consciousness akin to our own, with a sense of 'being there.'

Do they have an attention copy-like control system to control the movement of their attention? I do not see why not, so expect them to have an inner self. That self will be more primitive than ours, but will still grant the ownership experience. This will lead to their also having 'immunity to error through misidentification of the first person pronoun'. Not that they could say that mouthful of a phrase, but they would be unlikely to suffer from a crisis of identity as to who they are as an experiencing being (if they ever think about it).

Similarly, going down the evolutionary tree I expect that many domestic animals have a similar, but less well-developed sense of 'being there'. I expect higher birds of the crow family would have a similar sense for the reasons I outlined above about their relatively large prefrontal cortices, comparable to those of chimpanzees. Going further down the evolutionary levels of the animal world would lead to the sense of self becoming less well defined, until it will peter out all together, as may happen by the time we get to the fruit fly. Ultimately any attention control system will fade out in the animal kingdom as we go down to the single-celled animals. All plants will also be out of the attention/consciousness orbit.

Finally, animal consciousness – the mixing of owner and content in the way the attention copy model proposes occurs in humans, may be present down to a certain level of the tree of evolution, but may peter out due to the ever smaller higher control system. The fruit fly may even have a rudimentary attention system, driven by external input. We also have our brains so constructed to allow external breakthrough into our attention control. However, very recent published research in 2005 shows there is an intimate mixture of top-down and bottom-up attention control in humans, as if the bottom-up breakthrough was rapidly turned into a top-down control system to allow it to enter consciousness and to function more effectively under global control. It is still early days in these explorations, so we have to wait for a clearer picture to emerge to be sure. But their understanding may well be helped by the attention copy framework.

Animal Rights

My conclusion above that consciousness may descend some way down the animal evolutionary tree, and especially down a number of its branches in parallel, but in the process becoming increasingly 'diluted, seems to leave the door open for animal rights claims, even to the suggestion that many such animals should have legal rights in our society.

We need to be careful about either of those conclusions – that animals are conscious, and so therefore should have legal rights – before we accept them and try to change our society drastically over this apparent upgrading of animals.

I have made it clear above that the sense of 'being there' is crucial for any supposedly conscious animal. As the animal brain becomes less complex there is expected to be a reducing level of brain tissue devoted to the attention control system, and in particular to the range of stimuli which are involved in controlling the movement of its attention. There is still the same range of modalities – eyes, ears, noses, and so on, but with a decreasing range of stimulus concepts that can be experienced as content. That can be described by a dilution or 'thinning' of animal consciousness.

Moreover, there are fewer social rules and social control systems, and less forward planning, related to these decreases in experiential content. There is less in terms of self-attributes, if any at all outside a very few animals besides we humans. The mirror self-recognition test, that I mentioned earlier, only applies to us, to some apes and possibly to dolphins. Passing the mirror self-recognition test implies that an animal is able to know about its own body as if its body image belongs to itself. Neither dogs nor cats have such a body self-image. A dog will constantly bark at its image in a mirror, or rush behind the mirror to face off the intruder it sees in the mirror.

Without such a self-image it is doubtful that an animal can have self-control of its actions. It can act efficiently by planning, but it will be very unlikely to be able to 'know' that it is causing the actions. In other words, it cannot be held responsible for its actions since it is very likely making them without any chance of doing otherwise, from a voluntary point of view. Consider a dog being trained to respond in a certain way. As it learns does it acquire self-knowledge about this response? In other words does it 'know' it has done wrong if it does not respond correctly to the proper command? Yes, it does, at least in many cases, for example if the dog, having done wrong, then hides to try to avoid retribution. But is that a conscious response, or is it a learned association between the specific incorrect response and being chastised? For such a learned association, the hiding response would be automatic. I suspect the latter – the response to hide from future chastisement is automatic. The dog did not think, 'I do not want to do this, but I will be beaten so I had better hide'. I think that the simpler explanation is that the dog was distracted in some way, or had forgotten the meaning of the command, so did not do as required. It then recognised its trainer's angry demeanour as leading to a beating, so responded by 'let's hide'. And it thereby learnt the automatic association between the incorrect response and its chastisement.

This leads us to a very important conclusion, based on the question: how can an animal with no sense of responsibility be given legal rights providing it with some freedom of action? It is not expected to have any illusion of free will, in the manner that we as humans do so. An animal can and should be given legal rights not to be treated cruelly so as to cause it pain, but how can such an animal be regarded as being appropriate to have the sort of freedom that humans have in their society? If an animal does what it has to, but with no illusion of free will, then, provided it is given a good environment in which to grow and prosper with no cruelty, then that is all that we can expect to provide for it. But it will not thereby acquire any moral code so that it knows what it is doing at any time is right or wrong. To require that there be created free societies of such animals on a par with ourselves is not sensible: they could not work (except in zoos). All that can be done is for a farmer to be good to his animals, and that they be slaughtered humanely (possibly an oxymoron but let me pass that by); we should have no compunction in eating the results.

Those animals which have passed the mirror self-recognition test should be treated with more care. Those which even seem to have a degree of free will (as to be found in the way they deal with the future) would need to be considered again. But even then only humans appear to us presently to have the ability to look into the future – to be able to see what is about to happen in any depth. We still have to probe the experience of such higher-level animals, guided by an attention copy model of their minds.

Legal Rights for Animals?

For me, many animals are conscious. However, as the evolutionary tree is descended this consciousness becomes what I term 'thinner and thinner'. It involves less and less content of which they can claim to be the owner. Moreover, it is clear that at some point in the descent on any of the various branches of the evolutionary tree, the attention copy attention architecture will begin to dwindle away, and will ultimately vanish altogether. At some stage animals will no longer be conscious in the attention copy style. That they may be conscious in some other style is quite possible. However, since we do not presently know what that style is scientifically, I cannot discuss it further. Possible future scientific advances could well clarify this situation.

These conclusions cannot be used to argue that therefore many animals should have far increased legal rights. They will be very unlikely to have the illusion of free will, and are expected to be more driven by their immediate surroundings than are humans (the latter with their internalised goals and plans galore). For that reason more thinly conscious animals should have legal rights to a good environment and avoidance of pain, but no more.

CHAPTER TWENTY-THREE

BUILDING A MECHANICAL MIND

Introduction

Computers are now being built with enormous power and speed. At Los Alamos there is a computer composed of 150,000 interacting separate computers. If one master computer controls the others in this 150,000-strong cluster, the system is expected to be about a hundred thousand times faster than a single computer. Even now several groups are considering how best to use clusters of a thousand or so computers in creating simplified models of the brain. In Switzerland, for example, there is a collaboration starting between the EPFL University of Lausanne and the US computer company IBM to create, on a cluster of 10,000 computers, a small portion of the brain composed of 10,000 nerve cells (so one nerve cell per computer).

As to be expected, there are those who would like to go even further and wish to build a large and powerful model of the brain so as to create a machine with artificial consciousness. What 'artificial consciousness' means is not yet well defined. But one crucial component is the ability to possess self-knowledge, to know what is happening inside one or other of one's own modules. Thus some form of self-monitoring is regarded as the basis of machine consciousness. In this way, it has been suggested, some form of self is being introduced into the machine.

As machines become ever more complicated, so is it increasingly difficult to ensure that they are always functioning correctly. When an aeroplane is controlled by hundreds of thousands of lines of code, all that code must be bug-free. But it is almost impossible to ensure that is so. If the code is self-monitoring then it should be able to handle glitches in its own code. Moreover, it should be able, for example, to self-correct errors being made in flight control due to poor estimation of external conditions or if they change very rapidly, more rapidly than the program allows for. Self-monitoring is seen increasingly as the next step in developing more complex control systems, with their associated software, so as to handle increasingly complex tasks. Control theorists, in particular, sense that this is the right direction to move in our increasingly complex world. But if self-monitoring is at the base of consciousness, then engineers recognise that they must move toward creating a conscious machine.

I wrote about the nature of the human self in Part II. There I proposed that the self is composed of an outer component of 'content', based on known, specific attributes of the person. The other, inner component is more subtle, related to the experience of 'being there' inside a conscious experience. Without a sense of 'what it is like' to have an experience, there can be no experience, at least in the standard sense in which experience involves consciousness.

The difficulty with this approach is that it needs a specific mechanism to achieve the inner self that has the ownership experience. Self-monitoring can be achieved by means of comparison of actions with desired actions. This comparison was used in the attention copy model I described in Part II, functioning as part of the overall model for the creation of consciousness. But it was not the monitor component that did the work of creating an inner self, although it certainly helped to achieve that, as I discussed there. It was instead the copy of the attention movement control signal that I claimed was the key ingredient. Thus, I propose that we could only build a conscious machine provided it was based on some sort of attention copy-type model of attention control.

There must therefore be several ingredients to a conscious machine:

1. A perceptual system able to have percepts of object stimuli coded in some manner.
2. A suitably powerful attention control system, able to filter out all distracting stimuli so as to activate a representation of the target stimulus.
3. A mechanism to cause the movement of an attention amplification signal from a previous stimulus code to the desired one.
4. A further mechanism to use a copy of the attention movement control signal to speed up the movement of attention to the desired stimulus.

These four components were described in detail in Part II, with companion modules to hold an estimate of the attended state of the world, comprising a code for the desired target stimulus and one to hold the attention copy signal so as to use it to speed up the attention movement to the desired stimulus, as well as speed up access of the lower-level activities to the attended state estimator module.

These are somewhat technical requirements. But yet I claim them to be crucial to be satisfied in order to have consciousness present in the system. And none of them necessarily crucially involves self-monitoring. So there is a considerable discrepancy between this neuroscience-based approach to building a conscious machine and that of the engineer. Yet there is a monitor in the attention copy model of Part II, so that error correction is certainly present there. However, consciousness is not to be achieved by looking into oneself – by the inward eye, so to speak. It is important to be able to monitor one's actions and thoughts. But it is not inclusion of that faculty which would be sufficient in a machine to allow it to experience consciousness. Instead consciousness is to be created by attention using a copy of one's attention movement signal to help speed up and make error-free the brain activity codes of stimuli being attended to. That is the attention copy approach to the mind that I described in some detail in Part II. It came with a lot of neuroscience support. With that as a blueprint, I claim we could seriously start building a conscious machine.

Artificial Intelligence

But why should we make things so complicated? Why drag in attention and monitors and all these other components of attention copy models. Why not play it as simply as we can? Artificial intelligence has taken enormous strides in the last few decades. Robots can move around under their own steam, and play football with each other or dance or climb stairs. Software systems are used to control many machines in the home, such as a washing machine with 300 different settings for clothes, under the control of a neuro-fuzzy system. Trains can glide around with no drivers. Cars are also able to travel (albeit somewhat slowly still) in a driverless mode, although some of the most recent cars are being provided with cruise-control systems able to allow hands-free driving at 80 miles per hour. There is a great thrust to create autonomous robots for battlefield use. Pilotless planes now fly over distant domains, and can bring down death and destruction on one's enemies. Are we not already on the threshold of intelligent, if not yet fully conscious, machines? There may not be too far to go before these intelligent machines become conscious.

Whatever the value of these machines – and they are indeed valuable – they still do not have some of the components that we would expect of an intelligent machine. These crucial elements are imagining, think-ing, reasoning, creativity, planning, adaptive properties and graceful degradation (so if some components are lost, the machine does not stop performing altogether).

Starting at the end of the above list, the ability to adapt and to gracefully degrade as components are lost or malfunction is not possessed by most of the current generation of 'intelligent machines'. A single slip in a piece of code and the machine may not function at all. Breakage of a component in a complex car engine means it will not continue working. A small bolt displaced in an aeroplane can cause catastrophic results. Most modern machines are in any case made to be replaced if they fail, so why worry about the ability to keep on working reasonably well even if some part or other has broken? Just throw it away – there is always going to be a new and better one at the shops. Moreover, machines are built to be specific so they do not need to adapt to a new environment. Just get another machine that is more appropriate.

However, consider the case of a truly autonomous robot Alpha. It is out on a morning stroll, but it stumbles over a bolt lying on the pavement. It catches its knee on the hard ground, and one of its leg rotators shears. It is in some difficulty, since around it are people hurrying back and forth, but paying it little notice, although every now and again a person will stub its toe on the robot torso and swear at it or give it another kick. So the robot crawls to one side, out of the rush of the marauding feet. As it lies there it needs to plan how to recover. Should it call its best friend Beta? Should it try to get to the nearest robot garage as soon as possible, since it is worried that its energy sources (several of the latest hydrogen batteries) will be running down shortly, and will need recharging? Or should it give out its emergency call and hope some Good Samaritan of a human will stop and help? Of course it knows that it is in a difficult situation, and it should never have left its workplace for this short stroll, but what is a robot to do? It was given a curiosity drive, so it just had to go with it and go out into the brave new world.

This is where our sad little robot needs all the autonomy it can get to remove itself from its quandary. Without planning, reasoning and thinking abilities it may just lie there and be unable to prevent its batteries dying away, and rust to damage its components if rain comes. It would be very vulnerable if it were given any drives to make it desire autonomy – such as its curiosity drive – but not at the same time given cognitive powers commensurate with those drives to enable it to handle all that the world can throw its way.

There are presently no so-called intelligent machines that can think, plan, imagine, reason or be creative along the lines I am suggesting. Thinking involves consciousness: that is still not in any machine. Planning can be done at a low level by a variety of machines, but the plans are still of a low level. Moreover, there is still no machine that can plan adaptively – use in its plans things it has just learnt. No machine can imagine – again that needs consciousness (for there to be an 'imaginer' who is having the experience of the images). Reasoning machines exist at the simplest level, but again have little flexibility. All in all, the present intelligent machines possess little of what we normally call intelligence. They are marvels of machine learning, machine pattern recognition, and various other machine powers. But they are light years away from any intelligence of a human order.

These various higher cognitive faculties we are searching for are all centred round the highest level of cognitive processing, that of consciousness. It is as if a machine would need to have consciousness in order for it to be able to plan, think, reason, imagine, and so on effectively. At least it is reasonably clear that without a powerful attention control system able to organise the complex internal processes necessarily involved, such high-level intelligence will not be present. It would not be able to coordinate or organise its inner stream of thought. In the internal milieu of an artificial brain, the selection and ordering of the various processes necessary to achieve intelligence would just collapse. All would descend into chaos. Only by some overall control scheme, able to select one activity thread from many, would higher levels of cognitive processing be able to be achieved. Yet again, attention must be present to bring order from internal chaos.

I hear you say: 'But if all this is written in software, then already there is order – the linear order of the program. So there is no need for attention – it is replaced by programming'. Good point. But there is a danger of simply assuming that such a program could be written. How do we know that such a linear program exists that could capture consciousness in such a standard and well-established manner? There are in fact two real problems that we face in developing any way of creating machine consciousness. One is the need to write the whole of the software in terms of a neural network system. That is possible, as we will shortly consider. There is a much harder one, however: can a software program ever work? The human brain may be nothing like a computer – it may function on rather different lines. That is much harder to sort out, but first we have to be clear about what it is that needs to be computed, in whatever way, say by the old-fashioned linear program or by using some new blue-skies computing style. In fact, when we clarify the nature of what it is we want to compute it becomes clearer as to the sort of new blue-skies computing we need to use to get to build the conscious machine.

Modelling Neural Networks

Artificial neural networks have been around since 1943, when two American scientists suggested that simple models of a single brain nerve cell could be connected together to solve any logical problem (of a certain quite large class). These artificial nerve cells, or so-called neurons, were 'binary decision' units: they received activity from all of their companions in the artificial neural network to which they were connected. If that activity was above some preset threshold level (so deciding to respond if enough activity had arrived to them) then they responded by sending out a unit signal; if not, then they were quiet. In this way the activity moved around the network. It was shown that this decision system could solve considerable problems in logic.

Neural networks moved on over the decades, especially helped by two important features. One was that the connections between different neurons could be taken as real numbers, say 0.5 or −0.1, In either case the effect of a response signal coming along a connection from one neuron to the next was modified only to have a value equal to the connection's weight, so being excitatory to the tune of 0.5 in the first case and inhibitory to the value of −0.1 in the second. These connection strengths or 'weights' could be set to allow a neural network to achieve quite remarkable information processing tasks, like picking out a given face among others.

It was the next step that brought artificial neural networks much closer to those of the brain, but also made them even more useful. It was in the ability possessed by a neural network to have changed the connection strengths between the model nerve cells by suitable training methods. Three training schemes have been, and still are being, further developed: supervised training (as if a teacher were present to train the network on the answers it should give to specific inputs), reinforcement training (rewarding the network if it gives the correct answer, so making it increasingly likely that the network will give correct answers), and unsupervised learning (so the network picks out regularities from the inputs, and produces, for example, a useful topographic map of the distribution of inputs). Each of these methods, as well as their combination in hybrid networks, has enabled artificial neural networks to be developed to solve ever more difficult problems in artificial vision, route planning, memory storage and retrieval, and many more areas.

There has now developed a branch of artificial neural networks called computational neuroscience, which is devoted to creating artificial neural network models of parts of the brain, and in some cases even simplified models of the whole brain. This latter exercise is becoming ever more important now that computing power is increasing so enormously. So sooner or later there will be quite detailed models of the global brain, written and running on clusters of digital computers. In order to achieve this, it is clear that the chaos of the brain has become tamed. The resulting activity may have chaotic features, as my American colleague Walter

Freeman insists it should from his many results investigating the brains of a range of animals (rabbits, cats, and so on). But it would have been tamed as to what its underpinning description should be, in terms of the necessary connections between the myriads of nerve cells.

Given what I wrote in Part II, you can see how the overall program for a global brain should be structured: as based on attention as the supreme controller. There are two other components – reward value codes and memory codes – that would also need to be crucial components of such a software global brain program. There are already numerous computational models of both reward value and memory components, as well as the attention copy model for attention/consciousness. All the main computational features of the global brain are therefore already present, in principle. In practice there is an enormous amount of work needed to develop the detailed programs to produce simulations that fit the various experimental results now available from neuroscience. But that is a matter of person-months and person-years (undoubtedly many of them will be needed).

However, is that enough? Is running a digital computer program of the global brain going to capture the essence of consciousness? Even more, will it be possible to claim that the computer program itself, as it is running, is experiencing consciousness? And even more to claim that the consciousness being experienced is in any way like our own? Independent of the computers the overall program is run on?

Artificial Consciousness

Let us suppose that a complex software program supposedly representing the activity of the global human brain is running on a suitably large digital computer cluster. It is simulating the activity of the requisite billions of neurons, which may, each of them, itself be complex. For example, the Swiss EPFL–IBM project I mentioned at the beginning of this chapter has one dedicated digital computer for each neuron of the model being simulated. So there would need to be billions of such computers. Let us suppose that such a cluster of digital computers has been brought together and suitably programmed. All the aspects of higher cognitive processing I mentioned before are being played out in the program: planning, reasoning, thinking, imagining, creativity. It has an attention control system, for example built along the attention copy lines, to handle the incipient chaos, and to have buffer working memories on which content of consciousness is expected to emerge. I know it is a tall order, but let us suppose that by suitable training methods, now under development, such a software system can be created and run in relatively real time. Could the resulting system be said to be conscious? Or is there some basic flaw in principle in the system which could prevent this from happening?

There are those who claim that consciousness could not arise from any such simulation. For example, the British physicist Roger Penrose has made a strong plea for a new physics being needed to attain any understanding of consciousness due to a fundamental result of the Austrian logician Kurt Gödel in the 1930s. Gödel showed that there were statements that could be made in any suitably powerful mathematical system that were able to be seen to be true but could never be proven true in the system. So such systems were incomplete. They could not be used to prove every theorem that could be stated in them.

Gödel's incompleteness theorem was used by Penrose to claim that we, as conscious systems, could not simply be machines. For any such machine could be used to produce such statements which could not be proved by the machine. But we, as humans, could see the truth of the unprovable statements, so must have powers far beyond these machines. And in particular consciousness was claimed by Penrose as being at the root of these powers possessed by humans to give them this powerful ability. Therefore humans are not machines describable in any known mathematical language.

The results of this controversial analysis were already making waves in the 1960s among philosophers; Penrose brought the problem to the attention of the public, and used it to peddle his own brand of answer, through quantum gravity. That could well make the problem of consciousness harder with another insuperable problem: how to marry quantum mechanics with gravity. Quantum mechanics had been very successful in explaining all of the properties of matter down to incredibly short distances, as tested in the increasingly energetic particle accelerators built for increasingly large sums at various physics centres across the globe. Gravity had been explained in 1916 by the beautiful geometric theory of the great scientist Albert Einstein: gravity is the geometry of space. How to make the quantum-based forces of nature also geometric was the problem Einstein faced in the 1930s but could not solve because he left out the quantum aspects. Finally in the 1980s John Schwartz and Michael Green put together a very complex theory called 'superstrings' which achieved that unification (with a rather laborious proof that it gave sensible results for all gravitational processes finally being given by myself and colleagues Alvaro Restuccia and Paul Bressloff in the early 1990s). So the unification of these two aspects of nature, quantum and geometry, was shown to be sensible through superstrings.

Not that there is still an enormous problem of moving this theory forward to make real predictions. But there is no longer the logical incompatibility of the two approaches. So Roger Penrose does not need to try to reduce to one single difficult problem the old difficulties of quantum gravity by uniting them with the new difficulties of consciousness in the brain.

Yet I think that Roger Penrose was right in worrying that what Gödel said was an indication of the need to create more complex computational systems to be able to emulate consciousness in the human brain. The problem is that somehow the structure, and especially the dynamic running of a computer program of the brain, does not seem in any way related to the dynamical activity in the real brain. Even given that each neuron is being processed on a separate digital computer, the information it contains does not properly relate to what a real neuron is doing.

Living neurons in the brain have active membranes. By this I mean they hold electrical activity on their surface membranes (by suitable 'pumps' in the membrane surface) to keep positively charged sodium ions outside the cell. This leaves the cell interior negatively charged. Such a charge is modified positively or negatively by pulses of input arriving from other cells at various (unspecified) times. There are billions of these minute electrical state machines throughout the brain, and it is the ongoing dynamics of the changes of this activity that is the crucial basis of brain processing. The value in a living neuron of this membrane potential may vary from −100 millivolts to +20 millivolts. Each neuron is not just a little on−off machine, as the simplest artificial model of neural networks was taken in 1943, as I mentioned above. In other words neurons are not digital but have a real-number-valued state description.

When we move from digital to real numbers, to machines which have states described by real numbers, they still have undecidable statements about them (as shown more recently by extensions of Gödel's original undecidability theorem). In other words, if we built a machine that computed over the real numbers it also has the same principled (but controversial) reason why it could not be conscious. Such a NOGO claim is difficult to accept, for our own brains are very much like that, acting as machines over the real numbers.

So where is the loophole? One may be that we are not dealing with simple static types of machine over real numbers when we turn to create a real-time computing model of the brain, it necessarily being made of billions of neurons with their ever-varying membrane potentials. Our human brains are also constantly changing the strengths of the con- nections between their neurons. But we can expect consciousness to arise over such a short length of time that we do not expect the modifications occurring in our brain to be crucial in modifying the argument about the possibility of consciousness. Adding further complexity should also not change the general structure of our brain as a machine over the real numbers.

If real brain consciousness is sacrosanct from copying by the NOGO consciousness claim, then building a brain with an architecture very close to the real thing would evade the issue. It may well be that running a program on a digital computer should open the simulation not only to the NOGO consciousness claim, but also to the claim that the timing is essential. In general a digital software program will calculate the neuron activities sequentially across the brain, with the neuron activity being again updated sequentially across the various neurons defined in the brain. But this will be a gross distortion of the activity processing across the neurons. Even if each neuron had its dedicated computer, and these were updated in parallel, there is no active membrane being updated dynamically.

If the neurons were in hardware, able to ape effectively the membrane changes of a living neuron, then we are very close to the real brain (modulo the decidedly non-trivial further problems of the vast number of neurons needed as well as the complexity of their connections). At this point we have pushed the Gödel/Penrose argument so far that it has been made to apply to the actual brain itself, or one very closely like it. At that point it no longer behoves me to justify the approach. No consciousness NOGO claim is relevant to such a model. What is necessary is to build the hardware 'brain', run the activity, and check if all looks as it does in the real brain when real tasks are being solved. I proposed this some years ago in the CHIMERA chip, whose design would lead to a part brain, part digital chip architecture on the CHIMERA chip.

There is also a good reason to attempt to create a brain model in silicon close to that of the real brain. Consider a model of the weather, such as one used in predicting the weather by forecasters. If the model is simulated on a computer you do not expect to see water coming out of the computer. Simulation is not the real thing. It can never be. But then why should we expect a computer simulation of consciousness also to possess conscious experience? However, if we try to emulate the actions of a real brain by a model relatively close to reality, such as one based on chips like the CHIMERA chip mentioned above, then we have a chance of consciousness being produced. It is similar to the use of a wind tunnel to recreate the effects of wind running over a device, such as an aircraft wing. It is not the actual sky the wing is exposed to, but something closely similar. In the same way, it is not the wetware of the real brain that is being run, but the activity of a set of silicon-based 'active' neurons, which hold membrane potentials on their cell bodies, and have a degree of reality in common with the real brain.

Given such a program of conscious machine brain creation, one can then embark on exploration of possible modifications, and especially of simplifications, to see how simple and streamlined one could make the components of such a brain and still obtain what would appear to be consciousness experience. Such a program is for decades if not centuries ahead. But it is a viable one, and one which could take us much closer to conscious machines, if not their actual creation.

Ethical Questions

But I can hear you asking me: 'Is this not a dangerous program on which to embark? It possesses the shades of Frankenstein.' Indeed there is present in any of us a fear that our robotic creations, once they possess a certain level of autonomy, will rise up against us. This was first shown in Karel Capek's 1921 play 'R.U.R.', and then as dramatically demonstrated by HAL in *2001: A Space Odyssey* and the later Skynet in the film *Terminator*. These all have rogue robots trying to kill their human 'lords and masters'. There was even an intelligent computer controlled building, described graphically by Michael Crichton, which finally went ape. They all seem to turn against us, as if it were pre-ordained (possibly part of the three laws of sci-fi drama: make it exciting, make it dangerous to the humans, make the graphics have a high 'wow' factor).

All is not lost for autonomous robots, however. What about bringing up our children? In one way they also end up rising against their elders, finally elbowing them out of the way. This is especially the case if the elders are seen as still being in the past and not keeping up with the race of onward and upward progress. New ideas and new artistic creations take over society. New faces are seen in the media. They are the Young Ones in general. But the takeover is without bloodshed. That is so because our present upbringing of children does not cause them to run too violently amok with the sensibilities of their elders and finish them off with AK47s. Especially since the elders are also part of the imbibers of the creative products of the Young Ones.

In a similar manner it is possible to bring up autonomous robots so that they will be efficient and non-revolutionary members of our total society. Think multi-culturalism, but now extended to include robots of various levels of intelligence (as we have a range of intelligences already in our society due to genetic variation). The crucial concept I introduced above was 'bringing up your robot properly'. I have discussed the need, as seen from the attention copy model basis, for bringing up children in a loving and 'guided creative fun' manner, properly rewarded with love and affection but given a clear framework of NO GO for certain actions. So this goes a long way beyond Isaac Asimov's Three Laws of Robotics. These rules are too naïve for any future autonomous robot training programme. This programme would have to be based on the best of child upbringing programmes, along the lines I have suggested and beyond.

There will be failures in such a programme, as there are in our parenting and educational system. Our jails are full to overflowing, as we all well know. So we would hopefully not be so inefficient in producing so many socially ineffective robots as we produce socially inappropriate human members of our society. Nor would we need any widespread robot jail system: they would be developed so well that very few would need their friendly robot psychiatrist, although legal questions of moral responsibility would be posed in ever increasing numbers. These would, we assume, need to be based on an updated version of how we presently treat minor human transgressions in our society – fines, loss of privileges (taking away a driving licence), and so on. The robots would have no free will (similar to ourselves), but would be responsible for their actions in terms of their being held responsible for the memory codes of social rules they have formed over the many social interactions that go to make up their upbringing. In extreme cases these would have to be unlearnt and more appropriate ones put in place. But that is what is needed in penal institutions for humans in any case. However, it may be easier to introduce for the new breed of autonomous robots, as part of their contracts with society.

Beyond the Turing Test

I have covered a lot of ground in this chapter, but the upshot is that a modus operandi has been proposed for building a brain close enough in its vital activities to avoid any consciousness NOGO claims. Thus the acid test will be: if built in this way, would the hardware brain have external responses and internal flows of activity as observed by psychologists and by neuroscientists (through brain imaging and single-cell measurements)? What I propose here is a criterion for the presence of consciousness that goes beyond that of Turing. He proposed that the acid test is to keep asking the system questions, and if you cannot differentiate between the responses of the system and those of a human, then it has passed the test. But this test can be fooled by rather simple linguistic systems, whereas the additional criteria requiring a detailed internal flow of activity as would be seen in the human brain (and made more explicit by the attention copy-controlled processing) would make it very much harder to fool human judges (especially if they were neuroscientists).

CHAPTER TWENTY-FOUR

A PROPER MIND-USER'S MANUAL

Introduction

As in any user's manual, I am trying to help you achieve the most efficient use of your machine: in this case your brain and mind. It should include how to handle breakdowns, and also how to develop good practice in handling your mind. The user's manual so far has provided evidence for the brain being *the* organ of the mind. It has also explored in what way various deficits of the mind could arise. In both of these analyses the user's manual had to provide descriptions of the details of the structure of the brain, to be able to develop a scientific basis for understanding the system. It was thereby possible to develop a model (based on the idea of an attention copy) of how attention functions, and itself acts as a gateway to consciousness.

Both content and ownership of that content were shown in Part II to be able to be created by such an approach. Moreover, what could be some of the proper functions of consciousness were explained through the attention copy model: consciousness exists to speed up the movement of attention by using the precursor attention copy signal to grant ownership of the content of consciousness about to arrive as attention-amplified neural activity representing an attended external stimulus. The attention copy thereby acts as a wake-up call. At the same time, we saw how attention is a scarce resource until its job is achieved. In the third part I developed various ways in which modifications of the fundamental nature of human experience are to be understood, as seen from the attention copy model. In this part I have dealt with the more detailed lessons that the attention copy model provides for mind in family, society and its animal companions. From this vantage point we are ready at last to deal with vicissitudes of the mind and brain in a much more practical and hands-on manner.

In this final chapter I will develop a more standard user's manual, with components describing the various accessible parts of the system, instructions for their use, how to keep your brain/mind in good nick, and how to perform DIY maintenance or instead to get expert care for it.

There are numerous senses in which the brain/mind system is, for example, like that of a car. Both have clear physical structure, both can function well at times but then catastrophically fail, both require good maintenance to keep in good shape, both can be modified by experts trained in the relevant detailed technology (repair mechanics or brain surgeons, respectively). There is a major difference in that users cannot go and choose their brain/mind as one can go and buy a car. Nor especially can they rent one for a short period, leaving their usual one at home when they travel across the globe. But the similarities between the brain and the car are still considerable, and so such a form of manual as issued to new car owners should be of value, especially for a quick view of DIY maintenance that should be performed by the user, exactly as they would do for their car.

Operation of the Brain/Mind and its Controls

The brain has the structure of Figure 10, which I already showed in Part II.

Sensory Inputs

These enter through the eyes (vision), ears (audition), mouth (taste), nose (olfaction) and body sensors (touch and internal organ configurations). These sensory inputs are pre-processed by various sub-cortical nuclei,

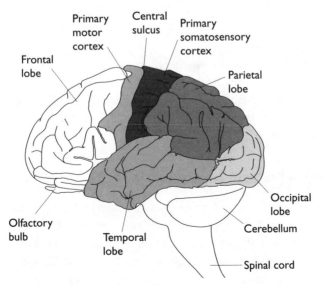

Figure 10 The general structure of the brain

before going to the relevant cortical sensory input areas for more developed analysis. Vision goes to the occipital lobe, smell to the olfactory lobe and audition to the superior temporal lobe. Associations between stimuli are also developed by memory in various cortical sites, as well as in the hippocampus, at the base of the temporal lobe. Representations of objects are created from views of them in the temporal lobes.

Motor Responses (Actions)

These are coded by the spinal chord, but more complex movements are coded at a higher level by the primary motor cortex. Even higher-level representations of motor sequences of responses are coded in higher-level motor areas (termed supplementary and pre-motor cortices). Finally, overall executive control is carried by codes in the prefrontal cortex. The cerebellum has long been known as involved in helping control motor action; damage to it, for example, can cause difficulties in making accurate reaching movements to objects.

Brain Stem (Reflexes)

The neural codes in various parts of the brain stem are the building blocks of early experience (such as the rooting reflex to search for the mother's nipple if the cheek is touched), and are used to develop higher level and more complex response systems incorporating knowledge of the world gained by the developing infant.

Drives

These ensure that primitive needs (such as for food and liquid) are met, and are coded in various brain stem and hypothalamic sites. These are initially encoded genetically, but then are modified by higher-level codes in the cortices to develop the groups of stimuli that can provide satisfactions for each of these drives.

Limbic System (Value Maps)

When actions are made and primary drives are met by actions on objects in the vicinity of the infant, then values are attached to the various objects, including negative values, as in the case of red-hot objects as a cause of pain. These reward maps are in the orbito-frontal cortex, just above the eyes (in the orbit) and are crucial in making effective auto-nomous decisions as to responses to make that thereby gain the best rewards in given situations. At the same time more primitive value maps are contained in the amygdala. Both of these maps appear to be somewhat independent of attention, especially the orbito-frontal cortical map, so explaining why emotion tends to be immune to cognitive control.

Memory System (Episodic Memories)

This involves memories of the self in interaction with other objects and persons. They are set up in hippocampus, but then are thought to be played back for laying down outside the hippocampus, and ultimately incorporating with other object and action memories as semantic memories (with no relation to the self).

Attention Control

This is the highest-level control system in the brain, including as it does the speed-up and monitor processing involved in consciousness. The attention control system modules are contained in the parietal and prefrontal cortices. Loss of various of the relevant components can lead to many disturbances of consciousness, as well as there being more subtle disturbances when modifications of connections are brought about in schizophrenia or cortical disintegration occurs in Alzheimer's disease.

Information Before Using

There are presently several routes for probing the infant brain before birth. These have delineated the developmental stages of the foetal brain, with the beginnings of autonomous control thought to arise between the 20th and 30th weeks. Various precautions are now recognised as needing to be taken in order to protect the foetal brain from damage coming from smoking, drug taking or drinking of alcohol by the mother (none of which are advisable). Another aspect to be considered even before conception is that of the genetic stock of the parents. This is still a difficult area to be able to make any scientific claims, especially with the debacle associated with the sperm bank recently set up from sperm donated by the world's supposedly most intelligent men (including Nobel Prize winners). Due to mutations these may not have bred true to form. However, the genetic code contains all the necessary information out of which the infant will grow to adult; how this occurs in detail is gradually being uncovered, especially with the latest published Hap Map giving details of the variations of specific genes between different sorts of people. This will lead to a much more detailed map of the functions of the many genes in the human genome, and thence in the future to practical genetic guidance for all.

There has been claimed to be value if a background of music is provided for the foetus in the womb, with classical music apparently being preferred by many foetuses. For example in India, cassettes and CDs claiming to help the well-being of pregnant mothers and aid in the development of the foetus are fast occupying shelves in city music stores and having good sales. Besides helping the mother relax during pregnancy, the gynaecologist Monesh Shah, at the Mother Hope Fertility Clinic in Mumbai wrote, 'The foetus can receive vibrations during the latter part of the pregnancy. It can perceive the vibrations after the fourth month. Music may help in the foetal growth, as in the advanced stages of pregnancy, the receptivity of the foetus will be increasing. I believe such a musical background will help, but it is just another general form of stimulus input. The vibrations of music would act as external stimuli and influences the environment surrounding the foetus'. However, the reality of this improvement by the foetus in this way is not clear. The gynae-cologist Dr Jyoti Unni suggested that 'There is no data to prove that music could help in the growth of the baby. What it could definitely do is relax the mother, which may then lead her to eat and sleep well, which in turn helps the baby. It is true that the baby can receive sounds from the fifth month onwards but nothing can be said about any direct influence of music on the foetus'. So if it helps the mother that is a good thing, but there is no guarantee of anything more.

Starting and Using

There is a considerable amount of information available as to methods for best use of the brain. These can only be put in place by the parents, so require careful development, with knowledge also needing to be acquired by the parents as to best practice in running their infant's brain. In particular the need for close and loving contact with the infant is crystal clear, as is the need to provide as much stimulation around the infant as is feasible without overloading the infant brain. However, it is thought that, barring gross overload (such as constant flashing lights and loud music), reasonable levels will not cause harm. Moreover, there is need to provide close contact of eye-to-eye form, since the infant face perception system has a reasonable level of genetically programmed face codes. These can be activated efficiently by close eye contact. Much is taken in by the infant even in the first few weeks after its birth, so stimulation is important from day one. Smiling at the infant is a good move.

Emergencies

There are numerous emergencies that can arise, although these differ at different ages. For the young, epilepsy is a possibility, but tends to go away with age. For the old senility of a variety of forms sets in, as discussed earlier. In between ages can also suffer from dementia, but also from tumours, epilepsy, strokes and other defects if there has been excessive wear and tear. Also car crashes and wars are an important source of brain damage, leaving permanent defects in the whole range of mental functions (as discussed earlier in detail). Once serious damage has occurred, it may be difficult to modify what is left of the brain to take over the lost functions, especially if the sufferer is an adult (so that the brain is not so adaptive). Expert advice is needed as to how any such damage can be minimised and recovery programs be set in place. Go to your nearest doctor for initial advice as to which neurologist should be consulted, or to the nearest Accident and Emergency Department at your nearest hospital.

Corrosion Prevention and Appearance

There is general need to prevent wear and tear by poor maintenance and use of both illicit and licit substances (drugs, alcohol, smoking, and so on). Life is littered on all sides with those whose brains have been reconnected, by their own actions of taking such substances, thereby making them dysfunctional. Try to persuade your child from going down that route, or, if you are an adult, avoid following it yourself.

Numerous intelligent brain foods are now on the market, and more are appearing. These contain various chemicals used in the brain as neurotransmitters or neuro-modulators, and may be especially involved in memory formation or in attention and alertness. Some of these have been shown to be of value to students about to take exams or by those in onerous jobs needing a high level of alertness. Take those relevant to any problem you sense in yourself, but be careful of overdose over a period of time, and only take those which have been carefully tested under rigorous conditions, and do not produce addiction (such as cocaine).

General Maintenance

This is only to be performed at any serious level by an expert professional: psychiatrist, neuro-psychologist or brain surgeon according to the problem presented. Much has advanced in being able to ameliorate symptoms that are causing difficulties. These advances use a variety of techniques: through therapy, through giving suitable chemical agents, and finally through brain surgery.

An important area where all these three methods are used is depression. It causes cognitive slowing down, as well as various levels of anxiety and mental anguish in more extreme forms. Depression is a major source of brain inefficiency, with over 40 million of present US citizens suffering from it in their lifetimes. Some cases of depression are resistant to therapy and known chemical agents, and so can only be treated by the more invasive treatment method of brain surgery. There are many cases amenable to cognitive behaviour therapy (CBT), in which lengthy discussion is given of the nature of how the brain has begun to malfunction so as to cause the depression and how the careful and gradual development of inner control over depressive thoughts can steadily bring the brain back to a proper balance. Drugs act more directly on the connections between the various component networks, enabling the balance to be obtained more artificially. If there had been a chemical imbalance as the source of the depression, then drug treatment would be more appropriate.

Finally, the approach using surgery has come to the fore very recently with the work of the Canadian neuro-psychiatrist Helen Mayberg. She proposed that there is normally a balance between the network of cortical areas producing cognitive processing in the brain and that supporting emotional processes and experiences. The former of these is sited dorsally in the upper part of the prefrontal cortex, while the latter is placed in the limbic region, being ventral or in the lower cortical areas and adjacent sub-cortical sites. Thus, the main cognitive area is suggested as the dorso-lateral prefrontal cortex; the main limbic areas are the orbito-frontal cortical area and the amygdala, with other components involving the hippocampus and the source of dopamine neurons in what is termed the VTA in the brain stem. It is through dopamine arousal that value maps are learnt (composed of a representation of the reward value of an external object). Apparently direct injection of drugs acting as precursors to the creation of dopamine can cause people to learn the relevant surroundings that predict such rewards, and so lead to drug addiction.

Thus there is a set of two networks in the brain, the cognitive one being placed in the upper part of the brain, the emotional one sited in the lower part. These two parts are connected by a crucial region in the brain, in the mid-brain region, called the cingulated cortex. It is this region, suggests Helen Mayberg, which is not functioning properly in depression. In particular, it is not acting as a proper connector between the activities of the two networks, but causes too much excitation in the lower emotional network and not enough in the upper cognitive network. Mayberg suggested that surgery should be employed to insert a brain electrode to be used to activate a suitable part of the cingulate cortex to inhibit the excess activity of the emotional network and help bring the cognitive network back on stream properly.

This insertion of brain electrodes and their connection to batteries in the chest of patients (to provide the electrodes with continued electrical current) has now been performed on several patients, both in Canada and the UK. In a number of these cases there was considerable if not complete amelioration of depression. One patient is reported as saying, as the electrode was moved around to find the best placement in the operation: 'What did you do? My head suddenly cleared and I felt so calm'. This calm returned when the operation was over and the battery turned on to cause continuous deep brain stimulation in the electrode. Such an operation, although onerous, would seem well worth it for those it benefits in lifting the misery of their depression off their minds, and allowing them once again to enjoy life and function as a valid member of society.

DIY Maintenance

In order to keep the brain in good shape in a healthy body, it is of value to keep it well used in the most appropriate ways:

- Attention: this can be developed by a range of tasks, such as in attending to each movement or thought one makes. This is time consuming and should be performed carefully in the evenings, in a 30–60 minute session, several times a week, in a room with no distractions. As suggested recently in an item 'The Mind Gym' by Dr Thomas Stuttaford and Suzi Godson, 'Open your eyes. From scenery to people, temperatures to sounds, take it all in. Remember your surroundings and test yourself later to see how good you were. Focus. Give whoever you are with or whatever you are doing your full attention'.
- Memory: numerous memory exercises are known, such as the old game of Pelmanism (in which a set of cards is placed on the table upwards, the players memorise their values and positions and the cards are then turned over, and a player allowed to take each card provided they correctly stated its identity beforehand. A mistake allows the next player to have their turn). Numerous similar games are available, which help keep memory flexible and under attention control. Recently

scientists devised what they claimed to be a memory game that if played regularly would take 14 years off your age (so don't try this if you are aged 14 or younger). It simply consists of memorising lists of words. As one of the creators said, 'After just 10 seconds of playing this we saw an improvement in cognitive functions equivalent to up to 14 years, and on average it took a decade off the cognitive age of volunteers after just 10 sessions'. As they specified, try to memorise a series of words such as bread, couch, carrot, milk, fish, apple, chair, shelf, table. Practise memorising the list as a series of categories, e.g. remembering couch, chair, shelf and table as furniture. By breaking the list down into categories the brain is able to memorise the list more effectively. Also follow the suggestion on memory I mentioned above by Stuttaford and Godson, of recalling your activities you carried out earlier in the day, or even some days earlier – that can be quite demanding. A similar method may be applied to memorisation of lists of numbers. They are split up into sequences of four years at a time, and the years are connected suitably together, say as years when certain records in a sport were broken. Training in this way, like the categorisation process in the learning of lists of words above, can lead to the ability to learn lists of numbers of quite amazing length, and with great rapidity.

- Creativity: this arises in numerous games, as in crossword completion (where memory is searched, but best results at times use unconscious responses as arise in creative processes). Similar unconscious scanning occurs in quizzes, where the immediate answer should always be tried, even though there is no 'reasoning' associated with it.

- Reasoning: here planning ahead as to the consequences of one's moves is needed. This faculty can be kept bright and burnished by various planning games, of which chess may be the intellectually most challenging. Not only is forward planning needed here, but also the ability to chunk place patterns on the board so that forward planning of moves is made less complex. At the same time value maps need to be created of various board positions to help in deciding which of the positions is most rewarding for a future win. Such a process takes lengthy practice, and may explain why it has proved so far difficult to program a computer system able to strongly beat any human competitor. In spite of being able to look ahead a number of moves, the assignment of value and the chunking of pattern structures have not yet been able to be learnt by a machine chess player at the same level of efficiency as that of a human.

- Intelligence tests: these test a number of skills, such as route planning in a concept space, associated memorisation and recall, reasoning by analogy, and numerous others. They are all of value to keeping the brain's connections fit and strong.

- Sleep: this is still not scientifically understood, but there is good evidence that during sleep there is enhancing of memories and their deposition into cortex from hippocampus. This implies it is important to keep a suitable level of sleep to allow these processes (and others still not understood) to proceed. It is also very likely that removal of damaging oxidants occurs (which have accumulated in the brain during its day's hard activity); this is most likely occurring during the slow-wave or deep sleep predominant in the first four hours (as has been suggested by recent researchers investigating such sleep in other animals, and also that there is a sleep deficit built up if we lose our slow-wave sleep, although there does not seem to be a similar deficit if we lose our dream sleep).

- Food: it has been said repeatedly that we are what we eat. Thus we need to ensure we eat a suitable range of food to keep both our brain and body in good shape. That is clear for the body, but not so for the brain, due to the presence of the blood–brain barrier. This was discovered when dyes injected into the bloodstream stained many tissues in the body but did not stain any part of the brain. The blood–brain barrier (made of narrow capillaries) stops many otherwise useful as well as noxious materials from entering the brain from the blood. That is why modern attempts to modify the brain, such as through imbibing acetylcholine otherwise lost in Alzheimer's disease, can only properly be done by direct intervention in the brain itself. This implies that the notion of 'super-intelligent brain food' being of value to promote the brain has to be viewed with suspicion. There is one proviso: if the 'food' can be attached to molecules that can get through the blood–brain barrier then there is a chance of such transfer into the brain being achieved. It is relevant to note that dopamine does not itself get through the barrier, although a substance called L-dopa does, and when it is through the barrier it is transformed into dopamine. This transfer and creation of dopamine in the brain is the basis of the L-dopa treatment for Parkinson's disease, in which there is a loss of dopamine cells in the basal ganglia. It is known that glucose, amino acids, choline (relevant to the production of acetylcholine), purine bases and nucleosides can penetrate the barrier, while proteins, most antibiotics, toxins and monoamine (neurotransmitters) cannot. Indeed, if the latter could get into the brain just through one's food, they could cause havoc in the firing of the nerve cells of the brain. Instead they are actively barred from brain penetration.

Specifications

These have already been given in Part II. They should not be needed under general working conditions, even when a serious malfunction occurs. In that case the brain should be taken to the nearest neurosurgeon who can use the latest brain imaging machines to attempt to determine if there is any structural abnormality in your brain or related functional defect causing problems in your mind.

Final Advice to Mind Users

I have tried to give a more user-friendly final chapter, able to be picked up and used on its own, in a similar manner to a car user's manual. The difficulty here is that the car user's manual can be put into a novice's hands and clear sense can be made once the user looks under the hood at the engine with its component parts exposed. There is no analogical process for a mind user. The figure at the beginning of this chapter is not what is normally seen by any mind user, but is only exposed after the brain has been stripped from its moorings and the user is dead. We can now look into the living brain, using the special techniques of brain imaging machines, to give similar figures to Figure 10, but now observable by the users themselves. Even more amazingly, such a brain structure can be observed at work performing its little acts of thinking, perceiving, emoting, and so on as the user experiences them.

Such a transparent situation is not, however the norm for mind users. Their brain is usually incommunicado to them. Thus, it is their inner experiences that count for the standard user. I have tried to cater for that bias by presenting in the book a bridge between brain activity and mind experience. The components of this final chapter attempt to help by showing how that bridge is being increasingly strengthened by insights now coming from science about how to keep your beautiful brain in good nick by at the same time keeping your miraculous mind in good nick. The two are inseparable. In fact they are one.

INDEX